WOMEN'S FOLKLORE, WOMEN'S CULTURE

Publications of the American Folklore Society
New Series

General Editor, Marta Weigle
Volume 8

WOMEN'S FOLKLORE, WOMEN'S CULTURE

Edited by

ROSAN A. JORDAN · SUSAN J. KALČIK

upp

University of Pennsylvania Press · Philadelphia

The quotation on page 137 from the poem by Anne Sexton entitled "Cinderella" is from Transformations *by Anne Sexton. Copyright © 1971 by Anne Sexton. Reprinted by permission of Houghton Mifflin Company.*

The photographs in chapter 5 are by Geraldine N. Johnson and the photographs in chapter 9 by Karen Baldwin.

Library of Congress Cataloging in Publication Data

Main entry under title:

Women's folklore, women's culture.

   Bibliography: p.
   Includes index.
   1. Women—Folklore—Addresses, essays, lectures.
2. Women—United States—Folklore—Addresses, essays,
lectures.   I. Jordan, R. A. (Rosan A.)   II. Kalčik,
Susan J.
GR470.W66   1985   398'.088042   84-12019
ISBN 0–8122–1206–1

Printed in the United States of America

Third printing, 1985

To Linda Dégh, Bess Hawes, and Ellen Stekert

CONTENTS

Introduction · *ix*

Part One

WOMEN IN PRIVATE / WOMEN WITH WOMEN

1. Dial a Story, Dial an Audience:
Two Rural Women Narrators in an Urban Setting · *3*
LINDA DÉGH

2. The Vaginal Serpent and Other Themes
from Mexican-American Women's Lore · *26*
ROSAN A. JORDAN

3. Woman to Woman: Fieldwork and the Private Sphere · *45*
MARGARET R. YOCOM

4. The Kinship Quilt: An Ethnographic Semiotic
Analysis of a Quilting Bee · *54*
SUSAN ROACH

5. It's a Sin to Waste a Rag: Rug-Weaving
in Western Maryland · *65*
GERALDINE NIVA JOHNSON

CONTENTS

Part Two

WOMEN IN PUBLIC

6. *Women's Handles and the Performance
of Identity in the CB Community* · 99
SUSAN J. KALČIK

7. *Belle Gunness, the Lady Bluebeard:
Narrative Use of a Deviant Woman* · 109
JANET L. LANGLOIS

8. *The Misuses of Enchantment:
Controversies on the Significance of Fairy Tales* · 125
KAY F. STONE

Part Three

TWO WORLDS/ONE WORLD

9. *"Woof!" A Word on Women's Roles in Family Storytelling* · 149
KAREN BALDWIN

10. *Some Differences in Male and Female Joke-Telling* · 163
CAROL MITCHELL

11. *Sex Role Reversals, Sex Changes, and Transvestite Disguise
in the Oral Tradition of a Conservative Muslim
Community in Afghanistan* · 187
MARGARET MILLS

12. *Woman Remembering: Life History as Exemplary Pattern* · 214
ELAINE JAHNER

References · 234

Contributors · 244

INTRODUCTION

U NTIL RECENTLY, folklorists have concentrated their efforts on performances that are characteristically male-oriented in that they are highly individualistic or competitive and take place in public or formalized arenas—the pub, the street corner—while ignoring folklore that is more collaborative and enacted in the privacy of the domestic sphere or as part of ordinary conversation. Consequently, such genres as personal experience narratives, popular beliefs, and various kinds of humor have often been dismissed as "minor genres" or, less formally, "old wives' tales" or "just gossip." In other words, genres and performance contexts that are especially characteristic of men have most interested folklorists as worthy of study, while folklore that flourishes within the private domain of women has been underrated and ignored. One term for this sort of bias is "sexism," defined by Bernard (1971:37) as the "unquestioned, unexamined, and unchallenged acceptance of the belief that the world as it looked to men was the only world, that the way of dealing with it that men had created was the only way, that the values men had evolved were the only ones. . . ."

This volume has been assembled in an attempt to help change this lopsided orientation in folklore scholarship by giving attention to women performers and women's genres, which need to be examined along with the more frequently studied, often more public, forms of folklore used extensively by men. In looking at women's folklore, however, we are finding that our studies also yield new insights into the realm of men's folklore and into the ways in which the two domains affect each other—whether the relationship be one of contrast or one of complementarity.

Rosaldo and Lamphere argue that "anthropologists in writing about human culture have followed our own culture's ideological bias in treating women as relatively invisible and describing what are largely the activities and interests of men," and they point to the resultant dearth of ethnographies taking the women's perspective (1974:1–2). Murphy and Murphy point out that the bias of the anthropologist fits the bias of the male informant, who also sees the world in male terms (1974:209). And Ardener argues that until recently anthropologists have felt quite comfortable in writing an ethnography based mainly or entirely on what male informants have told them, because

> those trained in ethnography evidently have a bias towards the kinds of models that men are ready to provide (or to concur in) rather than towards any that women might provide. If the men appear "articulate" compared with the women, it is a case of like speaking to like. To pursue the logic where it leads us: if ethnographers (male and female) want only what the men can give, I suggest it is because the men consistently tend, when pressed, to give a bounded model of society such as ethnographers are attracted to. But the awareness that women appear as lay figures in the men's drama . . . is always dimly present in the ethnographer's mind. (1972:136–137)

Farrer (1975a, 1975b) and Weigle (1978), in their introductions to collections of essays about women's lore, have already pointed to the same bias in the discipline of folklore. The gender of the folklore fieldworker influences what he or she looks for; it affects his or her relationship with informants, and what he or she is ready and able to see and hear and understand as important. Ethnocentric or sexist preconceptions about appropriate gender roles have limited the lines of inquiry pursued by folklore fieldworkers studying groups with gender assignments different from those the investigator has learned to consider usual. For example, Abrahams (1976) has related how his own culturally determined expectations about gender and cooking caused him to overlook for a while an important aspect of West Indian culture having to do with both male and female involvement with foodways, an area of inquiry which eventually proved extremely useful to him. This kind of bias, and the fact that until recently most field-workers were male and did not have free access to women's culture, have naturally affected folklore research and fieldwork, in its concep-tualization, in its application, and in the interpretation of data. In general, this male orientation has meant that women's expressive culture is ignored or viewed as insignificant and limited. Farrer (1975a) points out that women's folklore genres have been accorded attention only if they fit the prevailing image of women, that data has been collected from female informants on a very limited range of subjects, and that folklore theories and models are based on half (the male half) of the relevant data.

> Usually in Western societies it is the male genres that have been used to define the recognized universe of artistic expression within a group. These recognized, usually male, genres assume the status of "legitimate" folklore genres. Female expressive forms either fit the male mold or they are relegated to a non-legitimate, less-than-expressive category. (Farrer 1975a:xv–xvi)

Folklore studies, then, like anthropological studies, have de-scribed women as men see (or don't see) them. A tendency to see the world in male terms has influenced what kind of data folklorists have looked for and from whom, and also what data they have actually collected and from whom.

The chapters in this volume focus on the folklore and culture of women. One result of this focus is the uneasy (for some) feeling that all is not as it seems, that the student must look beyond ready as-sumptions and superficial interpretations. A number of chapters in this collection point to aspects of the culture being studied which could be misinterpreted if not examined carefully. Margaret Yocom warns that her female informant might easily be overlooked. Margaret Mills outlines assumptions that men make about women in Muslim society which are not borne out by women's storytelling. Susan Kalčik's women CBers do not fit the neat stereotypes their "handles" imply. Susan Roach asks us to look at the quilt and its context to see the rich layers of communication involved in a simple quilting bee. And Carol Mitchell's own informants, male and female, make statements about their joke-telling that are belied by her study of their joke-telling activities.

One assumption that a thoughtful examination of women's culture disproves is that women are necessarily powerless. The chapters in this book do not depict women as victims or as failures in an essentially male world. Despite male domination of one sort or another, many of the women studied here are very much in control of themselves and their worlds, and a sense of real power is communicated by their folklore. Geraldine Johnson's rugmaker has arranged the time and space of her life to suit herself. Yocom's female storyteller influences her family despite her noncompetitive style. Elaine Jahner points out that Sioux women as designers and storytellers have a significant effect on the basic direction of Sioux culture change; women's abstract designs represent potentialities for action, and therefore for change.

Many of the women presented in these chapters also communicate a sense of control over their worlds in terms of the rules and models of those worlds. This is especially true in the aesthetic expressed in many of the chapters. Geraldine Johnson describes the aesthetic criteria that her informant employs in rugmaking, and the compromises she must make in certain situations. Susan Roach tells us how aesthetics may be subordinated in some circumstances to other considerations, such as bringing skilled and unskilled women together to work on a quilt. Elaine Jahner's narrator sacrifices one kind of truth for another as she edits the story of her own life. Karen Baldwin, Margaret Yocom, Carol Mitchell, Linda Dégh, and Margaret Mills offer observations on aesthetics in women's storytelling.

Because of the void created by bias against the women's viewpoint, which we have discussed above, many studies of women's culture and folklore have begun to explore such subjects as women's aesthetics in an effort to see women as they see themselves and their world. As Weigle (1978:3) and Farrer (1975a:xi) have pointed out, this has often meant looking at a private world, a world of women with women, rather than the public world outside the intimate circle of family and in-group members. In the present volume we have grouped together chapters that deal predominantly with the world of women as expressed in folklore. In Part One, Linda Dégh describes the use of the telephone by two immigrant women narrators and analyzes the sources of their lore in Hungarian tradition, in their own life stories, and in their observations of everyday life. Rosan Jordan examines narratives told by Mexican-American women for a sense of how they view their world and their place in men's world. Margaret Yocom's detailed analysis of the private sphere of folklore study is also helpful for understanding the private world of women. Susan Roach examines a collaborative family quilting bee as a communicative event that affirms values and relationships within a family and between its womenfolk. Geraldine Johnson describes the context and process of one informant's rag-rug-making and explores the informant's own views on her craft.

Of course, women also can and do appear in the public arena (Weigle 1978:5–6), and the chapters in Part Two explore this aspect of women's culture. Susan Kalčik studies women as strategists manipulating identity and stereotypes in the public arena. Janet Langlois offers us a multifaceted view of a female villain-heroine. Kay Stone examines the public images of women in fairy tales and the reactions to them by men and women. Also pertinent here, however, are Geraldine Johnson's discussion of her informant's manipulation of the public and private worlds, and Carol Mitchell's look at stereotypes of women in jokes and at women as joke-tellers.

Women's activities in the public and private arenas are related, just as the activities of men and women are related. An approach that allows for looking at all these interrelationships would give students a clearer, less one-sided picture of how a culture actually operates. The chapters in Part Three take a step in that direction by focusing on cultural and sexual asymmetry and complementarity. Karen Baldwin examines the complementarity of male and female storytelling and shows how the two produce together a family's history. Carol Mitchell looks at the different performance styles and contents of male and female joking and male and female uses of public and private settings. Margaret Mills's study of sex change and sex role reversal in Muslim storytelling reveals the markedly differing views of women's world and women's roles held by men and by women. And finally, Elaine Jahner's study points to the interdependence of masculine and feminine in the rituals of the Lakota Sioux, an interdependence that is also apparent in everyday life, the role of Sioux women being to integrate "the forces of change into the fabric of daily life." In a sense, however, all the chapters in this volume explore to some extent the relationship between male and female worlds and views. Margaret

Yocom compares the private world in which many women narrators tell their stories with the public domain and style of male narrators. And Stone, Kalčik, Langlois, Jordan, Roach, and Jahner also comment on the male world and its relationship with the female world.

Ardener urges us to realize that "we are all lay figures in someone else's play" (1972:153). This idea is common in the study of other kinds of folklore. Both the editors of this volume, for example, have worked with ethnic material in which esoteric and exoteric views of ethnic groups are commonly discussed. It is easy for folklorists to accept the importance of distinguishing between how one ethnic group is described by another and how it describes itself, and also between behavior that is reserved for in-group gatherings and behavior that predominates at public presentations of group identity. Scholars have not, however, always applied the same rigor to descriptions of sex groups. Since the male view has been predominant, it is probably very difficult for men, even folklorists, to see themselves as women see them: to see themselves, in Ardener's terms, as actors in a woman's play. Women are more likely to be aware that there are two points of view, and women's studies have often included men, although from a perspective that men may be unfamiliar or uncomfortable with.

Farrer (1975a:viii) points to the need for studies examining "similarities or differences between male and female expressive behavior." And Weigle urges the reconciliation of male and female models of verbal art (1978:6–7). She suggests that the investigation of women's genres will lead to new insights into little-studied areas of verbal performance, such as conversation (ibid.:3–6). Thus the study of women's folklore, and folklore studies made by women, seem a likely starting point for enlarging our view of the world, enabling us to appreciate more fully the complexities of human culture as seen from multiple perspectives.

· PART ONE ·

WOMEN IN PRIVATE/
WOMEN WITH WOMEN

DIAL A STORY, DIAL AN AUDIENCE: TWO RURAL WOMEN NARRATORS IN AN URBAN SETTING
Linda Dégh

SITUATED ON Lake Michigan southeast of Chicago, Gary, Indiana, is one of the giant industrial cities in the United States (Moore 1959). Gary and vicinity accommodate the world's largest steel mills, and almost all the residents of Gary work in the plants or cater to the needs of their employees. Besides the majority black population, there are about twenty sizable and another thirty smaller nationalities residing in Gary. Huge freighters and tankers ply the lake, thousands of trucks and automobiles congest the superhighways cutting across the city, and the network of tracks within the city run freight trains day and night. The wind blowing perpetually above the Great Lakes whirls black smoke and mixes yellow and purplish-pink poisonous steam into the air. It is an unlikely scene for peaceful traditional storytelling.

But "Aunt" Marge and "Aunt" Katie, both residents of Gary, are born village storytellers. What can they do, how can they make use of their talents, their fantasy, sense of humor, pleasure of narration, in this most unlikely spot of the world?

It was in the fall of 1964 when I first met them. I had ample opportunity to study the anachronistic manifestation of their many-sided gift within the limits of the industrial city. I was able to observe them as their houseguest and also as a participant in the communal life of the Hungarian ethnic enclave to which they belong. It was easy to explore their way of life on both workdays and holidays, and their contacts with the outside world as means of expressing themselves. Nevertheless, evaluating their oral folklore and their personalities required comprehension of their cultural environment, so I had to familiarize myself with the worldview, value system, and aesthetic standards of the ethnic community. The dominant Hungarian peasant tradition I knew had gone through considerable modification. Hence, the function and quality of the actual oral literature would have been difficult to understand without knowledge of the ambiguous, uneven, and variable processes of this modification.

Sociologists dealing with immigration to the United States have come to an agreement concerning the sequence of the stages of acculturation, assimilation, and integration. When immigrants, attracted to this country by economic opportunity, decided to stay for good, they settled in ethnic communities, but within these communities there have been unlimited variables due to ethnic, situational, and positional differences (Hough 1920:18–19; Moore 1959:356–357; Dégh 1966:551–552).

The history of the steel industry in Gary and in the neighboring steel cities belonging to the larger Calumet Region can be traced in the life history of the Hungarians and the other ethnic communities in the area. The pioneer group that transformed the marshland around the Little and the Grand Calumet rivers and on the sand dunes on the banks of the lake was composed of the masses of Southeastern and Central European peasantry (Handlin 1951:7–36; 1959:26–29). They were the builders of the industrial plants in which they acquired jobs, and they were the builders of the cities in which their dreams of comfortable living came true. Among the cities in the area, Gary was the last to be built, following the construction of the plants of the U.S. Steel Corporation in 1906. The company settled its employees close to the workshops and named the new city after Judge Elbert H. Gary, chairman of the board of directors (Moore 1959:254). Because the ethnic settlements were established on uninhabited land and could therefore develop more or less by themselves, they were able to retain their ethnic character.

> The Calumet Region became a mixing bowl, rather than a melting pot, of races and nationalities. Melting pot suggests a oneness of

features and characteristics produced by a simultaneous amalgamation of different elements. This did not occur in the Calumet area. Instead, the movement of the population groups into the region during the first fifty years was such that each had the opportunity to make its presence felt. . . . The presence of so many nationalities and races produced a variety of flavors almost unique. (Moore 1959:244)

Both our storytellers were "charter members" of the Hungarian ethnic colony of Gary that has been dissolved now for some time. Both remember the initial hardships in the barren land and can tell when and in what succession the main buildings were constructed. The fate of the Hungarian community and other ethnic communities was shaped by the fluctuation of economic conditions. Depression, war boom, the importation of new workers, and other factors transformed the ethnic composition of the city. Broadway, the fifteen-mile-long main street and business district of Gary, is today inhabited almost exclusively by blacks. The folklorist who wants to visit more than one of his informants of European extraction during the day has to travel some fifty to eighty miles from house to house within the limits of the city.

Gradually, new cultural features accumulated in different layers on the dominant peasant heritage. In spite of outward appearance, the immigrant generation did not change its essentially peasant worldview and behavior. The commonly acknowledged attributes of the initial phase of immigrant readjustment, such as language learning, adoption of different food and dress habits, and acquisition of new technical skills (Willems 1955:225–226; Park 1950:138–151), remain imperfect up to this day and have not affected important cultural traits. The process of assimilation followed an uneven course, depending largely on the need for individual adjustment. At the time of their retirement, even those who were exposed to the impact of the dominant culture returned to the Old World lifestyle abandoned in early youth.[1] We can speak only of attitudinal changes, which affect mostly the material life of the immigrant generation. Yet these changes are extremely meaningful, since they react on the essential values of the subculture itself. Assimilation generally occurs with the first American-born generation, whereas integration becomes complete with the second.

The acculturation of the Gary settlers is the result of two parallel processes: the substitution of the urban-industrial way of life for that of the rural-peasant, and the accommodation of national minority groups to a multiethnic environment. Consequently, the form, role, and function of folklore underwent a basic transformation from its peasant model.

Mrs. Katie Kis and Mrs. Marge Kovács today live quite a distance from each other in neighborhoods to the east and west of Broadway. Mrs. Kis is eighty-six, and Mrs. Kovács is seventy-five. They came from the same Hungarian ethnic region and brought the same linguistic and cultural backgrounds to the United States. Like many other peasant immigrants prior to World War I, neither Mrs. Kis's husband nor Mrs. Kovács's father saw New York except for the landing port, Ellis Island. Typically, immigrants traveled by train directly to one of the industrial cities on the East Coast, where earlier immigrants helped them find places to live and work. Their jobs were in factories and mines. Meanwhile, the dream of making enough money to return and buy land in the Old Country faded because of the war and the Depression (Lengyel 1948:127). Our informants, Mrs. Kis and Mrs. Kovács, followed their elders and settled with their families in the Hungarian ethnic neighborhood of the newly erected midwestern industrial metropolis. Neither of them has ever seen any of the big cities, the skyscrapers, and the various technological wonders that are characteristic of urban America.[2] Having left the familiar environment of their home village, they sought protection in a neighborhood similar to what they knew. Mrs. Kis and Mrs. Kovács were next-door neighbors in the Hungarian community of Gary and were related by marriage. They belonged to the same Hungarian Protestant church (Church of Christ) that acted as the protector of the national identity and became the center of social activities for the group (Handlin 1959:77–84; 1951:117–143; Fishman 1966:15–16, 20–22).

As long as the Hungarian community did not exceed its original four-block area in downtown Gary, its population was not forced to learn English or to adjust to an urban way of life.[3] When the steelworkers' earnings became steady and the typical Hungarian peasant frugality and hard work bore fruit, the families prospered and the old community began to disperse. One by one, families moved to a healthier location in the "green belt" within the city limits, away from the congested, polluted streets. They built their comfortable homes according to the standard of respectable American workingmen: the three-bedroom type with a roomy basement, one bathroom, a screened or open porch, and a handsome garden. The homes were well equipped with modern conveniences. In such homes the "front room" has wall-to-wall carpet, and the kitchen is large and bright with big windows, built-in cabinets, a freezer, and other household appliances. Who would ever compare this home to that of a Hungarian peasant family? Yet this house represents the fulfillment of a peasant dream. It is roomier and certainly more luxurious than the house of the biggest farmer in the Old Country, but its interior arrangement and decoration and its functions are very much the same.

Taking the homes of Mrs. Kis and Mrs. Kovács as models, we find similarities to their Old Country homes. As in the Hungarian peasant's home, the center is the kitchen, not only as a place where food is prepared and consumed but also as a place of relaxation for the members of the household and a favorite gathering spot for neighbors, relatives, and intimate friends. The heavy decoration of the kitchen walls is remarkable. Colorful ceramic plaques, plastic fruit, flying birds, framed artificial flowers, and other cheap ornaments from the supermarket replace the earthenware plates of the peasant kitchen. The embroidered prayers, the "house blessings" made by the lady of the house, are as popular as in the Old Country. The function of the living room is the same as that of the "clean room" of old. It is crammed with the most cherished knickknacks but is not used much. American in-laws, acquaintances, and other callers are seated here. Mrs. Kis still has the traditional chest of drawers full of trinkets on the top and surrounded by family photographs. Mrs. Kovács, on the other hand, has replaced the chest with a vanity that gives more room for family snapshots and keepsakes. Besides the objects in this "sacred corner," the walls of the living room are decorated with pictures of her parents on their wedding day and of her father in his military attire, framed certificates of citizenship, and a faded wreath from her father's grave. It is also interesting to note that the porch, like its Hungarian equivalent the "tornác," serves as the farewell place where visitors are shown out and kept for a while, to emphasize hospitality.[4] Outside the home is the garden, not the spotless smooth lawn of suburban American homes but the colorful carpet of flowers in front of the windows. It is a source of pride to grow a Hungarian flower garden, and the women are eager to get the seeds of the favorite geranium, petunia, mignonette, rosemary, rose mallow, and gilly-flower. They order the seeds from the Old Country, and they exchange breeds with friends. The backyard, on the other hand, displays a touching holdover of the peasant vegetable patch, evidence of the tenacity of the traditional ethnic diet. The care of vegetables is normally in the hands of the master of the house. Since both the informants are widows, they tend and renew faithfully year after year the plant stock on the patch built by their husbands, giving away the excess of herbs and vegetables.

Mrs. Kis and Mrs. Kovács reside today in their comfortable homes completely alone. They have no financial difficulties, since their pensions and Social Security benefits cover their immediate needs. All the extras are well taken care of by their children and grandchildren. However, their lives are marked by isolation and solitude, largely because of the dissolution of the old ethnic community, the dissemination of the neighbor families, and their inability to adjust to this new environment. Those above the age of sixty who lived through their active years within the ethnic ghetto found themselves in a strange neighborhood at old age. The lively system of kinship and neighborhood contacts had been replaced by an environment in which there are neighbors whose customs and language they do not understand. At the same time, their old family ties had fallen apart. Their children prefer to speak English with their American-born spouses of diverse origin, and their grandchildren, as a rule, do not speak Hungarian at all. Meanwhile, the most prominent cause of isolation is the enormous distances within the city. It is difficult for relatives to spend their little spare time after working hours on the busy rush-hour highways in order to pay a short visit. The relatives of Mrs. Kis and Mrs. Kovács are more devoted than the average, but their visits are still usually limited to Sunday afternoons, except for occasional calls to deliver essential foods or medicine or to do some urgent repair.

Both the elderly women remain by themselves almost every day of the week and almost every hour of the day. Aunt Marge told me once: "Sometimes I do not talk to anyone for a whole week, only to myself." The size of the city condemns them to solitude and to boredom. They do not own cars, as women of the immigrant generation; they never even learned how to drive a car. They are too old for long hikes, and even if they were able to walk there would be no place to go in the big noisy city full of unknown people. The ethnic church still stands in the old neighborhood, but the neighborhood itself is no longer Hungarian. Church services would be still available to them if there were someone to drive them there. Occasionally the minister does gather the senior members for the Hungarian language services, since their relatives participate in the English service—if they have not relinquished membership in the ethnic church entirely in order to increase their status by joining a more attractive suburban church.

All these facts suggest a hopelessly bleak and useless existence, almost like being in a prison. Nevertheless, the lives of Mrs. Kis and Mrs. Kovács are anything but bleak. Their solitude does not mean apathy or desperation or merely waiting for the years to pass. Loneliness shows itself when they warmly welcome even occasional visitors, such as a repairman, the mailman, the deliveryman, or the insurance agent. Once in the kitchen, visitors are overwhelmed by funny stories, which can be enjoyed despite the language deficiency. But except for the rare pleasure of telling stories for a live audience, what makes life bearable, even pleasant, for these women of cheerful disposition? In other words, how do they spend their time?

The telephone plays the predominant role in maintaining and transmitting folklore, as well as in keeping Mrs. Kis and Mrs. Kovács in touch with the outside world and passing on news. Their children call them daily, and they may talk more than once a day if a problem arises. In such cases, the telephone substitutes for personal visits, but a call lasts only for minutes.

The telephone is also almost the exclusive communication link between members of the immigrant generation. Our storytellers discuss with their friends, who are as isolated as themselves in their own homes, the social rites in which they participated or of which they have learned. They exchange opinions on weddings, birthday parties, meetings of the ladies' aid association, and bingo parties. They enjoy gossiping, and the telephone is an excellent outlet for discussing the behavior of the others. Unusual events affecting the life of the ethnic community are passed around in minutes through the telephone. Following a report about a sudden illness or death, female members of the community call all their acquaintances and stay up all night to enjoy the pleasure of passing on the sensational event embellished by naturalistic details. The telephone spreads personal news on health and everyday trifles and is a means of comparing notes on events from the outside world as understood, or more often misunderstood, through television.

Besides the usual exchange of opinions, our informants use the telephone for telling stories, although they limit their talk with busy younger people to the minimum. Experience has taught them telephone etiquette prescribing who can call whom and when, and how to refuse an unwanted call.[5] But Mrs. Kovács and Mrs. Kis converse for hours and never exhaust their pleasure in narration.

As is proper, it is usually Mrs. Kovács, the younger, who greets her older partner each morning with: "Good morning, Godmother, how did you sleep?" "All right. And how about you?" Thus, storytelling is usually launched. These telephone narratives almost without exception begin with an actual experience: a dream, a strange feeling bringing up old memories, something seen on television or heard on the radio, a funny spectacle observed through the window. This is usually linked to an anecdote formalized as real event. Mrs. Kovács, for example, mentioned that an old fool bragged about his readiness to wed her. "Just like the gypsy who talked about marrying the princess. . . ." On another occasion, Mrs. Kis told me about the latest visit of the minister. Giving a lively presentation of their talk, Mrs. Kis reproduced her answer to the minister's question whether young girls in her hometown used to wear short skirts like girls do nowadays. The short skirt reminded her of a well-known obscene joke concerning the short skirt of the lady teacher and the view of the little boy, and she reshaped the story as a truthful event involving her own grandson. In this fashion, the two narrators exchange folk narratives in long succession over the phone. Obscene anecdotes alternate with jokes and witch stories in turn.

Mrs. Kis and Mrs. Kovács love to laugh, and they laugh freely, totally relaxed by their phone stories. One can hardly wait for the other to finish a story, having an even better story to tell. They do not hesitate to ridicule their acquaintances, and they do not spare themselves either, once they begin to joke. They know very well that it does not fit their age to laugh loudly. Their daughters are quite critical of their long phone conversations. Mrs. Kis's daughter does not like phone gossips. "You two understand each other!" remarks Mrs. Kovác's daughter-in-law. A good source of laughter is one of Mrs. Kovác's neighbors, Mrs. Nagy, a nosy old woman, a real paragon of virtue. Because of her barbed words directed against the hilarity of Mrs. Kovács and Mrs. Kis and their "laughing with their mouth open," Mrs. Kovács compares Mrs. Nagy to the woman in one tale who fixed her mouth in front of the mirror before going to a wedding party, then had to talk to someone on her way, so she returned home to fix her mouth again.

I have observed and recorded telephone narration sessions with Mrs. Kis and in turn with Mrs. Kovács. Although I always questioned the caller about the responses at the other end of the line, this one-sided recording did not give me a total picture of the joint performance of the two informants. The only way to find out about their cooperative storytelling was to bring them together at the home of one or the other. During the period of observation, I found the standard repertoire of the two narrators to be variable and continuously renewed by actual experiences.

While the telephone functions as a means of acquisition and trans-mission of knowledge and also as a means of keeping up communi-cation with the ethnic group, television opens a window into the unknown world in the intimate surroundings of their comfortable homes. The set is on almost all day, and its presence is felt even unconsciously through its little noises. It is on while the women perform daily chores and receive guests; even if they relax in the lounge chair in front of the set, it does not matter what is on the screen. They are not at all disturbed that they do not fully understand what is happening there. Both Mrs. Kis and Mrs. Kovács were able to list the shows they favor, but they were unable to describe the con-tents. Colorful action, spectacular scenes, dancing and singing, and buffoonery entertain them well enough without dialogue. Misconcep-tions arise because of their inability to distinguish fiction from reality. The traditional realm of folk belief is reaffirmed through science fiction, modern ghost stories, and supernatural mysteries. Mrs. Kis is especially sensitive to TV witch stories. When watching the serial "Bewitched" she immediately responded: "As I saw this witch last night, you know the witches of our village came to my mind. Oh my God, I left the village because I was so scared of them. . . ." Here she tuned in a well-shaped belief legend about the witch who was caught and shod with horseshoes when she pursued young people in the shape of a yellow filly.

Information about the outside world transmitted by television in the United States is hardly stranger and less intelligible than the language of the newspapers, the sermon of the minister, or the speech of the intelligentsia even in the Hungarian village where Mrs. Kis and Mrs. Kovács were born. The attitude of peasant immigrants in the New

World is very similar to that of Old Country villagers, who were content with only a partial understanding of the world beyond their own, taking it for granted that the affairs of the masters are none of their business.

Neighborhood relationships of our two narrators are quite different from those in the Old Country or in the original ethnic community of Gary. Friendship and kinship affiliations formed in the old neighborhood proved to be tenacious when people set up houses in different places, while new ties in the new locations had to remain superficial because of the diversity of ethnic origins among the new neighbors. Mrs. Kovács has two Hungarian neighbors, both of them Catholics and therefore members of another ethnic nucleus. One of the families is second generation and speaks only English. Except for the senile ninety-year-old grandfather, there is no one worth talking to. With the other aged couple, however, Mrs. Kovács is in a continual village squabble. Mrs. Nagy, a seventy-nine-year-old "fussbudget" with a snappy tongue, has been mentioned already. She never stops scrubbing floors, polishing doorknobs, or repainting kitchen walls. Whenever she takes a break in her self-imposed work, she keenly watches the window of her neighbor and usually finds what she is looking for: something she disapproves of.

Mrs. Nagy has lived for sixty years in the United States and never learned to speak English. Still, only the oldest three of her nine children speak a broken Hungarian. She still lives by the norms of Veszprém County,[6] according to which Mrs. Kovács does not behave as she should. As already noted with regard to telephone narration, Mrs. Nagy objects to Mrs. Kovács's loud laughter and bad conduct. Mrs. Nagy even objects to Mrs. Kovács's guests, her way of treating them, her way of cleaning house. Mrs. Kovács is both annoyed and amused by all this. She never stops talking about it, and as a born entertainer she imitates Mrs. Nagy, makes fun of her criticism, and incorporates her sayings in her racy anecdotes. Listening to Mrs. Kovács, one would believe that the two women see each other often. In truth, they usually observe each other through closed windows, and except for accidental encounters meet only once or twice a year.

Mrs. Kovács's closest relationship in the neighborhood is with a Rumanian couple. She knew them before they moved out here, and she learned from them most of the charms, magic prayers, and home cures she knows. The husband understands some Hungarian, and they converse in the scanty English they both possess. Other neighbors—a "hillbilly" family, a Polish couple, an Irish couple, and a Croatian-German couple—are the topics of conversation rather than acquaintances. Mrs. Kovács is well aware of ethnic differences and collects every little bit of information about the neighbors, whatever she overhears from behind the closed doors and what she can conclude from the behavior of household members.

There are no Hungarians in the neighborhood of Mrs. Kis. She must content herself with what goes on in the home of the "hillbilly" across the alley, what the many children of the Croatian family across the street do, and how the love affair stands between the boy and the girl in the two American households down the street. She takes notice of unusual sounds and motions, and shapes exciting, horrible, or funny stories out of the meager facts. Contrary to the Hungarian peasant attitude, compulsory for elderly women, neither Mrs. Kis nor Mrs. Kovács breaks her back with housework. They consider themselves entertainers, and thus differ from those retired people who cook and wash and clean all day with an almost fanatic sense of duty in order to justify the usefulness of their own lives. Our informants find other pleasures. This does not mean that they are sloppy and neglect their homes. They take particular care to prepare traditional ethnic dishes for themselves and their visitors. For example, it is most repulsive to them to buy noodles in the store instead of making their own.

Under the circumstances it is small wonder that the arrival of a guest is welcomed by these village raconteurs who are forced to limit their natural talents to telephone conversation. When relatives announce their intent to stay longer than usual, or if the visitor is in no hurry, like the minister, a church elder, or myself, both storytellers return to the long-abandoned style and tempo of village narration. Once again they live in the environs of their happy youths in the ethnic community where they played leading parts in entertaining at social occasions.[7] Nowadays, if there is a chance, they give generously of the rich store of the folk narratives accumulated in their memories. They incorporate both old and new and retain at the same time the body of their traditional narratives. Always on these rare occasions traditional food is offered with the proverbial Hungarian hospitality. One can visualize the past glory of these two born entertainers in the happier days of the Hungarian community in Gary.

Occasionally Mrs. Kis and Mrs. Kovács leave their homes, usually to attend church and meet old friends in the congregation. Besides attending church services now and then, they occasionally meet their contemporaries in the church hall at benefit bingo parties, baby showers,[8] birthday parties, wedding dinners, and more often at funerals. Women of the immigrant generation contribute their ethnic cooking to the get-togethers. Mrs. Kis is especially popular for her sausage- and noodle-making. The communal preparation of well-liked ethnic specialties is a favorite pastime in the Hungarian churches of the area. The women of the church sell the delicacies in order to increase the meager parish budget. At the same time, the communal work of twenty to thirty women is a unique survival of customary social work of women in the Old Country. While the dull manual work is being performed, the women sing songs; tell tales, jokes, and legends; gossip; and trade home remedies and ethnic kitchen recipes.

Visits to the doctor for checkups also yield experiences with which our storytellers enrich their narrative stock. They love to talk to doctors and nurses about the condition of their health, and they enjoy medical attention, especially since Medicare is free for them. Receiving "shots," taking medication, undressing in the doctor's office, and watching other patients all generate countless humorous stories with both women. They also like to talk about diseases and cures. In spite of their frequent visits to doctors and nurses, Mrs. Kis and Mrs. Kovács are profoundly interested in traditional home remedies and occasionally resort to them in addition to modern health care.

Traditional entertainers of a diminishing immigrant generation, Mrs. Kis and Mrs. Kovács live happily and enjoy every minute of their limited possibilities to display their talents. They prepare themselves with special enthusiasm for their last public appearance. They look forward to the day when they will receive all their beloved friends and relatives. They will then be dressed up in their Sunday best, with new hairdos and scarlet nailpolish; beautifully rejuvenated by the expert hand of the embalmer, surrounded by flowers, they will be awaiting their guests in the reception room of the funeral home. As in the Old Country village, the farewell reception of the acculturated Hungarian-American in the funeral chapel is of extreme importance. No one regrets saving for the funeral what they would never spend on doctors' bills. Mrs. Kovács, for example, has two thousand dollars in her bank account, but her sons have a hard time making her accept money for her medicine.

When I helped the two narrators to meet personally, they were thoroughly delighted. They did not run out of wordplay, jokes, and witty quibbling. Verbal sparring continued for hours until they were quite out of breath. They were grateful for the afternoon full of laughter. They recalled storytelling in the Old Country and in the Gary of their youth. "It isn't worth bringing us together," said Mrs. Kis in a brief pause of laughter. "Once we start cracking jokes, nice and ugly come one after the other." Upon which Mrs. Kovács poured out a load of dirty jokes which she allegedly had told to people in the church hall during a bingo party break. "You are a hell of a woman, Mrs. Kovács!" said the men, and the minister avoided looking in her eyes because of embarrassment. Both Mrs. Kis and Mrs. Kovács are typical village jokesters. Their style of narration is similar in many respects, but it also differs.

Mrs. Kis was born in 1882 in a village in southern Hungary. "Born on New Year's Eve," she says with emphasis, "I was the thirteenth child of my mother." She likes to stress the peculiarities of her childhood. The father, an old widower, married the young midwife of the community, who seemed to be the target of village gossip because of her profession, which caused her to be away mostly at night. "People told me, I do not belong to my father. My real father was a big millionaire." Telling about her mother, Aunt Katie pictures an outgoing young woman who liked to dance and sing. She has told the episodes of her mother's life so many times that each has become a refined, well-rounded narrative. She indicates her mother's voice modulation, sings her favorite songs, and shows how she danced. Because her mother did not love her, Mrs. Kis was brought up by her father's sister, an unwed mother whose tragic fate is one of Mrs. Kis's fine epics. Mrs. Kis finished two years in grade school and took up work as a kitchen helper at the estate of the local squire. She was seventeen when the young coachman married her. "Not because of the property," she explained. "Father owned four acres—he was too proud to become a slave of the earth as peasants are."

Her husband left Mrs. Kis with two girls when he went to the United States in 1909. She joined him in Gary in 1913. Her disappointment at beholding the barren land for which she had abandoned house and property is the source of another dramatic story. The daughters did not recognize their father waiting at the depot. There were only shacks on the barren sand hills, and stakes marked the line of the future Broadway. Had she come here to live in misery? Mrs. Kis raised her hands above her head, wringing them with emotion, and said, "I will not stay here. I will go back home." But there was no place to go, because the war broke out. The Kis family shared two rooms with another Hungarian family. Mr. Kis worked in the foundry; Katie went to do housework in American homes. She tells a whole cycle of dialect jokes about the troubles of Hungarian women not knowing English, including many familiar ones, as if they happened to her. But, in fact, neither she nor her husband needed to learn English, because all their contacts at the factory and in the neighborhood were with Hungarians. They bought the lot and built the house in which Mrs. Kis now lives. Everything was paid off by the time Mr. Kis planned to retire, but he was not to enjoy the fruits of hard labor. He was sixty when a mishap in the foundry caused his death. Two years later a good friend of Mrs. Kis, a widower, proposed to the widow. Their adherence to different faiths, however, caused trouble. The husband-to-be, a Catholic, did not want to give up his religion, nor did Mrs. Kis. The Hungarian Catholic congregation denounced them because they had set up house together without getting married, whereas the Hungarian Church of Christ accepted them as they were. Mrs. Kis relates the story of her second marriage in funny and exciting episodes. She never even acknowledged her mate of ten years as a real husband, but consistently talked about "my Kis" with whom she spent the happiest years of her life.

This sketchy life history shows how Mrs. Kis usually formulates her narratives as episodes of her own life. This does not mean that her stories are not in traditional folklore form. On the contrary, Mrs. Kis's stories, as shown in repeated recordings, are well-shaped traditional and variable folk narratives rooted in actual facts. The wealthiest body of her stories seems to come from the old home village and is based on childhood memories. She reshapes them over and over again, describing village life with an almost ethnographic authenticity. She often inserts her stories into the frame of a ceremony, visualizing a baptism, a wedding party, a pig-killing dinner, or a dance she once attended. Getting involved with her narration, she brings the typical village characters to life. She plays the parts of each, imitating the tipsy, the haughty, the bashful, and the braggart.

As for anecdotes, Mrs. Kis prefers the spicy and the lewd, if not the definitely obscene. However, she is most at home in the realm of the supernatural. She firmly believes in magic healing, the curative power of herbs, the evil eye, and the wisdom of seers and fortune-tellers. She also believes in witchcraft. Her favorite stories are genuine folk legends, and in telling them she pictures the village community where she was born as a place plagued by malicious witches. She has known the witches who used to sit on the street corners around midnight spinning hemp and beating up young people who dared to be outside in the late hours. She herself was chased once by a witch who turned herself into a dog. Another time, a young woman fooled her husband by changing into a rooster, and another one tortured a young fellow who preferred another girl instead of her own daughter. Mrs. Kis's father also had firsthand experiences with the supernatural. He attempted to learn superhuman skills at the crossroads, and the fairy folk later made him dance with his own boat.[9]

The stories that originated in the United States differ from the earlier themes, and the scene and sources of inspiration have changed. These narratives reflect the experiences of immigrant and urban life. A group of stories in Mrs. Kis's repertoire focuses on hardship in adjusting to the unknown environment. Another group of stories is less homogeneous. It gives an idea of how and to what extent mass media replace folk tradition as a source of material for new folklore forms. The latest sensations from newspapers, magazines, radio, and television are passed on from mouth to mouth to create well-rounded oral narratives about the crimes, love affairs, and mysteries of the metropolis. The newer anecdotes of Mrs. Kis are partly old forms set in modern context and put in the first person. They tend to be more concerned with sexuality than are the older stories.

Mrs. Kis is a verbose narrator; she expands even brief jokes with a lengthy introduction. She meticulously prepares the comical situations to make the punch line more effective. Her manner of rendition is not only epic but dramatic. She acts out her stories, accompanying them with body and facial motions characterizing the actors. She involves herself in the narrative both as a spectator and as a participant in the event. In other words, she claims credence for her realistic narratives that shift between legend and anecdote. She easily improvises stories upon suggestion. It occasionally happened that she did not know a story I asked for, though she did not admit it. As an accomplished raconteur, in order to gain time until she could find something, she would begin: "It was long ago, to be sure, my lady

. . . I was a little girl when this happened . . . isn't that strange? Believe me, this really happened . . ." and so on. Then if she remembered something, often half-heard and half-improvised scraps, she happily recited it instead of what I asked for. Once I asked her whether she had heard of "Diana of the Dunes," the mystery woman who, according to historical sources, used to live on the sand dunes.[10] The story Mrs. Kis immediately started had nothing to do with this subject. On another occasion she gave the girl a different name, and the third time she told me the story, the heroine was a close acquaintance of hers who occasionally sought her advice. My interest inspired Mrs. Kis to spin a handsome sentimental story.

Mrs. Kis's narratives are characterized by her personal involvement. All of them stem from a direct experience. As already noted, she has an extremely lively imagination, which carries her far from everyday reality, from solitude and silence. At night or in the early morning, when she lingers between sleep and wakefulness, the moving shadows and the cracking of old furniture acquire meaning. Her dreams and hallucinations are of great importance to her. She remembers the happy and the sorrowful days of the past and lives them again in her memories, and she tells about the colorful play of her fantasy if there is anyone around to listen. Even if she is alone during the day, she might recite a wordplay or a rhyme, sing an old song, or tell a story aloud and laugh or cry at its outcome. Things going on in the neighborhood also stimulate her imagination. Even one example demonstrates her ability to build up a story around mere observations. Mrs. Kis in this case tells about the death of a neighbor with whom she was never actually on speaking terms. The story begins at noon, with the neighbor walking his dog around his grape arbor. Mrs. Kis yells at him jokingly from her porch, "Hi, neighbor! When can I come to the grape harvest?" "You just wait," came the answer, "we will have a dance, you and me!" This jolly conversation was shaped by our narrator only to sharpen the contrasting gloom of the second part of the story. The sound of an unusual vehicle makes her look out some time later, and who is there but the undertaker with a hearse. He is a familiar person, a prominent character in Gary; everyone knows him. Mrs. Kis converses with him, and the surprise turn ends on a tragic note: the same neighbor she joked with earlier had died.

Mrs. Kovács was born in 1894, not far from the hometown of Mrs. Kis. Her father came to the United States in 1906, and a year later her mother and the children followed. Margie, the oldest, went to work in a cigar factory at thirteen because the family, with four small children, needed the money. Worried about the young girl living as a roomer in a big city, her parents gave her in marriage at fifteen. Her short girlhood was the happiest season of her life. She bought nice dresses for herself and went to dances with other girls. She was reluctant to accept her parents' decision, but had learned to obey. The thirty-one-year-old factory foreman of Hungarian background meant security and well-being. A family picture made at the wedding shows her silent revolt: she has obscured the face of her husband and that of herself with the bridal veil.

As soon as the construction work in the Gary region had started, the family moved there. The father worked for U.S. Steel, the husband for Inland Steel Company. All the brothers and sisters of Mrs. Kovács stayed in Gary, and soon an extended family grew up around her. Six children were born to her, and today she has twenty grandchildren. Most of them are hardworking skilled laborers, respected in the community. Some of the grandchildren attend colleges and universities. They all want to help "Grandma," to make her life happy. But she does not want modern luxuries and the gadgets they bring her. She was definitely angry when her youngest daughter "wasted her money" on a bathroom scale. The elegant dresses, shoes, and hats they give her rest among mothballs in the closet. She does not need them, and maybe sometime her grandchildren might like to have them. She ardently opposes the wastefulness so typical among young Americans. Her house is full of odds and ends that she refuses to throw away.

Mr. Kovács, an obstinate carouser and a boozer, was not easy to live with. Often on paydays he came home from the tavern, beat his wife, and chased his children from the house. However, Mrs. Kovács overcame hard times because of her happy disposition and her strong inclination to humor. One tragedy overshadowed her life: her youngest son was accidentally shot to death at fourteen by a schoolmate. She still cannot speak of it without tears, remembering the fatal afternoon. Even if it was difficult for her to cope with her husband's whims, she treated him with the care and reverence required in the traditional peasant family. Fortunately, her husband's love for convivial evenings sometimes gave her the opportunity to attend parties and have a good time in the Hungarian community. Mr. Kovács was an outstanding singer, and his wife learned all the songs he knew and has sung at the Hungarian festivals in Gary. She does not have a musical ear, but she insisted on singing some two hundred folksongs into the tape recorder as they came back to her while she was telling stories. Some of the wives of Mr. Kovacs's drinking partners became lifetime friends because of their common lot. The couple spent much time with the Tóths, for example, and their relationship was based mainly on their mutual interest in joke-telling.[11] In the old system it was not becoming for women to leave their homes without their husbands. Mrs. Kovács and her friends, however, always found an excuse to have fun. Whenever they wanted to see a movie or a show, or play cards, they would stop briefly at the get-togethers of the church ladies and then take off. They were always eager to assist with food preparation for the festive occasions of the community.

The social life and the rituals of the Hungarian community were the framework within which the personality of Mrs. Kovács could find its expression. She is much more a social entertainer than Mrs. Kis, the epic narrator with a vivid imagination and a deep feeling for the supernatural. Mrs. Kovács, in contrast, does not lose herself in lengthy dreams; she likes action. She loves company, and the more people around the better she performs. To make fun, even to play practical jokes, is natural for her, even if the audience can be reached today only by telephone. As soon as she thinks of something worth telling, she calls her acquaintances and tells it.

Mrs. Kovács has been a widow for fourteen years. The first few years brought her the freedom and relief she dreamed of, and she quickly became an enthusiastic organizer of social activities and an accomplished performer in the Hungarian community. She recited poems at national celebrations, wrote verses and greetings for name days, and taught Hungarian dances to the girls. The schoolchildren learned from her how to greet their teacher in traditional verse. She joined the carol singers at Christmas from house to house. Mrs. Kovács likes to masquerade above all and seizes every opportunity to dress up and act. As other informants tell us, she was always ready to put on her husband's suit, hat, and boots, paint a mustache with soot, and fool around at Halloween, at pig-killing dinners, and at wedding parties. Many people still laugh at the fun they had when she appeared at a wedding with a carrot fastened to the zipper of her pants and danced in the traditional bridal dance. However, she did not need a special occasion to put on an act. Another time, for example, she visited a neighbor who complained that the tinker did not come to fix her pots and pans. Masquerading as the tinker, she hammered flat all the useless pots beyond repair. When the neighbor complained to her about the clumsy tinker, she gave her some of her own pots. She would do such things even today if she had the opportunity.

Mrs. Kovács is an intelligent woman, still interested in increasing her knowledge. She is especially concerned with medical terms and with the "secrets" of the English language. She learned from the schoolbooks of her children, but her speech is poor and she tries to widen her vocabulary by noting words and idioms not heard before. She keeps a diary, she writes poems, and she learned how to write letters from a popular book of correspondence. She likes to watch TV shows, especially the comedies ("The Red Skelton Hour") and the spectacles ("The Ball-Dance"). She avoids anything violent, exciting, or horrible.

Cracking jokes is Mrs. Kovács's favorite pastime. Her humorous skills range from the descriptions of comical situations to the well-developed anecdote. All genres are represented in her repertoire. Life is full of funny turns for her, and whether she experienced these herself or heard them from others, she tells the stories with much pleasure. The older part of her repertoire contains traditional jokes and anecdotes that she brought along from her home village, or heard from older immigrants in Gary, or bartered from joke-telling part-ners. Besides a valuable body of gypsy anecdotes, numbskull stories (Kovács and Maróti 1966), and "slippery" parson jokes, she has a fine set of dialect stories on words mistaken for something else and oddities of the different ethnic groups. She does not hesitate to make fun of her own ignorance, and tells a "true story" about how she allowed her children to stay away from school by not knowing what it meant to "play hookey."[12]

The great majority of Mrs. Kovács's stories are pithy jokes, how-ever, sometimes even reduced to the minimum explanation of a pro-verbial saying. These color her conversation, as do her anecdotes. As already noted, it is her technique to insert jokes into everyday speech, to illustrate how she or someone else fared. When she could not open a door that was stuck, for example, and I offered a knife to force it open, she was immediately ready with a saying, leading to a joke: "Let's try, as the man in the tale said," and then came an obscene joke. Her improvised jokes are as innumerable as her sources, most often everyday events and her talks with and observations of whoever happens to come by.

Mrs. Kovács does not have too many biographical stories. Her memories of the Old Country are fading, so she does not have more than a couple of episodes of her childhood. The stories formulated on her experiences in the United States are also quite weak. She has some stories about her girlhood in the cigar factory, about the life of the family during the Depression when they tried farming and went bankrupt, about the horrible ordeal of the family when gangsters tried to force her oldest son to enter their gang. There are also some horror stories from neighborhood gossip, radio, television, and newspapers. But as we have seen already, Mrs. Kovács does not like to see the tragic aspects of life. She is extremely sensitive; she laughs easily but also sheds her tears easily.

In spite of her rational worldview she has told me many legends and items of folk medicine. She does not believe in them but she has heard them from relatives, friends, and neighbors all her life. She does not pass them on voluntarily; she told them only at my request. However, she believes that dreams come true and that experiences of pregnant women can result in markings on their unborn children. She has tried magic formulas for getting rid of styes and warts on herself and on her children. "I do not believe in it, but it cannot do harm," she explained to me.

We conclude from this survey that the two storytellers remain as two traditional types mainly because of their constant contact with each other (Dégh 1969). Both of them are community narrators who draw inspiration from and depend heavily on the immediate response of an audience. In their present situation, however, they do not have an actual audience. Resorting to the only means to overcome isolation and the loss of storytelling opportunities caused by the distances in the city, they use the telephone as the vehicle for exchanging stories. Mrs. Kis is a very imaginative raconteur. Her style is rich and abundant; she improvises easily and switches skillfully from the epic to the dramatic presentation. Mrs. Kovács, on the other hand, is a high-spirited performer and jester, with a strong feeling for the humorous. Uprooted from their original setting, both narrators were compelled to avail themselves of whatever materials they could find in an environment hostile to traditional folklore. The composition of their repertoire thus became a mixture of old and new elements, each of them choosing whatever suited her personality best. Autobiographical stories usually become particularly important with migrating workers who enter a new community, because newcomers can always tell something interesting and different from the usual.[13] This is also true of Mrs. Kis, whose old memories were polished by the many retellings into magnificent prose narratives, as refined as her most archaic belief legends.

The common ground between Mrs. Kis and Mrs. Kovács is mainly their preference for dialect jokes, their keen sense of the comical in human errors and frailties. Their abilities to observe people, others as well as themselves, and to express themselves in jokes and jocular wordplays are based on common experiences. Both women also have a remarkable interest in erotic themes. They surpass the usual amount of obscenity that occurs in the jokes and talk of old peasant women. Both of them favor discussing sexual affairs, and above all they love to tell about their own past erotic experiences and project them to the present. Jocular remarks about a "boyfriend," an old fool, real and imaginary marriage proposals, and indecent passes are often the topic of phone talks, winding up in sensual laughter.

Our Gary phone narrators raise a question that was not a problem when storytelling was observed exclusively in traditional communities. We took it for granted that tradition, performer, and a participating audience had an equal share in the creation of oral narratives (Dégh 1969). It was difficult to imagine how the quality of the narrative would be affected by the dominance of one of the three. However, assuming that the tale audience strongly influences the creative personality of the narrator, the case of Mrs. Kis and Mrs. Kovács demonstrates that the creative individual can overcome unfavorable conditions, can survive and find her means of expression. It is definitely worthwhile to investigate storytelling situations in modern urban life.[14]

NOTES

1. I recently visited one of my most outstanding folklore informants, who had retired and moved with his wife to Florida. Their newly built home, their thrifty economy, their Weltanschauung, and their folk medicine were those of the farmer who never left his home village on the Great Hungarian Plains. The couple had

entered a community of Hungarians of similar extraction on the west coast of Florida whose members reinforced the old values retrieved after fifty to sixty years.

2. Mrs. Kis, who had lived in Gary for fifty-four years, has never seen the center of Chicago, just twenty-seven miles away. "I had no relatives or acquaintances there," she explained. Mrs. Kovács and her husband used to visit the Hungarian ethnic section "Burnside" in South Chicago almost every weekend. They had a good time in the settlement created for the workers of the Pullman plant, but they never went downtown. Only recently, when her youngest daughter, the wife of a successful businessman, took her to a good restaurant, has she seen the Loop. She still speaks about this experience, incorporating what she saw into a märchen-like story embellished by traditional motifs.

3. One example of the unanimous statement of our informants will suffice: "Everybody was Hungarian at that time. The store owner, the saloon keeper, the butcher—and there were no church services in any other language but Hungarian. The mailman was Hungarian and the policeman was Hungarian. Even the bosses, the foremen in the workshop, were Hungarians. When my auntie died at seventy-five, she could not say more than 'good morning' in English, though she had been here for forty-five years."

4. Mrs. Kovács told me once how she had to teach her American daughter-in-law good manners. The young woman used to open the door for departing guests, which could be understood as an insult—as if she were urging them to go.

5. Mrs. Kovács once called a woman who apologized and cut her short because she was busy baking a cake. The storyteller was too embarrassed to repeat the call because "she had the same excuse a month ago, so she obviously does not want to talk to me."

6. Veszprém County is in western Hungary. Mrs. Nagy is an excellent informant in folk religion and in folk medicine. She claims to cure by magic. She told us that Americans are not so "well educated" as the folks in her hometown used to be, when she was a girl.

7. Elderly people usually idealize the life of the old community and blame affluence for its dissolution. Both Mrs. Kis and Mrs. Kovács stated, "We were all brothers and sisters during the Depression. And now? Everyone wants to cut the throat of the other, even if they are related by blood. Men were out of work, and they built their own church together in 1932. Women did the cooking and we talked, played cards, and sang all day long. But today? Everyone is busy making more money than they ever can spend but everyone wants to beat the other. There is no friendship anymore."

8. Hungarian-Americans have adapted baby showers and bridal showers, according to their standards. The godmother of the bride or expectant young mother throws a party for female relatives, who donate basic necessities in the form of a gift.

9. This legend has a wide distribution in Hungary, and Berze Nagy (1957) included it in his tale type classification under No. 814*. More recently, Balassa assessed the unpublished versions (1963:531).

10. This eccentric recluse caught the fancy of local news reporters around 1916 (Moore 1959:601–605).

11. At a single session the couple told me 120 jokes, most of them traditional Aarne-Thompson types.

12. To play hookey is to skip school. In the story, Mrs. Kovác's children asked their mother every morning if they could play hookey. Not knowing, she always told them: "All right, dears, you be good boys and take care of yourselves."

13. The realistic rendition of human experiences has long been known to students of the folk narrative. These were given different names: "Geschichte" (Wesselski), "Memorabile" (Jolles), "Memorat" (Sydow), "Bylichki" (Sokolov), "Erzählung wirklicher Ereignisse" (Pomeranceva), "Alltagserzählung" (Bausinger), "True stories" (Dobos), and so on. However, the interest in the genre—or rather the mixture of genres, cutting across more recognized and more stable forms—is rather recent, having begun when urban folklore became a major issue (Bausinger 1958, 1968, 1975; Dobos 1964; Neumann 1967).

14. This study is based on fieldwork research of the Calumet Hungarians carried out jointly with Andrew Vázsonyi from 1964 to 1967.

This essay has been published in slightly different form under the title "Two Old World Narrators in Urban Setting" in a volume entitled *Kontakte und Grenzen: Probleme der Volks-, Kultur- und Socialforschung, Festschrift für Gerhard Heilfurth zum 60. Gebenstag* (Göttingen: Verlag Otto Schwartz, 1969).

· 2 ·
THE VAGINAL SERPENT
AND OTHER THEMES FROM
MEXICAN-AMERICAN WOMEN'S LORE
Rosan A. Jordan

T HE HISPANIC ideal of modest and submissive behavior for women and dominant, aggressive behavior for males is a familiar one (see Alvirez and Bean 1976:278–279; Grebler, Moore, and Guzman 1970:366; Senour 1977:329–330). Within the family, the husband/father's authority is seen as absolute. The wife/mother's role is characterized by self-sacrifice, service to the needs of others, and nurturance. Her activities are narrowly confined to home and family, and mothering—bearing and raising children—is seen as her primary function. For men, sexual relations outside marriage are permitted or even encouraged, and fathering children (legitimate or illegitimate) is considered proof of virility. Training for these adult roles begins in childhood, as girls are given much less freedom than boys and are expected to help with housework and child care. As adolescents, girls are watched over carefully to ensure their sexual purity, while boys are encouraged to begin developing sexual prowess, which is thought to be proof of masculinity. In a summary of the literature on the psychology of Mexican-American women, Maria Nieto Senour writes: "In comparison with people of other cultures in the United States, Chicanos are said to dominate their wives, overprotect their daughters, and expect passive compliance in return" (1977:330).

While the patterns described above are generalized and tell us little about how people actually live their lives, they do give us some indication of the cultural pressures to which individual behavior is a response. It is my purpose in this chapter to use folklore as a source of information for examining how Mexican-American women actually view their culturally assigned roles and how they respond to cultural pressures of the sort just mentioned—that is, respond symbolically if not in individual actions. Folklore is an important means of expressing attitudes, ideology, and worldview, whether consciously or unconsciously. And if folklore is sometimes indirect and in need of analysis to interpret its encoded message, so too it may be a vehicle for learning aspects of a culture which are seldom or never stated in other ways. Women's folklore tells us things that social strictures or psychological repression prevent women from otherwise saying—things at variance with the official ideal of the culture. Narratives sometimes express ideas and feelings that would never emerge from a questionnaire or an interview, or they may express them more powerfully.

For example, in 1967–68 I collected from three sisters named Mary, Betty, and Janie—all Mexican-American women born and still living in Texas—a number of legends, memorates, and family sagas that present a picture of the world as a precarious place for women, a world where women are vulnerable, fearful, and often mistreated or despised. Circulating among Mexican-American women in Texas, there is a body of lore that centers on what I have referred to elsewhere as the "vaginal serpent" theme (Jordan de Caro 1973). This lore consists of legendary and personal narratives about snakes or lizards pursuing and sexually assaulting women and reveals much about the sexual fears and fantasies of the Mexican-American women who tell them. I first became aware of the vaginal serpent tradition when one of the sisters, Mary, decided to help me with a collecting project by recording some stories she had heard as a child in West Texas while listening to older women talk:

> This is about the things that old ladies talk about, you know, when they're out in the country. And they said that before there was any outhouses and you had to go to the bathroom behind the bushes, you had to be very careful because there was kinds of animals that liked women and would get inside.
>
> And there was this girl that was real young, and some kind of animal got inside of her, and so she got pregnant; and she was *like*

she was pregnant. She had morning sickness and she started getting fat, so her parents thought that she had been running around with a boy, you know, that somebody had gotten her pregnant. They used to beat her up and try to get her to tell who the boy was that was responsible for her condition. But she didn't know what they were talking about, because, you know, in those days they would never tell their children about the facts of life or anything.

So this went on for some time, a few months, and so one day they went out to town or someplace and they locked her in the house, and when they came back—they were gone I guess a couple of days or so—and when they came back they found it, that she had given birth to a whole bunch of little animals, and they were eating her up. And she was dead.

Mary then told the following story:

And there's this type of snake. It has many different names, and the people in West Texas call them *chirrioneras*.[1] And this is a real funny snake—grows real long and likes women. And they whistle, you know, like regular men—wolf whistle, you know. They whistle to women as they go by.

And there's this story that was told also, about this lady that was pregnant. And this was a bunch of families that lived out in the country. These families lived out in the country, and the men would work out in the fields. And the ladies would stay at home and take care of the children and, oh, at a certain hour they would go and take their husbands their lunch. So all the women would walk together, and as they went by a certain tree out in the woods, there was one of these snakes, you know, *chirrioneras*. And it would whistle at the women as they went by. And so they didn't like that, and they would tell their husbands. They said, "Well, stay together and he won't bother you."

So this lady that was pregnant, she was getting pretty fat and she couldn't walk as fast as the other ladies, and so every day she would get a little further behind. So toward the end before she had her baby, she was walking and all the ladies walked faster, so they left her behind because she walked too slowly. And they got over there where the men were, and her husband said, "Where's my wife?" And they said, "Well, she was walking too slow and so we just left her behind because we were going to late"—you know, if they didn't hurry. So he said, "Where did you leave her?" And they said, "Well, just as we went through the woods. As we were going through the woods she got behind, so we just came on without her."

So he went out to the woods to look for his wife, and when he got to that tree he could see that she was laying down under that tree that they complained that the snake would whistle at. And so when he got there . . . , the baby had been born, and the snake had choked the baby, was wrapped around the baby. And she was dead.

Questioned about the source of this story, Mary said that her older sister Janie had told it to her recently.

A few months later I had the chance to expand this information. Mary's sister Betty was temporarily living with her, and Mary asked her if she remembered hearing a story about some little animal that liked women. Their conversation went like this:

Betty: It's just like a water dog, is what it is.[2] Only it's real slimy. It's not a snake; it's a lizard. Well, it's more like a water dog. I don't exactly remember what they're called in Spanish.

Mary: And one of those crawled inside some girl. I guess she was supposed to have been asleep, wasn't she?

Betty: She was asleep close to a barnyard, 'cause that's where they are. Around where there's lots of manure and filth. You've seen them haven't you? They're brown and about so long [eight inches]. They're water dogs.

Mary: And when one got inside this girl they thought she was pregnant.

Betty: Everyone thought she had been playing around. And they condemned her and everything. The whole town shamed her. But this one old woman, she noticed that the girl was real pale and unhealthy, and she said, "That girl's still a virgin. Something's wrong." And so she took the girl and had her lie down, and she applied hot towels on her stomach and drew out a whole litter of those things.

Mary: Who told you about that?

Betty: Do you remember Doña Jovita who lived near us in Colorado? There was a whole bunch of those things over there, and that Doña Jovita told us not to go over there. I was about thirteen. And we used to go over there and throw rocks at them.

Author: Was that really supposed to have happened?

Betty: She said that it happened a long time ago when she was young, to a girl in her village who was about fourteen.

Betty, a few years older than her sister and a rich source of narrative material, then asked Mary, "Did you tell her about the *Negro* and the *chirrionera?*" and proceeded to relate the following three stories, two of them supposedly accounts of personal encounters:

The *chirrioneras* are snakes that chase girls. One time Great-grand-mother—you know, Nanita—she was walking out in the field and a *chirrionera* got in her skirt. She was having her period and he could smell that. And he got in her skirt and she couldn't get him out, and finally she had to take off her skirt and leave it there. She came home in her pettiskirt. Yeah, they can smell it when a woman is having her period, and they like it, and they try to get up there.

And then, when Grandmother first came from Mexico there was this white woman that a *chirrionera* got up her vagina and almost drove her crazy. Yeah, you can imagine it wiggling around in there. They finally got this *Negro* to come and do it to her, and that snake bit him, you know, on the end of his thing, and that is how they got it out. And that happened out there. I guess Mother could tell you who the woman was it happened to. And a dirty old *Negro* did it to her to get it out. They paid him a hundred dollars to do it to her. . . .

Oh, I don't know if I should tell this story or not. It's about Grandmother. She told me once I better take her seriously when she told me this. 'Cause you know I'm skeptical about a lot of the stuff she says. In spite of all I've seen, I still don't always believe a lot of things. But anyway, she told me that this is true. When she was nursing Cosme, she used to wake up in the morning and she was dry. And she wouldn't have nothing to give Cosme. She had blisters around her nipples, and she was dry. And she'd mix up some *atole* [corn flour gruel] to feed him in the mornings, but he would still be hungry, and she didn't have enough to give him.

And so someone said something about *chirrioneras*. Do you believe that—you know—what they say that *chirrioneras* milk the cows? The encyclopedia says that's not true, that bull snakes do not milk cows—a *chirrionera* is a bull snake. But they do.

Anyway, she stayed up late one time, and she didn't think she could get much sleep before daylight, but decided just to lie down and rest a little. And so she was just laying there, and she felt it get on top of the covers. And Tío Neo got up and killed it. That was about a half hour before dawn, when people sleep their soundest sleep. And so that's when the snake was coming in. And they say that when the *chirrionera* gets close to you, it hypnotizes you.

So after that the blisters disappeared, after they killed that snake. This really happened. I mean, some of the things may be made up, but I know that to be true.[3]

I learned from talking to other women that the belief in and fear of snakes, lizards, and water dogs which seek to enter women's vaginas is common among Mexican-American women and young girls in West Texas (and elsewhere, although I am not able to judge the extent of the tradition in other places). In 1894, John G. Bourke reported in the *Journal of American Folklore* the existence along the Texas-Mexico border of this tradition associated with the axolotl, which is another name for the water dog, both names referring to the larvae of the salamander. The axolotl, writes Bourke, frequents damp, slimy places, near pools of water and garbage, and "will enter the person of a woman, at certain times, and will remain just as long as would a human foetus. Young girls, at their first change of life, are especially exposed, and will manifest all the symptoms of pregnancy (Bourke 1894:120). A modern Mexican author, Juan José Arreola, cites the chronicles of Bernardo Sahagún as the source of similar warnings about the dangers of bathing in waters inhabited by axolotls. Arreola (1964:32–33) himself notes, "In a town near ours my mother treated a woman who was mortally impregnated with axolotls,"[4] a reference to an event that appears to be identical to Mary's and Betty's stories.

In addition, I found one close analogue from Afro-American tradition in Richard M. Dorson's collection, *American Negro Folktales*, "Girl Swallows Lizard," contributed by a female narrator, Mrs. E. L. Smith. In this text a girl swallows a spring lizard, which "growed inside of her, and got so large till they thought she'd got 'in the wrong path.' And back in those days they mistreated you for anything like that." When the snake is discovered choking the girl, she is rushed to the hospital, and her family "was so ashamed of having 'bused and dogged her" (Dorson 1967:277–278).[5] And from the Ozarks we have a tale recorded by Vance Randolph, as told by Mrs. Marie Wilbur, in which a woman "birthed a live water-moccasin six foot long and nearly ten inches thick" after having swallowed some "balls" her husband found in the creek. She was, we are told, never again the same in the head (Randolph 1958: 31–32). Both the Negro and the Ozark texts have been identified with the extensive tradition of swallowed animals living inside their victims. But they seem also to represent a female rendering of that tradition (both informants are female). Like the narratives and beliefs of Mexican-American women about reptiles penetrating and destroying female bodies, these tales reflect fears and anxieties concerning women's vulnerability to sexual assault, and also pregnancy anxieties. Psychiatrist Karen Horney (1967:129) writes, for example, in reference to the typical fears of early childhood, "What else could be the meaning of the fears of burglars, snakes, wild animals, and thunderstorms, if not the feminine fear of overwhelming forces that can vanquish, penetrate, and destroy?"[6]

The same material may be rendered so that it reflects a male viewpoint. For example, a tale collection by Arkansas folklorist Randolph (1976:34–35) contains a story called "The Half-Wit and the Eel" which is essentially the same story Betty told about the *negro* and the *chirrionera*. The story in the Randolph collection concerns the foolishness of the rich man's daughter who had been playing with eels, and the use of the village half-wit, because no one would be likely to believe him, to retrieve the eel from the girl's vagina by copulating with her. Much is made of the laughter of the good-old-boys in the bar, who scarcely know whether or not to believe the half-wit's story. The narrator of the tale is male, and the details of the story would indicate that its intended audience was male; it may very well, then, reflect concerns of the male psyche. Another example of an obviously male-oriented narrative about a woman with a dangerous snake in her vagina is the Rugby song "Charlotte the Harlot":

Way out in the West where the cactus grows thick,
Where the women are women, and the cowboys come quick,
There lives a fair maiden of forty or more—
Charlotte the Harlot, the cowpuncher's whore.

One night on the prairie her legs opened wide.
A rattlesnake saw it and climbed up inside.
All the cowboys assembled on Saturday nite,
Just to see the vagina that rattles and bites.

CHORUS:

She's filthy, she's nasty, she spits on the floor.
Charlotte the Harlot, the cowpuncher's whore.

One night on the prairie while riding along,
One hand on my saddle and one on my dong,
Who should I spy but that maid I adore—
Charlotte the Harlot the cowpuncher's whore.

I leapt from my saddle and leapt for her crack,
But the damned thing kept rattling and biting me back.
I pulled out my six-gun and aimed for its head.
I pulled the trigger, shot Charlotte instead.

CHORUS REPEATED

The funeral procession was forty miles long,
And all the cowpunchers were singing this song:
Here lies a maiden who never kept score—
Charlotte the Harlot the cowpuncher's whore. *Amen.*[7]

As Betty told the story about the *negro* and the *chirrionera*, however, the emphasis was placed on the discomfort, helplessness, and humiliation of the woman. And Betty grouped the tale with others that emphasize women's vulnerability to physical assault. For example, she led into the tale with an account of her great-grandmother's being pursued by a snake intent on violating her person. Thus when Gershon Legman (1964:490–491) refers to the tale in the Randolph collection as "a vagina dentata story rationalized as of a serpent 'lost' in the woman's body," his comment can apply only to the male version of the story. In fact, the major point here may be that the story itself means nothing separated from its cultural context, and scholars have not often noticed that the male culture is not universal.

The texts cited above were grouped together by Mary and Betty themselves, and the picture the stories present of life for Mexican-American women is a bleak one indeed. The women in the stories exist in a world where their sexuality makes them constantly vulnerable. They are liable to sexual assault by snakes or lizards and are mistreated by their families, who wish to restrict their sexual activities. They suffer, are humiliated, and are vindicated only in dying. Demonstrations of female sexuality such as pregnancy or menstruation make them even more vulnerable. They die giving birth; snakes steal their mother's milk. In several of the stories, other women turn their backs on the suffering of the victim.

The repertoires of the three sisters, Mary, Betty, and Janie, include other personal narratives that also reflect a vision of the world as a precarious place for females. A bit of family saga related by Betty, for example, tells of Indians in Mexico abducting her great-grandmother:

> This band of Indians rode through the village and stole all the women, you know. And this Indian had Nanita up on a horse. And she was nursing a baby at that time, and so when he was riding away with her he squeezed her and the milk squirted out of her breasts. The Indian got so mad he threw her off into an old *nopal* [prickly-pear cactus]. When she got back she was all scratched up. [*Laughs.*] Nurse your babies! You never know when you may be stolen by an Indian.

In a more somber vein, all three sisters told me separately about their grandmother's experiences in Mexico. Mary told me, "Grandmother's earliest recollection was that her sister was killed on the road. Her sister was stoned. And she kept seeing her come up to her, all bloody. Later they found her." Betty gives more details of the same story, which she heard from her mother:

> Grandmother's sister was married, and her husband went away and was gone for a long time. Eventually she met another man she liked, and he was nice to her, and so she was living with him and she was expecting a baby when her husband returned. And her husband and her lover took her out on the *barranca* and killed her. They stoned her. Her husband and her lover.
>
> Anyway, Mother was playing outside and she saw her aunt appear all battered and bleeding. But when she told her mother, she told her not to say any more about it, that she was imagining things. But then the next day they came and told her her sister was dead. [Mother] thinks it was her *alma* [soul], you know, that [her aunt] came to say goodbye to Mother because she loved her.

The grandmother also had painful memories of her own marriage as a girl in Mexico. She told Mary that her husband had gotten tired of her and kicked her out, whereupon she took her children and lived up in the mountains in a lean-to. In Janie's words:

> Grandma once told me she used to lie in a cave. And that man, her husband, liked to go with women. Once he went by where she could see him. And he was real mean to her. I thought it was awful. She said one time a bear came in the cave and she was afraid he would eat her and her children. One time we were by ourselves, and she started telling me about the kind of life she used to lead. That man would hit her and Nanita. She cried. She said she was happy we had a good way of life compared to what she had known.

Parallels to the young girl in Mary's story who gives birth to a litter of "little animals" and dies after being falsely suspected by her family of sexual misbehavior may be detected in several other of Mary's stories. Speaking of other relatives who live in rural West Texas, Mary told me that one teenage girl, accused of flirtatious behavior by her parents, was subsequently not allowed out of the house, not even to attend school. Similarly, Mary remembered from her high school days in the city a girl who had stayed overnight with a girlfriend, with her father's permission. Since her parents were separating, however, the mother remained suspicious of her daughter and took her the next morning to a doctor to have her examined. Mary could imagine the girl's shame, for "everyone at school the next day knew what had happened." It is significant that the only märchen Mary remembered from her youth (told originally by her grandmother) had a similar theme (the misunderstood daughter cast out and denigrated but later vindicated—basically Type 533 with the Love Like Salt framework).

If women learn early to fear sexual violation, apparently they are never expected to enjoy sex. Ari Kiev, in his study of Mexican-Americans in San Antonio, writes that "a wife's enjoyment of sexual relations is often considered a justifiable cause for suspicion of infidelity. . . . The sexual exploits of men occur with unrespectable women or prostitutes, never with wives" (1968:59). The dangers of not repressing one's sexuality are expressed in the following narrative of Betty's:

> Mother told me about a woman in Mexico who had relations with a dog and gave birth to a litter of animals with human faces. They killed them; and they had to take the girl out and kill her because she was more animal than human by then.

Gershon Legman writes that stories about women having sexual relations with animals are told to demonstrate "the sexual greediness and depraved appetites of women in general" (1968:212). They function among women as a reminder of the necessity of maintaining control over and of suppressing sexual feelings.[8]

Thus, in addition to portraying women as abused and misused by others, the narratives we have been discussing also reveal a certain degree of self-hatred in women and a distrust of their own sexuality; woman's sexual nature, they seem to say, is instrumental in bringing about her suffering. In another of the sisters' stories, which they remembered being told by their mother, the punishment of a woman who refused to feed her infant was that each time she refused, her breast would grow longer until she finally had to sling it over her shoulder. The obvious message of the story is that women who resent having to breast-feed their babies are courting disaster (and perhaps that they are abnormal), but it is interesting that the punishment takes the form of an accentuated and grotesque distortion of the mother's female appearance. However, Mary's joke about an ignorant farm girl whose display of sexuality frightened away her boyfriend, while ridiculing the girl's ignorance of properly modest behavior, also reveals the potency inherent in the female sexuality it denigrates. In this story, told to Mary by a female friend from Mexico, a naive farm girl lifts her skirt and boasts that she has three more of "these," referring to the underpants her city cousin has brought her, but not realizing she has forgotten to put them on. Her boyfriend faints.

The women's narratives we have looked at so far, then, show women to be not so much passive and submissive as helpless and vulnerable, and not so much modest and pure as fearful and self-loathing where sexuality is concerned. But what about the emphasis in Hispanic cultures on bearing and raising children as women's primary function? The vaginal serpent cycle of stories almost certainly reflects anxieties related to bearing children as well as sexual anxieties. The widely known narratives about the legendary figure known as La Llorona, or the Weeping Woman, give us some insight into Mexican-American cultural attitudes toward mothering activities and into the conflicts and stresses that Mexican-American women experience in relation to the mother role.

Bacil F. Kirtley wrote, "Probably the legend of 'La Llorona'—'The Weeping Woman'—has permeated Mexican folklore more thoroughly than any similar theme" (1960:155). The legend concerns a poor and humble woman who, grief-stricken at being cast off by her rich lover who is intent on marrying a woman of his own class, murders her children, commits suicide, and ever afterward roams the streets mourning their loss and frightening those who hear her. The memorate form concerns the narrators' accounts of encounters with the figure of La Llorona but may allude to her history incidentally.

The figure (and the name) of La Llorona is almost universally known to Mexican-Americans in the Southwest also. Elaine Miller testifies to the popularity of the legend complex in Los Angeles but notes that the most easily collected texts have to do with encounters with La Llorona rather than with biographical information about her. She states, "It seems to be a rare individual who can offer any information beyond the fact that the *llorona* was a woman who drowned (or killed) her children and was subsequently condemned by God to wander in search of them [Q211.4:Q503]" (1973:66). In her wanderings she is said to be dangerous to children—particularly to crying children. (For additional texts from the American Southwest, see Leddy 1948 and 1950, and Perez 1951:71–127). Bess Lomax Hawes lists the most stable elements associated with the tradition as "the name 'La Llorona' itself, the associated act of weeping, and her appearance as a ghost in the form of a woman, almost always dangerous, if not wicked."

> Closely associated additional motifs include white clothing, walking at night, appearance near water or during a rainfall, continuous searching, betrayal (sometimes *by* and sometimes of the central figure), and, what is the most emotionally impressive attribute, the loss or murder of the child who is the object of the search. (Hawes 1968:161)

When Mary asked her sister Betty to tell me about La Llorona, Betty's response was two different origin stories:

> There's two stories about La Llorona. According to one, this woman was married and everything, but every time she had a baby she would kill it. She would feed it to the hogs or something, until finally they caught her and punished her. They sent her to prison or something. After she died she would come back and haunt people. She goes where she hears a baby crying. She tries to get near crying babies— you know, whenever a child is neglected or anything. And she's supposed to always be dressed in white, and she has long black hair, and people say when they see her she just stands and looks at crying babies with real sad eyes.
>
> According to the other story her baby was always crying and she didn't like it. And then one time it rained and rained and she threw it in the river and drowned it. And her punishment was that she had to find that baby. So every time it rains a lot she appears around rivers and ponds looking for her baby. This is the creepy one.

Both stories portray La Llorona as a wicked child-killer (although in much of the published material about her she is portrayed as being first a victim herself or as having merely "lost" her children). In Betty's first story, moreover, the woman had no motivation at all for committing infanticide (a form of the story which Hawes 1968:162 labels unusual). Betty emphasizes the woman's lack of motivation by explaining, "This woman was married and everything," lest the listener think the babies were killed because they were born out of wedlock. The method of murder—feeding the infants to the hogs— seems horribly grotesque, although the same motif was noted by Hawes in her study of La Llorona narratives collected from inmates of a California school for delinquent girls (1968:162). The woman in this text, moreover, remains unequivocally evil, as we have no sign of her repentance (in some texts she commits suicide) and find that she continues doing harm after her death in coming back to haunt people. We should note, however, that she doesn't actually harm other people's babies; she is, in fact, drawn to babies who are already crying and who are neglected. These she merely looks at "with real sad eyes." The onus of the crime of harming children thus becomes shifted to all women who neglect their children, and the tale contains a powerful cultural directive to all who hear it.

In Betty's second story, the mother drowns her baby because "it was always crying and she didn't like it." Her search is then a punishment for her crime. It is implied here that crying children will attract her and that good mothers will not have crying children. Concerning La Llorona in Arizona, Betty Leddy has written, "Mothers threaten their children by saying, 'Stop crying, or La Llorona will come,' for she comes 'on the wind when she hears a baby cry'" (1948:274). The stories Betty told, however, seem designed to frighten mothers rather than children. Mary's statement about La Llorona demonstrates that she also associates La Llorona with frightening mothers:

> I just knew that she was looking for babies and always crying. She was trying to find her baby. But I never knew why. I was always scared to death of La Llorona. But when I was up there in Rhode Island by myself, with [my husband] gone out on duty and me taking care of [my baby] all by myself, can you imagine how scared I would have been if I'd thought about La Llorona?

In considering the function of La Llorona as a scare figure frightening young mothers, it is helpful to remember that there is a great deal of cultural pressure on Mexican-American women to have large families. Statistics reveal an incredibly high birthrate among Mexican-Americans (Moore 1967:22). Mexican-American women frequently continue to bear children into their forties, and the incidence of large families (six persons or more) is far larger than for any other population group in the United States (Moore 1967:18). Mexican-American men feel that fathering children is proof of potency and a reinforcement to their masculine pride. On the other hand, many women have unresolved fears about the dangers of childbearing; they are also aware of the difficulties poor women face in giving their children adequate care. It is likely that the La Llorona tradition serves as an expression of some of the fears and apprehensions they feel about being mothers and caring for children. The unresolved nature of La Llorona's plight makes her a pathetic figure even when her evil nature is stressed. And perhaps there is a parallel between the eternal nature of La Llorona's fate and the seemingly unending years of motherhood the Mexican-American woman undergoes. At the same time, however, the frightening figure is obviously intended as a cultural reinforcement to encourage conscientious maternal behavior in Mexican-American mothers.

Another form of the La Llorona complex projects hostility toward aggressive males. La Llorona narratives in this category center on men who encounter La Llorona while they are out on the town late at night. Thinking at first that she is a beautiful and unprotected young woman, they follow her, but they discover too late that she is hideous and frightful—and dangerous.[9]

This manifestation of La Llorona, the siren who attacks men, is said by various folklorists to be motivated by a desire "to avenge her experience with an unfaithful lover" (Miller 1973:67). Michael Kearney discusses at length the values embedded in this form of the La Llorona complex as it exists in the town of Ixtepeji, Oaxaca, Mexico; he writes that

> [The anger and desire for revenge that the wife suffers] from the husband's betrayal and abandonment generalizes to all members of his species; all men whom, by their actions, she identifies with her husband become subject to the controlled, directed release of her suppressed wrath. . . . The predatory male, or *macho* (from the woman's point of view) here appears in the legend almost as an archetype. But now, again, from the woman's point of view the time has come for his just reward which she is fated to mete out to him. (Kearney 1969:203)

None of my own informants ever mentioned this form of the La Llorona legend, and I do not know whether it is related primarily by men or by women. It could, however, reflect men's fear of women just as much as women's desire to retaliate against male sexual aggression. Bacil F. Kirtley wrote: "Likely the pale demon woman who fascinates and destroys is a primordial image, a symbol embodying the male's ambivalent feelings toward the mysterious female sex." (1960:163)

Women's resentment against male domination and treachery is expressed in other forms of their folklore. For example, a number of ethnographers note Mexican women's use of a drug called *toloache* (or *torvache*) (that is, *datura stramonium*, or jimpsonweed) to induce a narcotic effect in men, especially in errant lovers. Michael Kearney refers to this practice as retaliation against and control of husbands, especially unfaithful husbands (1969:203n).[10] Probably, however, the enjoyment of such retaliation is vicarious, through identification with the women of legend and rumor. Mary told me about a *torvache* plant that had grown in the yard of a house she formerly had lived in, and she repeated two personal narratives related to her by another woman:

> This lady from Mexico, she told me, you know, one time she came to my house? And she saw that and she says, "Oh, Mary, why do you have that plant?" And I said, "I like it. I think it's got pretty flowers." She says, "But that's a *brujo*'s [witch's] plant." She says that that's what they use to make people go crazy, and to kill people.
>
> And she told me about this lady that lived in Mexico, and her husband was going real crazy all the time, you know? And she was giving him this to drink every day little by little and was driving him out of his mind.
>
> And another lady had killed her husband like that. And they could never prove nothing, because this was just, you know, medicine that she was giving him.

The resentment of Mexican-American women against the cultural norms that define their role as women is more common than usually recognized. One woman from whom I have collected extensively complained about attitudes toward female sexuality that lead to over-protectiveness, male dominance, and possessiveness. She felt that her husband and his brother had been possessive and domineering toward their younger sister, even though by Hispanic standards their superior sex and age gave them a degree of authority over her:

> Mexican boys are very possessive with their sisters. Like this kid at church who wouldn't let his sister go to [church] camp. He told his parents, "Oh, she wouldn't act right." Of course, it's all right for other girls to flirt with him. My brother was bad about that sort of thing. He would say to Daddy, "I saw her talking to a *bolillo* [Anglo]. Don't let her talk to *bolillos*." I guess he expected me to lay down in the grass and take off my panties right there on the street corner.

The same woman also commented on the behavior of some of her conservative relatives, specifically mentioning the sexual promiscuity of the males and the passivity of their wives, about whom she remarked:

> But they know what their husbands do. And they just—you know— they just take it for granted. "That's the way they are, so what are you going to do? He's a man you know." So they get these silly ideas in their heads. They don't know any better. They think that's the way it should be.

Chicana activists joining the struggle against oppression in the majority culture have discovered that liberation for Mexican-American women must begin at home, and stereotyped sex role patterns have become subject to reexamination. Chicana activist and journalist Francisca Flores has protested angrily against those who push "the Chicano philosophy which believes that the Chicana woman's place is in the home and that her role is that of a mother with a large family":

> Women who do not accept this philosophy are charged with betrayal of "our culture and heritage." *Our culture hell!* . . . Mexican women who bear (large) families beyond the economic ability to support them, suffer the tortures of damnation when their children die of malnutrition, of tuberculosis and other illnesses which wipe out families in poverty stricken or marginal communities in the Southwest. . . . In the course of many pregnancies many mothers and children do not make it. The toll in human life is very great. If the promulgators of the "Chicana's role is in the home having large families" also projected concern with the health problems of abnormal or self-induced abortions and still-born births, we might accept their contentions as a basis for discussion. As it stands, however, we have to conclude that their belief on the role of the Mexican woman is based on erroneous cultural and historical understanding of what is meant by "our cultural heritage," as it relates to the family. (Flores 1971:1–2)

Another Chicana activist, Sylvia Delgado, has criticized restrictive cultural norms that keep young girls ignorant and unprepared for adult life. At a Chicana conference in 1971, Delgado warned against men who use those norms to control their girlfriends through guilt manipulation, even discouraging them from using birth control lest they feel free to go with other men. Most significant, she warned against cultural pressures that encourage early marriage and pregnancy:

> For he may leave, but now you have a baby . . . your life is no longer yours. Your youth died and now you are assuming a role handed down to you. *All because you say, "My boyfriend didn't want me to take the pill."* A whole new battle begins, now you are a woman with a child. Your mother's face will show you the struggle. (Delgado 1971:6–7)

Traditional roles, however, continue to exert strong cultural imperatives and may even be embodied with symbolic power. The editors of a publication called *El Rebozo*, for example, explain the significance of the name of their paper:

> The traditional garment of the Mexican woman symbolizes the three roles of the Chicana . . . '*la señorita*,' feminine, yet humble . . . '*la revolucionaria*,' ready to fight for *la causa* . . . '*la madre*,' radiant with life. (As quoted in Rendon 1973:360)

A male activist in the Chicano movement suggests that "what Chicanas have to answer for themselves, individually, is whether they can live with more than one of these roles at a time." However, he also notes models from Mexican tradition for women's revolutionary activities:

> Young girls are relating to the folk heroines of the Mexican Revolution—*La Adelita*, subject of a revolutionary *corrido*, who exemplified the *soldaderas* (women who accompanied the rebel armies as camp soldiers, sometimes taking arms themselves). They recall the name of Juana Gallo, a *mexicana* who led the men of her village to avenge a *federales* attack against her village, and of *La Marieta*, Maria del Carmen Rubio de la Llave, a *guerillera* under Francisco Villa. (Rendon 1973:358)

Women's folklore can be an important means of indicating differences in male and female ethos and worldview and exposing ideologies that have been accepted as representing the total culture as reflecting only a male ideal. The (male) picture of the ideal woman, which usually omits the role of revolutionary activist, is succinctly expressed in this poem by Abelardo, a Chicano *poeta de la gente*, or people's poet:

LA HEMBRA

No woman will cling to youth, the fast illusive,

With such tenacious abandon as she does,
carrying a niño in her womb is the crux
of all femininity that forever was.

Her joy, her love, her endurance is impressive,
but the way she suffers almost without a tear
makes her life fully mysterious yet so clear.

Your critics whisper your life is dull, reclusive,

deep down they envy your security,
you can give and take all with such maturity,
you can change pain to joy and lust to purity.

(Quoted by Rincón 1971:16)

This poem idealizes the almost mystical image of the passive, submissive female, suffering in silence, repressing her sexual needs and serving as a symbol of purity, stability, and fertility. She is defined primarily by her childbearing function and in relation to men. These are the very concerns of the folklore we have been discussing, but in the folklore we have seen reflections of the fears and anxieties that women experience because of these ideals, and we have seen glimpses of women's resentment of the repressive role given them.

NOTES

1. In Santamaría (1959:408) we find the following listing: "Chirrionera. (*Masticophis flagellum*, SHAW y otras especies de los géneros *Preustes* y *Drymarchon*). f. Nombre vulgar que se da comúnmente a una culebrilla de cola muy larga que emplea como flagelo cuando se ve acosada, enrollándose a la pantorilla. Es propia de los lugares donde hay vegetación, en el norte."

2. Strecker (1926:63) explains that the water dog of the plains region of West Texas is the larval stage of a large tiger salamander that breeds in the shallow lakes that form after the first heavy rain of the year. In the larval, or axolotl, stage the animals "have large, plump, light-colored bodies, external gills, finned tails, and large broad heads, and in general appearance look not unlike small catfish. In this

stage, the animal has a voracious appetite. . . . The axolotl form is so different in appearance from the adult animal that it is usually given another name, that of 'water dog.' "

3. This story has been noted elsewhere, usually with the added motif that the snake pacified the hungry infant with the tip of its tail while stealing the milk. Rosenberg (1946:91) reports the existence of this legend in Argentina (and also the belief in snakes impregnating women); he does not identify the sex of his informants. In J. Frank Dobie's folklore novel *Tongues of the Monte* (1935:90–91), an old Mexican woman tells a version of The Singing Bone in which the first incident concerns a snake (here identified as an *alicántara*, which Dobie notes is a coachwhip, also called a prairie racer) which has been stealing milk from the hero's mother's breasts. I also know of at least two unpublished Louisiana versions, both of which were told by women. See also Cardozo-Freeman 1978.

4. My thanks to Lysander Kemp of the University of Texas Press for calling this work to my attention. Arreola also credits Sahagún with reporting on the legendary origin of axolotls as a result of an important lady's douching in a lagoon named Axolitla after having been raped while having her period by a gentleman from another town (1964:33).

5. Two additional Negro-American texts heard in Chicago and in Missouri and collected by a female student at Fisk University were sent to me by Saundra Keyes.

6. Horney believed that such anxieties had a physiological basis in the vaginal organ sensations of even young, inexperienced girls and in the young girl's subsequent dread "that if her wishes were fulfilled, she herself or her genital would be destroyed" (1967:154). Horney further explains that fantasies, dreams, and anxieties betraying *instinctive* knowledge of sexual processes may assume various guises, including that of "animals that creep, fly or run inside some place (e.g., snakes, mice, moths)" (1967:142).

7. I collected this text of "Charlotte the Harlot" (at a party in Baton Rouge, Louisiana, in 1972) from Tom Sprott, Jr., of Winnsboro, South Carolina.

8. Kinsey, on the other hand, believed that accounts of women having sex with animals represent a projection of the male desire for a variety of sexual activities, especially in view of "the male capacity to be aroused erotically by a variety of psychosexual stimuli." One wonders, however, about his assumption that the creative expressions he refers to (from "ancient archives of folklore and mythology" to modern literature and art) reflect utterly and entirely male fantasies. He even states: "Females, because of their lesser dependence on psychologic stimulation, are less inclined to be interested in activities which lie beyond the immediately available techniques, and rarely, either in their conversation, in their written literature, or in their art, deal with fantastic or impossible sorts of sexual activity. Human males, and not the females themselves, are the ones who imagine that females are frequently involved in sexual contacts with animals of other species" (Kinsey et al. 1965:502).

9. Texts of this form of the legend are found in Miller (1973:99) and in Dorson (1964:438). The latter is reprinted from Perez (1951:73–74, 76). The text in Dorson is a memorate of a personal encounter with La Llorona; the text in Miller is merely explanatory or descriptive. Also see Toor (1947:531–532).

10. Others who mention this practice are Mendoza and Mendoza (1952:477) and Bourke (1894:140). Both sources note that Mexican women administer the drug to their lovers in potions; Mendoza and Mendoza say that it is the seed of the plant which produces confusion and that the potion is supposed to ensure that a woman's lover will never forget her.

3

WOMAN TO WOMAN: FIELDWORK AND THE PRIVATE SPHERE
Margaret R. Yocom

E VER SINCE I have been old enough to remember, my sense of family has grown out of the stories told by Grandmother Bertha Davidheiser Yocom, my father's mother, and Grandfather Elmer Christman Keck, my mother's father, both in their different ways fine tellers of personal experience and family narratives (Fig. 1). Bertha's stories about ice-skating with her brothers on the Schuylkill Canal near Douglassville, Pennsylvania, about leaving the countryside to work in Philadelphia, and about managing a farm family with her husband, Isaac, lived on in my imagination long after the telling. The people, places, and events in Elmer's stories also echoed in my mind: the men in his father's slaughterhouse who, wielding great knives, stuck belligerent hogs in the neck; the bright-eyed boy-men who sweated through freshman hazing at Pennsylvania State University; T. DeWitt Kyler's boundless farm near Whitehorse, Pennsylvania, where Elmer worked one college summer; and the explosion in the Emporium, Pennsylvania's World War I smokeless powder plant, where he stood helplessly by, watching brains bubble inside the charred heads of his fellow workers.

When I returned home to Pottstown, Pennsylvania, in the summer of 1975, I heard the stories once again, but this time as a fieldworker as well as a granddaughter. What surprised me was not the stories—I knew them so well I could tell parts of them myself—but the difference between the private and public settings where Bertha and Elmer told their stories and the contrasting ways that they, as storytellers within these settings, approached their listeners.

Elmer's stories, usually about himself or his relatives, provide the spice for many a family meal. Either before or during a meal, or lingering over a dessert, his tales ring out to everyone within earshot. "That's nothing," he said, laughing, after my father, Norman Yocom, mentioned that Great Uncle Rufus Keck as a wedding-day joke smeared Limburger cheese on the manifold and exhaust pipe of Uncle Donald Keck's car. "You should have seen what Wilmer Keck did when Bessie Keck married Wayne Kline," Elmer continued:

> Wilmer knew that they were getting married at the parsonage out at Reverend Kline's. So they had a cab there to take them wherever they wanted to go. Whether it was up to Reading to Wayne's place or whether it was to a railroad station, I don't know what it was. But anyhow, what Wilmer does was: he goes up, tips the cab driver, asks how much he was owed. So he paid him off and told him to get going. And he has the calf wagon from the abattoir that we hauled calves in . . . all decorated up and had it pulled up in front of Reverend Kline's. When they came out, they lowered them in the calf wagon and hauled them around town.[1]

If someone says, "Today's a cold day," Elmer will say that the coldest was that one day in 1911, when as a freshman at Penn State he found frozen water in his water basin. If someone mentions a friend of theirs, he knows that fellow's grandfather who used to live just down the block from him and who worked for years in the Arcade building where the parking lot is now. Garrulous and outspoken, he is the one whom all the family members seek out for information about his and his wife's relatives. Addresses, birthdays, anniversaries, and death dates—he knows them all, or he has them in his updated address book or among his chronologically arranged stack of funeral cards. At family reunions, it is he who recites the names of those who have come—and those who have not. And going to Grace Lutheran Church with Elmer is a combination of reverence, worship, and fun. As he walks inside the church and sees his friends milling about, he reaches for their hands. "Elmer, good morning," they say. "How're you doing today?" "Terrible, terrible," he says with a grin. One Sunday morning when Elmer saw Wellington Smith, he stood right in front of Smitty, smiled, and started brushing his own hair back on his forehead. "You better comb that hair out of your eyes," Elmer teased him. Smitty ran a fake comb across his bald head and laughed to those standing around him: "That's Elmer. It wouldn't be Elmer if he didn't give somebody a bad time."

His humor and his stories, told in front of his relatives and friends, are those of a man in the public sphere who revels in the attention of many listeners, who shows his friendship by giving people a "bad time," and who enjoys following someone else's story with one of his own that will top, he claims, the one that went before. Once, after an evening of talk on his son-in-law's back porch, he leaned back in his chair and after a moment of silence remarked more to himself than to anyone else, "You know, I suppose I have done some pretty interesting things. I should have written a book." A fieldworker could not ask for a more willing informant.

Bertha Yocom, like Elmer, was born to Pennsylvania German Lutheran farmers near Pottstown in the 1890s. She lived on Keck property when for a few years her father rented Elmer's father's farm. After high school both left home for a time. Bertha studied bookkeeping and traveled to Philadelphia, where she worked until her marriage in 1920 brought her back to farming. Elmer learned animal husbandry at Penn State, worked in a World War I powder plant, and brought his bride, Louisa, from the hills of northwestern Pennsylvania home to Pottstown in 1919 when he returned to his father's slaughterhouse.

But here the resemblances end, for to see Bertha at a family gathering is to see a woman carefully dressed in purples and blues who listens attentively, smiles constantly, and talks rarely—unless someone speaks to her. When she does talk in front of others, she rarely speaks about herself. The day I suggested that I might like to write down some of the things that happened to her, she cried out, "Oh, no, no."

A fieldworker who met both Bertha and Elmer in public might well think Bertha an overly shy and untalkative woman who would not make a rewarding informant. How wrong that fieldworker would be, for she does indeed talk about herself and her relatives: everyone in the family knows bits and pieces of her life story. And some of those bits, like her several-mile walk over the cornfields to the train that would take her to Pottstown and school, are famous.

The difference between the way Bertha appears, as a storyteller, and the way she is lies with the setting where she performs. Like most of the women in the Yocom-Keck family, she tells her personal experience narratives not in public, like Elmer, but very much in private. And the fieldworker who would like to work successfully with Bertha and the others must be prepared (as with many other women informants) to investigate and interview within the private sphere.

In the private sphere, with its atmosphere of intimacy, Bertha and her women relatives thrive (Fig. 4). When they feel close and comfortable with one another, when they perceive that everyone will listen and talk, their storytelling begins. This sphere of theirs may be indoors or outdoors, in any room or on any lawn; the location does not matter to their storytelling as much as the privacy that those locations afford.

Their privacy may come from natural isolation: they may be the only two people in the room. Or it may come from created isolation: amid a flock of relatives, several women turn and face one another, their bodies forming a circle as their arms reach toward one another; or they relax on a swing or a bench with only enough room for the two of them (Figs. 3,4).

The private sphere of women's storytelling has shared not only confidences and privacy but also work. No matter what the activity—whether slicing the ends off just-pulled scallions, searching in the spring grass for dandelions deserving enough to become a dinner vegetable, cutting parsley for a noonday meal, sewing a torn seam, recording the death of a relative in the family Bible, or packing her belongings after she sells her home to move in with her daughter (Figs. 5–8)—for the talk to flow a woman needs only another who will help, listen, and talk in turn.

Women's private storytelling sphere includes all those areas that feel not merely a woman's touch but also her dominant influence and control. In kitchens and dining rooms especially, women are the mistresses of many details that a careless or uncaring eye might overlook. Here, where they place several forks and spoons of varying sizes by each chair, where they arrange plates by paralleling the design and the lines of the table, and where they make their way between spatulas, potato mashers, dippers, and tea strainers, they work and talk together as other relatives and occasional guests go about chores or visit in the living room until the call to dinner comes (Figs. 9,10).

Many of the products of these labors are ephemeral. Paradoxically, they last for a brief period of time, but they are constantly re-created: dinner table decorations of multicolored flowers, dishes of roast beef garnished with onions and carrots. Yet these items as well as those that last longer live on in the women's storytelling sphere as women comment on their displays of table and food, of sewing and ceramics (Fig. 11). And after their work is done, the private sphere shifts to favorite sitting places, large overstuffed chairs and rockers within view of family photographs and strategically positioned so that the occupants can see out of several windows and onto the street beyond (Fig. 12).

There is no denying the very comfortable feeling that a female fieldworker experiences as she steps into this private sphere of women's storytelling. How many times has she been led in and out of rooms and been shown embroidery and photographs, quilts and books, dishes and special gifts? How many times has she come from a long journey to a woman's house, worried about how this stranger might respond to her, and heard her informant begin by complaining herself about the heat and the distance that the fieldworker has had to travel, and then watched this woman settle easily, cold non-alcoholic drink in hand, into a discussion of her latest illnesses. It feels like home.

And well it should, for women, when they meet, know that they have many common bonds, especially in the work they do to maintain both their homes and their bodies. They cook and trade recipes, bear children and raise them, worry about their relatives, clean and decorate, sew and make gifts, welcome guests, and share information about sicknesses, cures, and doctors.

What they do not or cannot do also bonds women together. Although they might keep the records in the family Bible up-to-date, for example, they will not inherit the book itself. Because women cannot pass on to their children the name they themselves received at birth, they often do not inherit family documents, furniture, or land. Women are what other families inherit: "Well, she was a Smith," a woman will hear about herself after her marriage, "but now she's a Jones." Because women have no voice in many decisions, they do not represent jobs, power, or money to one another. What a woman informant sees in a female fieldworker is largely a person who will face many of the same joys, sorrows, and challenges she herself did.

Women's personal narratives within the private storytelling sphere reflect these bonds, for the narratives have little competitive edge to them; few women talking in the private sphere begin their stories with, "That's nothing." Neither do their narratives exist primarily to entertain. Exemplum-like and liberally sprinkled with the marker "Now, not to brag or anything but . . . ," women's personal narratives provide support as they teach other women what is possible for them.

One rainy afternoon, for example, as Bertha Yocom and I sat in her bedroom, we spoke of one of our friends, a woman who had never been out of her hometown, and rarely out of her house, until she moved several hundred miles away with her husband. We spoke of her inability to adapt, of her unhappiness. "She wasn't like me, poor thing," Bertha observed:

> For twelve years I worked in the city [Philadelphia]. I was a book-keeper, not a stenographer. Why, do you know how I became a bookkeeper? I didn't even know what "bookkeeper" meant. I thought it was someone that took care of books, kept them, you know, something like a librarian. Then a friend of mine, a schoolteacher, told me that teachers made only forty-eight dollars a month and had only seven months' work and that bookkeepers made more, worked all year, and got two weeks' paid vacation. Well, I thought that was pretty good.

Bertha talked over an hour about business college, paying her father back, riding the train to Philadelphia, working in a necktie and clothing firm, teaching Sunday school, and saving money to help pay for the farm. "It's good," she remarked as she finished. "You never heard much about my past."

Similarly, on Mother's Day 1976, when the Kecks gathered to visit an ailing Grandmother Louisa, Great Aunt Martha and I sat on the back porch swing and talked about my fieldwork, Elmer Keck (her brother), and how Elmer was in college while Martha was growing up:

> *Martha:* Yes, well, I went away to college in 1925. *[She was looking at the pictures I took of Elmer.]* Do you know when they sold the farm?
> *Peggy:* I think it was around 1927.

Martha: That's when my father died.

Peggy: I'll have to check.

Martha: Yes, I went off to college knowing that my Dad had cancer. That wasn't easy. And in my dorm you couldn't get any phone calls except emergencies after eight. If the phone rang after eight, I'd be terrified. I couldn't study. . . . But I learned to overcome this fear gradually. This experience always stayed with me in many other situations. You can't let fear cripple you.

Although Bertha and Martha offered their experiences as good ones worthy of praise, they did not seek to praise themselves at their listener's or anyone else's expense. Bertha's closing remark ("It's good. You never heard much about my past.") links her to her audience. She does not present herself as one person who has done something much grander than her listeners could ever hope to accomplish. Likewise, through her conclusion ("You can't let fear cripple you"), Martha also bonds herself with her audience; she shows listeners how to interpret and use that story for themselves.

In contrast, when Elmer talks about himself in the public sphere, he entertains, informs, and competes, good-naturedly, with his audience. "That's nothing," he often begins. Once, for example, when I mentioned getting a work permit for my first job when I was sixteen, he laughed, "Work permit? Why I went to work when I was five, doing newspapers with Alan [Elmer's older brother]. I had my own route from the time I was six, mind you, till high school."

If told to children, this part of Elmer's life history might by its example lend support to their quest for a job, but the information itself, told as it was without narrative comments that bond, does not link narrator and listeners together in a common struggle. Instead, it points out the strengths of the narrator and challenges the listeners to put forth their own.

Although women rarely carry their personal experience narratives outside this private sphere with its emphasis on bonding, women certainly do not restrict their storytelling to that one sphere. Some women blossom before a public audience with tales about relatives, children, and friends (Fig. 13). Yet because women usually stay within the private sphere and because they are often in the company of other women when they share these narratives, it might be tempting to describe such storytelling as sexually exclusive.

Labeling such storytelling as sexually exclusive would also be aided by research that often applies the principle of exclusivity to women's traditions in general and to women's bawdy materials in particular.[2] Yet women exclude men when the material is far from bawdy, and women perform bawdy traditions in front of men (see Kalčik 1975; Johnson 1973; Green 1977). At issue in any discussion of women, fieldwork, and exclusivity must be not only the type of material being performed or the sexual composition of the group, but also the kind of atmosphere the participants want: public, with its attention and competition, or private, with its intimacy and bonding.

Women telling their personal experience narratives in the private sphere do not automatically exclude men; even the most public male storytellers can find a place in the private sphere (Figs. 14,15). A woman who feels a close bond, especially a family bond, with a man will share private information with him. "I never said this to anybody," explained Mrs. Carmel Iannone to her grandson who was collecting her life history. "I say it because you're her [Mrs. Iannone's daughter's] son" (Princiotto n.d.).

Women narrators, however, do exclude men and women who are unwilling or unable to adapt to the intimacy of their private sphere. They may also exclude people they do not know well enough; they would not want to invite those who might disrupt the privacy they desire.

The private sphere of women's personal experience narratives therefore does not depend on physical location, sexual exclusivity, type of material, or the number of participants. It is a mode of social interaction, a space where none need fear ridicule or embarrassment, where handwork often accompanies talk, where participants feel that they all share several bonds, where narratives emphasize those bonds, and where each participant is seen as equally capable of and willing to contribute personal information. Fieldworkers who would enter this sphere successfully need to be able to give of themselves, to share their own stories with others, and to participate in the thoughts, struggles, sorrows, and joys of women of all ages (Fig. 16).[3]

NOTES

1. These remarks are from a field journal entry for May 30, 1979, and from an interview of June 23, 1979. Subsequent comments of informants quoted are taken from field journal entries from 1975 and 1976.

2. Goldstein (1964:83) notes: "I was informed several times of obscene-story and song sessions which would take place during women's tea parties at a specific place and time; unfortunately, my sex eliminated me as a potential participant or onlooker . . . and I was forced to obtain my data about such sessions during interviews with one or more of its participants with whom I was on especially good terms."

3. All photographs except that of the author and Susan Supplee (which is the work of G. M. Vaught), were taken by Margaret Yocom. The author thanks her entire family for their help and support, especially the women of her family: Bertha Davidheiser Yocom, Louisa Zwald Keck (1898–1977), Martha Keck Fry, Betty Keck Yocom, Gladys Yocom Metka, Edie Yocom Boyer, Marie Rebecca Yocom, Jean Keck, Fern Keck, Janet Yocom Keck, Diane Yocom Supplee, and Nancy Mortensen Yocom; and her grandfather, Elmer Christman Keck (1893–1982).

1. *Elmer Christman Keck and Bertha Davidheiser Yocom.*

2. *Bertha Yocom talks with the author at a picnic table.*

3. *Jean Belman Keck and Martha Keck Fry talk.*

4. *Bertha Yocom talks with daughter-in-law Betty on porch swing.*

5. *Bertha Yocom talks
   as she works in
   hers and her
   daughter's garden.*

6. *Bertha Yocom cooks and answers an interviewer's questions.*

7. *Bertha Yocom records her brother's death and talks about her mother's Bible.*

8. *Bertha Yocom packs her belongings and talks about the items as the time to move nears.*

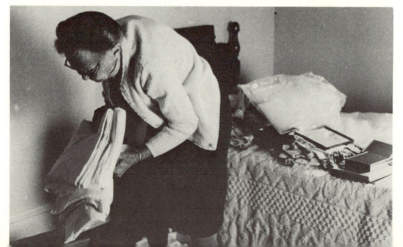

9. *The Yocom family table at Bertha and Isaac's fiftieth wedding anniversary party.*

10. *Sisters-in-law Gladys Yocom Metka, Betty Keck Yocom, and Edith Yocom Boyer.*

11. *Janet Yocom Keck shows Bertha Yocom her newly hand-made ceramic dishes.*

12. Louisa Zwald Keck talks in her living room.

13. Marie Yocom regales her husband David and family friend Dorothy Barkel Moyer with her stories.

14. *Above left: Public performer Elmer Keck talks to his daughter Betty in her kitchen.*

15. *Above right: Betty Keck Yocom listens to her father Elmer.*

16. *Susan Supplee reminds author Margaret Yocom about childhood games, yet another aspect of the private sphere of women's traditions.*

4

THE KINSHIP QUILT: AN ETHNOGRAPHIC SEMIOTIC ANALYSIS OF A QUILTING BEE
Susan Roach

H ERALDED AS a great American art form, the patchwork quilt has been analyzed and exhibited as both painting and sculpture (e.g., Holstein 1973; Mainardi 1973a, 1973b). In appreciating its graphic qualities, however, art critics isolate the quilt from its traditional sociocultural context. The social and technical complexity of quilt production, function, and meaning prohibits consideration of the quilt as merely an art object. But folklorists have yet to turn out any substantial body of quilting scholarship, even though quiltmaking has been acknowledged as a traditional American folk art form that has been transmitted through American culture for over three hundred years. The dearth of articles on quiltmaking in folklore journals (not one article on the subject has ever appeared in the *Journal of American Folklore*, for example) indicates this neglect.[1] The numerous popular books on quiltmaking are of limited folkloristic value because they deal primarily with quilting history (often romantically), quilting directions, and quilt patterns. The large number of quiltmaking articles in popular periodicals, especially in the early 1920s, 1930s,

This chapter is an expanded version of a paper entitled "The Quilting Bee: An Interrelationship Between Folk Art and Speech," presented at the annual meeting of the American Folklore Society, Philadelphia, 1976.

1940s, late 1960s, and the 1970s, is evidence of the almost continuous popularity of the craft with women, but like the books, these articles offer little more than basic instructions or patterns and provide no insight into the quiltmaker or the quiltmaking context. (See Roach and Weidlich 1974 for a detailed survey of quilt publications.)

Examining the quilt in its context will make it possible to understand the full significance of the quilt and its meaning in society. It is helpful to see the quilt as a communicative expressive form or sign that has a multiplicity of functions in the society that produces it. Such a contextual study must note the makers of the quilt, the occasions of its production, the functions of the quilt, the internal artistic form of the quilt, and the quilt's relations to other modes of communication in the society.[2] Since the form and function of a particular material culture object are linked intimately to the context of the object's production and use (Glassie 1974:343), the quilting bee, the traditional social context of quilt production, is a convenient place to observe many of these different functions, their interrelationships and importance to the group, and the symbolic messages and meaning of the quilt. This approach provides a framework to investigate an instance of quiltmaking which took place in the summer of 1974 in my own family, a politically conservative, religiously fundamentalistic, Anglo-Saxon Protestant group in rural north Louisiana.

There are still some scattered women's church groups and revivalist quilt guilds that hold quilting bees in the area, but traditional family-centered quilting gatherings have become rare. More commonly, the traditional quilter in north Louisiana quilts alone with occasional help from one or two relatives or neighbors. My own family's renewed interest in quilting began when my grandmother decided to gather some of her family to quilt a patchwork top she had pieced six years earlier. She suggested that we quilt this top when I was talking to her about helping me quilt one of several quilt tops that I had inherited.[3] Failing eyesight had kept her from completing the quilt or piecing additional ones, but a recent cataract operation that had improved her vision prompted her to try quilting again. She was no doubt also encouraged to revive her art by a recent visit from a sister-in-law, who was piecing quilts to sell, and also by her daughters, who were making polyester-knit baby quilts for their new grandchildren.

Although the family had not actively participated in a quilting bee for several years, my eighty-year-old grandmother and her daughters had quilted together frequently until about twenty years previously. My grandmother had also belonged for a few years to a home demonstration group that met weekly for "quilting parties," a custom that had eventually been discontinued, probably because of the convenience, practicality, and lowered cost of electric and synthetic blankets and because the participating women had moved away or, on growing older, had been deterred by health problems. Even though in 1974 the family no longer commonly gathered to make quilts, several members might get together to help put up vegetables and fruit or to help with some household chore such as upholstering a chair. Such occasions were social gatherings where news, opinions, and gossip were exchanged. With this established custom of helping out, it was no surprise when the women in the immediate family from nearby communities and towns responded to my grandmother's invitation, eager to help their mother "get the quilt out." Because of the seasonal heat, her daughter-in-law who lived just down the road volunteered her air-conditioned living room for the gathering.

Getting a large group such as this together for the quilting process greatly facilitates quiltmaking. The quilting process itself has the practical purpose of holding the filler or batting in place between the patchwork top and the lining. The lining, filler, and top are stretched tightly over a four-sided frame placed on chairs or suspended from the ceiling. Because of the unwieldiness of the quilt in the frame and the need to have the quilting stitches close enough to keep the cotton in place, quilting is most efficiently accomplished with several people working at once around the frame. At this particular quiltmaking session there were ten quilters quilting for about six hours; yet the quilting was not finished, or to put it in quilting jargon, the quilt was "rolled" only twice at the session, probably because of the inexperience of some of the participants. (The session began just after the quilt had been installed in the quilting frame, or "put in," and ended with the discontinuation of quilting for that day.) Since the quilt was not completed in one session, seven members of the group reassembled during the following two days and finished the quilt. Although I taped all three sessions, my analysis concentrates on the first session because of its complexity and because its conversation deals more directly with the quilt itself.

The participants in the first session included my grandmother ("Mamaw"[4]), who was once an expert but now a rusty quilter; her four daughters, aged forty-five to fifty-eight, three of them (Aunts A, B, and C) experienced seamstresses and quilters, and one (Aunt D) an inexperienced seamstress; and a daughter-in-law (Aunt E), who had not quilted for approximately fifteen years. These participants had all learned to quilt as children, and Aunts A, B, and D had recently been working on the baby quilts mentioned earlier. Three grand-daughters—two novice quilters (F and G) with some general sewing experience and the author (I), who had learned to quilt as a child—participated in the quilting session along with one grandson (H), who had no sewing experience. It is interesting to note that there was no hesitancy on the part of the women about allowing the twelve-year-old male (the daughter-in-law's son) to participate. He was the object of some gentle teasing evidenced in the following interaction:

> *H:* This is fun.
> *Aunt D:* H is having more fun than anyone at the quilting. *[Laughter.]*
> *Aunt C:* I tell you what, he can sure learn.
> *Aunt D:* You know what? If I had brought my wig and put it on H, he could have been the girl. *[Laughter.]*
> *Aunt A:* We don't have no sex discrimination.
> *Aunt D:* I know it. That's why we have the boy come in, because we cannot have sex discrimination, because at the office we have three boys workin' now because we cannot discriminate.

Aunt D's teasing remark suggesting that the nephew be wigged to accomplish his sex-role reversal implies that quilting is thought to be women's work predominantly. However, her stance is quickly modified to show the group's awareness and approval of sex discrimination rulings recently occurring in their area. In noting this socio-political sanction for the nephew's participation, the group also smoothes any hurt feelings caused by the teasing. Actually male participation in quilting in this family (and others) is not new. When Aunt A was asked about male participation in quilting, she recalled that her two brothers had quilted some as children and that it had given them something to do when the isolation of the farms in the area made it difficult for children to get together for play. It seems then that nephew H's presence at his home and his lack of other activities make him a potential participant. The men of the family who wandered in and out of the session did not seem to disapprove. In fact, two of the hus-bands, one of whom was the father of the boy, were coaxed into trying their hands at a few stitches. The men, staying only a few minutes,

and the boy, complaining throughout the session, voiced such difficulties with the task, however, that there was no doubt that the activity
was considered the exclusive domain of women. Thus the main participants in the event—my grandmother, her four daughters, a daughter-
in-law, and four grandchildren—spanned three generations and had
varying degrees of quilting experience.

If we approach this quilting session as a complex speech event—
considering both the components of the event and the specific recur-
rent conversation about the quilt, the quilting bee, and the quilting
process—we can learn much about the form, function, and meaning
of the quilt. First, as the setting and the participants indicate, the
quilt signals a social interaction and reveals cultural values. The
quiltmaking creates a situation that brings a woman, her daughters,
and her grandchildren together. Without the object and task, there
would probably have been no gathering of kin of this size on a non-
holiday. This quilting bee can be termed a variant of family visiting
rituals. Such occasions are held seasonally, usually during Christmas
and Thanksgiving holidays and on selected summer vacation days.
The usual pattern is for the grandmother of the family to receive word
that an out-of-town daughter or son is coming to visit, whereupon she
notifies all her other nearby children to meet on the designated day
for a midday meal ("dinner") and visiting. The quilting gathering here
is different only in that a task is the reason for the family's meeting.
Comments made by the participants showed an awareness that the
planned quilting drew everyone together:

> *Aunt E:* I'll bet everybody goin' by thinks, "What in the world's
> goin' on at E's?"
> *F:* A reunion!
> *Aunt E:* We planned it just right, didn't we? We got Aunt C in
> on it.

Awareness of the symbolic function of the quilt as the focus of a family
event was again evidenced beautifully later in the session when, following various participants' complaints about the poor quality of their
stitches, Aunt A, the daughter with the most quilting experience,
suggested, "Everybody has to write their name on the one they quilt."
Protests followed her idea. A granddaughter asked if there is a special
name for such a quilt, and Aunt E answered, "Friendship." The
grandmother tried to elaborate seriously on the friendship quilts she

used to make, but Aunt D, her daughter with the least quilting expertise, laughingly interrupted: "This is friendship, all right." Another daughter, Aunt C, responded, laughing, "Kinfolks, *kin*folkship." Aunt A answered, "It's *kin*ship," and Aunt D confirmed it: "It's kinship instead of friendship." All laughed and approved the clever wordplay by repeating the word "kinship." Thus the quilting bee took on the significance of a holiday that ritually draws the family together, reaffirming the cultural value of the extended family. The quilting bee functions like ritual visiting and also provides a chore for the visitors—to "get the quilt out." This incorporation of work with visiting reaffirms the group's cultural value of the Protestant work ethic.

In addition to reaffirming the Protestant work ethic, the quilt reveals the rural tradition of saving and recycling materials. In fact, one motivation for piecing a quilt is the accumulation of many fabric "scraps" which are "going to waste." Other recycling practices such as handing down clothes, reusing tinfoil and plastic bread wrappers for storage, saving vegetable peels and meal leftovers to feed various farm animals, or even making toys from empty thread spools support their belief that nothing should be allowed to go to waste. Likewise, pieces in the quilt are those saved from my grandmother's and her daughters' sewing remnants and old clothes, as revealed by the following conversation:

> *Aunt E:* Boy, I'll tell y'all what. This black and white checkered diamonds is somethin' else to try to do.
> *Aunt B:* Oh, that's Aunt D's. It was something to sew! Lord!
> *Aunt D:* The black checked?
> *I:* Oh, I had a dress out of that.
> *Aunt D:* Oh, I did too.
> *Aunt B:* Aunt D had a skirt and vest.
> *I:* I had a skirt and a top.
> *Aunt D:* I had a skirt and a vest for mine.
> *I:* I still have mine.
> *Aunt B [pointing out another scrap]:* Oh, I had my diamond jubilee dress out of this.

Since the quilt is pieced with remnants from some of their own clothes, it is also a means for the participants to interact with their past selves as well as with one another. As the above comments indicate, while the participants quilt they can discover those pieces that hold memories of past costumes, the places they wore them, and who they were at that time.

The participants' comments also reveal the practical functions of the quilt as a household object. In spite of the popularity of electric blankets in this group, the quilt still functions as an extra bed covering, as we are told by my grandmother's comment: "In the wintertime when the electricity goes off, you'll want this quilt. Somebody will."

The conversation also reveals another family use of the quilt as a "baby pallet," a pad or mat placed on the floor in a central position so that everyone can watch the family babies when they are brought to visit. This use was attributed to the present quilt when Aunt D, soon to be a grandmother herself, tried to reassure her mother that her stitches were all right: "Well, the little baby's not gon' have very much toenails for the pallet quilt." Aunt E responds, knowing three of the daughters have already been making baby quilts and blankets, "Is this a baby quilt too?" Aunt D answers, "It's the pallet quilt." Aunt C objects that my grandmother already has a pallet quilt, but Aunt D replies, "Oh, yes, but it's old. These new babies has to have a new quilt." Thus, in addition to providing a practical safe play area for babies, the pallet quilt functions to make the new children the focus of family attention and to emphasize the importance of the generational continuation of the family.[5]

In addition to its practical household functions, the quilt can be seen to be an art object made according to traditional ideal aesthetic norms of production. All the experienced quilters in the session were aware of these norms and tried to convey them to the novices. In order to interpret the quilt and its making, we need to examine these expressed norms of the quilting process and their functions.

According to informants who at one time quilted frequently, the woman giving the quilting bee always invited those friends or relatives who were noted for their good needlework. In this case, however, both good needlewomen and novices were allowed to participate, violating the norm for consistent, even stitches. Actually, it is more accurate to call this norm an ideal, since there were undoubtedly many quilting sessions where novices practiced in order to become skilled quilters. According to one participant, novices would be less welcome to quilt on a fancy quilt than on an "everyday" quilt. The present quilt was labeled "everyday" by its maker not only because of its plain cotton and cotton blend fabrics and its simple geometric star design, but also because of the maker's expressed disappointment in her execution of the pattern, noting that she should have planned her use of light and dark colored fabrics more carefully in order to contrast the overlapping star shapes. Nevertheless, even though the quilt was considered an "everyday" one, the participants still valued the ideal of neat, well-executed quilting stitches.

While use of inexperienced quilters violates traditional ideals somewhat, the selection of the quilting design—the stitching that holds the pieced top to the cotton and lining—followed standard procedures. Pieced six years prior to the quilting, the quilt piecing pattern was composed entirely of diamond shapes put together to form stars. The quilting design would be "by the piece," with stitching on the inside edge of each diamond-shaped patch. According to the conversation, quilting by the piece (besides being less confusing for the beginners) would emphasize the pattern and provide ample stitching to hold the cotton in place. Also, stitching around each diamond would produce a pleasing repetition of the patchwork design on the light-blue lining.

Much of the beginning conversation of the session made it somewhat atypical because it focused on the proper equipment for quilting, a topic that can be attributed to the varying degrees of quilting experience of the participants. Each participant had to have a thimble and the correct size needle and thread. Also, much conversation was devoted to the precise measuring of the distance of the stitching from the seams, thus indicating the importance of straight, even stitches on every diamond. After some disagreement, a half-inch seam was agreed on, and several participants attempted to find a seam guide or to construct measuring devices from the cover of a handy mail-order catalog. Then the experienced quilters showed the novices how to use the equipment. For example, my grandmother cautioned everyone, "When you start off, pull your knots through so there won't be no knot a-showin'." For the first couple of hours of the session, then, most of the conversation consisted of instructions with demonstrations of the process of quilting. For example, the grandson H asked: "Where do I start, right here? Do I start right here? And I come up right through the center, right?" accompanying his questions with the actions he described. He was answered and shown by an experienced quilter: "No, wait a minute, wait. Start right there, then you're gonna come down."

These detailed instructions are expected to give the novices quilting competence, but this is only part of the problem. As Aunt D, the daughter with the least quilting skill, put it, "I know how to quilt, but that's not the thing. I know *how,* but knowing how and doing it's two different things." The problem then is the performance of the skill, and several participants were dissatisfied with their performances. Their expressions of dissatisfaction served to emphasize their awareness of the norms that their hands had not yet mastered. For example, Aunt E complained, "It's gonna be hard for me to do. I can't if I got to measure all the time." She was answered by Aunt C, a more experienced quilter, "Well, come here and look. You don't have to measure all the time. Just get started on it and if it gets crooked, it's all right, it won't matter." Similarly, my grandmother, having trouble with her eyesight, said, "On this blue, I'm making stitches about two feet long." Her daughter, Aunt A, an experienced quilter, replied, "Well, that'll be all right." Using the idea of the pallet quilt again to express a method of aesthetic judgment, Aunt D said, "Well, I'm glad it's a pallet quilt, 'cause little bitty babies will not have— We'll put little socks on it, so it won't get its toenails hung in the stitches." When one of the novices questioned her about this statement, she explained, "That's what they always said, when they's quilting. They'd have a long stitch, they'd get their toenail hung in it."

Although all these comments indicate the number of actual inadequate normal performances, these performances were accepted and excused in this quilting context. These actual performances were also ridiculed at times in rural metaphors. For instance, in referring to some problem stitching, the grandson remarked, "This is crooked as a jay bird." The least skilled daughter, Aunt D, similarly remarked later, giggling over her own attempt, "Oh, that looks like a chicken scratch going over here. Wanna see my chicken scratch?" This last disclaimer caused the whole group to go into hysterical laughter, most laughing until they cried, making it the biggest joke of the event. Thus, not only were mistakes condoned, but they also provided the basis for group fun, a positive reward for a substandard performance.

This acceptance of novice quilters and substandard quilting does violate the demonstrated traditional aesthetic ideal, but in the case of the present quilt it was much more important to get the whole family involved in the fun and to get the quilt out than to produce a formally perfect quilt. To put it in Jan Mukarovsky's terms, the production of this piece of folk art is "marked" (in the linguistic sense of the word) because the aesthetic function is dominated by other functions. The dominance of the aesthetic function in art is always considered to be fundamental or "unmarked" (Mukarovsky 1970:7–8). Marked cases in folk art are quite common, according to Mukarovsky, as he further notes that in the folk stratum the aesthetic function and norm are usually subordinated to other functions and norms, even in objects that may be called art (1970:56).

But even though the aesthetic function of this quilt is subordinated to its social and identificational functions, the quilt has considerable value for the group. In fact, the quilt could be valued *because* of the normal violations, an idea suggested by the following interaction, which deals with my eighty-year-old grandmother's concern over the poor quality of her stitching:

> *Mamaw:* If they don't like the way we do ours—
> *Aunt A [interrupting]:* Mamaw, it's your quilt.
> *Aunt C:* It's your quilt, Mamaw.
> *Aunt D:* You can do it any way you want to. It is your quilt.
> *Mamaw:* Well, if it's not quilted good—
> *Aunt D [interrupting]:* And everybody is gonna want it, Mamaw. When they get through with it, everybody is gonna want it.
> *Mamaw:* Want the quilt?
> *Aunt D:* That's right, because it has your little quilting down there, and see, Mamaw, they can't tell it apart, 'cause you're on one side, and I'm on the other. *[Laughter.]* That'll be the best part about it.

The participants accepted the substandard quilting in order to include the family. In fact, the men who came in near the end of the session were encouraged to try a few stitches. As Aunt A explained to her brother: "It's the last one [quilt] Mamaw made, and her younguns all quilted it, and grandyounguns. That's why you and [brother-in-law] are supposed to be quilting on it." The inclusion of these unskilled men, even briefly, in the quilting session is highly uncommon even in this group, but it emphasizes the importance of the family's togetherness. Therefore, the quilt represents the efforts of a grandmother, five of her six children and their available spouses, and various grandchildren; it thus becomes a symbol of three generations of the family cooperating for a new fourth generation—ideas that certainly have great sentimental value in such a family-oriented group and make the quilt one that "everybody is gonna want." Hence an aesthetic transformation takes place in that the context of this quilt transforms an "everyday" quilt with substandard construction into a beautiful heir-loom that all the family members will cherish.

Our limited examination of a quilting bee provides a sample of the communicative aspects of the quilt in the overlapping semiotic sub-systems in which the quilt functions—as a practical household ob-ject, as an object or means of social interaction and family reaffirmation and continuation, as an art object, and as a vehicle to express cultural beliefs and worldview. We have also seen that a particular folk art object cannot be understood and appreciated fully without examining these overlapping functions and how they relate to other aspects of the culture, such as the communication system. The family's conversations in the quilting session indicate that in this specific folk art object the aesthetic function is dominated by socio-cultural functions, thus influencing the message of the quilt. As a symbolic form the patchwork quilt easily lent itself to carrying messages reaffirming the meaningfulness of family ties and the trans-mission of family values to new generations. Analysis of the quilting bee as a speech event allows us to interpret those messages in order to understand what the quilt says about itself, its makers, and their relationships.

NOTES

1. This void promises to be filled with several dissertations on the subject of quiltmaking, including Maude Wahlman's work on Afro-American quiltmakers (Yale University), Lorre Weidlich's work on Revivalist quiltmakers, Joyce Ice's work on Lytton Springs, Texas, quilters, and my own work on northern Louisiana quiltmakers (University of Texas). Ice and Shulimson (1979) offer the first published contextual study of quiltmakers.

2. This approach was adapted from Joel and Dina Sherzer's ethnographic se-miotic studies of Cuna molas (Sherzer and Sherzer 1976a, 1976b).

3. It is apparently quite common for women to make and store pieced tops for quilting later, as evidenced by numbers of quilt tops for sale in antique shops.

4. The terms of address, "Mamaw" for grandmother and "Aunt _____ " are the terms used by all members of the group; sisters address one another as "Aunt _____ ," and their mother as "Mamaw," the same terms their children use. I chose to use these terms in presenting actual conversation from the quilting session to give the original flavor of the event. Letters rather than actual names have been used to preserve the anonymity of the participants.

5. It may be that quilts function as a symbol of family involvement in various rites of passage because quilts have often been made as gifts to mark occasions such as births, weddings, children leaving home, and even deaths.

· 5 ·
IT'S A SIN TO WASTE A RAG:
RUG-WEAVING IN WESTERN MARYLAND
Geraldine Niva Johnson

"They have such neat-looking, clean-looking rags, and it's a shame to throw them away. I think it's a sin, so I take them."

T HE WOVEN rag rug found in far western Maryland today is the great-grandchild of America's oldest and most popular handmade floorcovering: the rag carpet. Sometimes known as "list" carpet, it covered bare Colonial floors long before other types of carpet—Turkey, Brussels, or Ingrain Scotch—were fashionable. Edward Jarvis of Massachusetts, a nineteenth-century diarist, remembers the wall-to-wall rag carpeting in his mother's parlor as the "common kind of carpet, for most farmer and mechanic families" (Little 1975:200–201).[1] Created in strips up to thirty-six inches wide, the pieces of carpet were tacked together and stretched across the length of a room. "We used the carpet tacks," a contemporary rug weaver recalls. "We got right down on our knees with the old hammer and . . . started right up the edge of it." After wall-to-wall rag carpeting lost its appeal, many women continued to weave strips of carpet or runners to use in bedrooms, kitchens, and hallways. Gradually rugs twenty-six by fifty-four inches became popular because they were easy to wash in the new automatic wringer washers.

No one can be sure of the origin of rag rugs. They are an important class of floorcovering in continental Europe and in Scandinavia, according to contemporary scholars. Among the French and French-Canadians, the rag carpet or "catalogne" is a treasured folk art object. A traveler who visited Leeds, England, in 1783 mentioned in his diary the existence of at least one small shop weaving yards of "list" carpet for commercial sale.[2] Such shops also existed in Philadelphia during the nineteenth century, where as many as eight looms were crowded into one small room to weave carpet, runners, and rugs for an eager American public (Cole 1932).

Weaving rag rugs is now a widespread American craft and could be called a vital home industry. Many women and some men weave on a regular basis, producing individually from four hundred to five hundred rugs each year. Although some may weave only a few rugs for their own use, many more weave on special order or for resale in local shops. They set up their looms in back porches, basements, or remodeled sheds, usually working alone. In some homes, however, up to three looms may be pounding away in one room. Even though times and tastes have changed, these weavers are creating a product of tremendous complexity in a manner that clearly links them to the past from which the craft emerged.

My own interest in rug-weaving began in 1975, when I participated in a crafts survey for the state of Maryland. I found woven rag rugs scattered on floors throughout the state, but in the far western Appalachian region almost every other home appeared to have rugs and a loom. During periodic visits to the region over the next three years, I frequented craft shops, county fairs, fiddle contests, and family reunions, searching for weavers. I talked to many women, conducted tape-recorded interviews with approximately twenty of them, and photographed hundreds of rugs on floors or pinned to a canvas hooked to the side of my Dodge van. What emerged from my survey was a sense of the history and vitality of the craft and the knowledge that at least three distinct rug-weaving communities existed in this small two-county area. One woman's approach to the craft is described in this chapter, and her techniques as well as her final products represent those of one weaving community in western Maryland.

Elaine is not the most skilled of the twenty rug weavers I have interviewed, nor is she the most unusual.[3] She has never created a strange "rug masterpiece," although one of her favorite woven rugs is made from funeral ribbons taken from the church cemetery.[4] That one of these and two other rugs made by Elaine have won blue ribbons at the county fair for the last three years, however, is one indicator of the community's acceptance of her product. Moreover, she is a cooperative informant—willing to be questioned, observed, recorded, and photographed by a persistent folklorist. Most important in making her an interesting subject for this kind of analysis is Elaine's serious professional attitude toward her weaving. She enjoys her craft and her rugs; she weaves almost daily and takes pride in her work.

This portion of my study combines Henry Glassie's (1967) interest in the "detailed description [of folk technology]" with Michael Owen Jones's concern for the "idiosyncratic personality of the creator" (1968:255).[5] Throughout the project, I used the techniques of oral history to gather the data of life history and the techniques of field observation to document the craft.[6] Describing the process is a valuable exercise because it tells us as much about the rug maker as it does about the rug. For this reason I have tried to include the informant's own comments on her tasks whenever appropriate (much as Roger Abrahams allows his informant to tell her own story in Riddle 1970). In fact, throughout the discussion I have opted for the informant's own language when possible in order to record, as did Jones, the craft worker's own speech patterns, her special terminology in its context, and her emphasis. The results of this investigation tell us something about that curious phenomenon we call tradition, illuminate the not-so-simple process of rug-weaving, and present the life of one woman as it is organized around her craft.

LIFE HISTORY

Elaine was born on a farm in western Maryland in 1907. Her father, who came into the region from Pennsylvania as part of a sawmill gang, was Scotch-Irish; her mother was Pennsylvania Dutch. Elaine completed one year of high school and attended summer normal school at a nearby college in hopes of teaching elementary students, but she was not assigned a school and "decided to do housework." Although she married in 1932, she continued to work "at housework" or in the textile plants located in western Maryland and southwestern Pennsylvania. Her husband, Harry, a carpenter by trade, worked in factories when he could, and farmed as well. In 1957, Elaine and her husband leased an Esso station near their farm. When Harry died in 1962, Elaine had to finish out the lease alone. She decided the rent was too high and the station too busy for one person to run. It was "too much for me to care for myself and not enough money coming in to hire help. In 1966, I located on our own place with a little filling station, a Texaco service station, where I'm living now."

Elaine's "little business place" is itself a fine example of salvage craft. She and her daughter, with the help of neighbors, built it from two burned-out trailers in 1966. They removed the most severely damaged sides of the eighteen-by-nine-and-a-half-foot trailers and built a twelve-foot section where the doorway is now located. Elaine added two rental trailers to the property, put up a sign for a frequently vacant campground, and thus had a thriving gas station/grocery/trailer rental business.

Elaine is vague about her earnings at the station; she claims it is "not much of an income." At the moment she is "in the red" and simply trying to make ends meet. Something is always breaking down, she claims, and because she trusts people too much, she gets "beat out of money." She probably covers most of her own living expenses through the station and uses the $1,000 she earns from the trailers and the $700 from her rugs for the extras she requires. She stays at the station because it is "something to do" and she "can meet some people" while she sells bait, rugs, gas, groceries, and ice. Right now bait is her best-selling item, because "all people can afford to do these days is fish."

The interior of the gas station is a combination grocery store, living quarters, and rug room. The total space available, eighteen by thirty feet, is roughly divided in half. Half functions as a store loaded with typical general-store items: cookies, candy, bread, dish soap, dog food, and canned goods, including some of Elaine's own canning. The aisles are narrow, and they are usually made even smaller by the number of boxes and bags, some filled with rug rags, stacked on the floor.

The other half of the station serves as a living area and rug room. Here Elaine has her Warm Morning stove, bathroom, cooking stove and sink, three refrigerators, two sewing machines, one rollaway bed, three cupboards, one kitchen table, and two chairs. Old clothes and

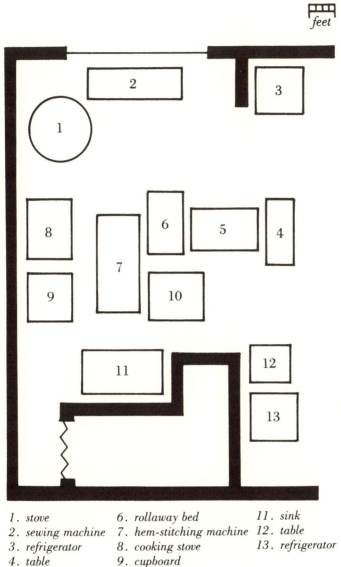

feet

1. stove
2. sewing machine
3. refrigerator
4. table
5. cupboard
6. rollaway bed
7. hem-stitching machine
8. cooking stove
9. cupboard
10. refrigerator
11. sink
12. table
13. refrigerator

Figure 1. Floor plan of the rug room portion of the gas station

boxes of rug rags are stacked everywhere. The aisles are narrow here too, and one must navigate carefully to avoid knocking anything over.

The station gives Elaine the social interaction she finds essential. Of her home, she says, "It's too lonely down there in the hollow. Here somebody comes in every little bit to talk to." The neighbors drop in to buy a carton of milk or a candy bar or a pack of cigarettes, and they stay and chat awhile. The breadman delivers his orders. Two young boys, strangers to Elaine, sit at her kitchen table while they try to convince her to buy their mother's embroidered pillowcases. Several customers come in on rug business; in fact, Elaine believes that most people who come into the station come for the rugs. The days are not lonely here. On the other hand, running this business is not as taxing as operating the other gas station had been. "If you don't have time to enjoy yourself, what good is it?" This station gives her the opportunity to meet people but still close up when she needs to run errands in town, work in her garden, or go on a picnic. It makes just the right demands on her time, "and it's better than living alone."

The station may be a "good bit of confinement" for Elaine, but it does not keep her from performing many other household and community tasks. From May to November she is busy planting, cultivating, and harvesting the garden. She cans peas, beans, tomatoes, pumpkin, cider when it is fresh, apple butter, and applesauce. She makes about three gallons each of dandelion, elder blossom, elderberry, and grape wine. She operates the hem-stitching machine for the church sewing circle and hems about 275 pillowcases a year. All these chores are squeezed in at the station when she is not pumping gas or fetching earthworms and ice.

Elaine has only one daughter, Millie, born in 1944. "I got a daughter late in life," she says, "and now I can't seem to keep her home. Seems everyone wants my Millie." Millie, who works at a local nursing home, moved out of her mother's household and into a neighbor's home ten years earlier. These neighbors have come to be "Aunt Elaine's" extended family; they perform chores for her on a daily basis, and she is included in all their family activities. More than anything else, however, Elaine wants Millie back home, and she still resents the neighbors with whom her daughter lives.[7]

Elaine's kinship network includes a sister, nephews, nieces, and cousins, many of whom live in the area. Through a common western Maryland tradition, the family reunion, these kinship networks are kept intact and family values are reinforced. Elaine used to attend three annual family reunions, and she still attends at least one or two a year, as well as her hometown picnic. Several years ago, Elaine, Millie, and a neighbor provided the music—primarily hymns—for several area reunions. Elaine played a portable organ while Millie accompanied her on the clarinet, and a neighbor played the trumpet. They stopped playing when the neighbor died and Millie began to work on weekends.

St. Paul's Lutheran Church in a nearby community provides another important source of support for Elaine. It still "seems like home" because her husband is buried there and because Millie was confirmed there. Elaine sings in the choir on Sundays and used to enjoy participating in the sewing circle. They would "visit, talk, and have a good time" while quilting. She does not attend the weekly circle meetings any more because Millie cannot take her, but she does participate in the "secret sister" activities. Each member of the circle is assigned a "secret sister" who sends presents and greeting cards on her sister's birthday and anniversary. Her identity is not revealed until the end of the year, when a new secret sister is selected. This extended family member is the source of much interest and excitement on Elaine's part.

Elaine's home is about half a mile from the gas station. It sits back from the road one-quarter of a mile and is indeed down in a hollow. The two-story I house is large but crowded with furniture, including some interesting pieces made by her husband and his brother. Her prize possession is the "organ in a piano case." She has a huge freezer and an ice-making machine on the porch so that she can make her own ice to sell at the store. The pathway through the rooms is narrow, and every piece of furniture is stacked with papers, boxes, and books.

Even though she has a large house, Elaine lives almost exclusively in the kitchen. In the winter she blocks off the rest of the house and heats only the kitchen, while the mice chew the fringes off the rugs in the living room. In the summer she still lives in the kitchen, where a big stove dominates the room. There she has a rollaway bed neatly made up for herself and a new chest of drawers for her clothing. A small table serves her well for the few meals she eats at home.

For a woman who values family and friends so much, that symbol of sociability, the dining room table, is strangely absent. Elaine never entertains her family or neighbors in her house; on major holidays she is invited to a relative's home. The gas station satisfies her social needs, and the large dining room table she had in her home was moved down to the rug room when Millie left. It now serves up rug rags instead of holiday dinners throughout the year.

As is often the case with those who are dissatisfied in some way with the present, the past assumes a rosy glow in Elaine's mind. She remembers "the old times" as times of sociability and conviviality:[8]

> An aunt would come. Maybe she'd stay a week because traveling was slow, and when she did come, she stayed and visited with us probably a week at a time, and we'd have spare bedrooms prepared for them. We'd have a nice sitting room for them because we had more company in them days than we have today to entertain.

Women were also more skillful in those days. "Oh, them old-timers had the most beautiful quilting that you ever looked at." It may well be this romantic attitude toward the past which makes Elaine believe the old-time rag carpet is going to return to popularity some day.

Finally, Elaine is a woman who has made some important decisions concerning her life. She is not the victim so many people like to find in the traditional pockets of our society. She has chosen to make a small, crowded gas station the center of her social and economic world. She has chosen a specific "business place" that gives her an adequate income with maximum freedom. She rejects some of society's blessings, such as television—"Nothing is more tiresome to me than that." Yet she has what she wants: four sewing machines, four refrigerators, three organs, two freezers, one ice machine, and one ice maker. Once we had a long, rambling conversation about the aggravating and odious nature of laundromats; I guess I should not have been surprised to find that Elaine has not one, not two, but three commercial-size clothes washers and dryers. While she can justify this luxury in practical terms, basically she is a woman who gets what she wants. Like Thoreau, she has simplified her life beyond what might be comfortable for most, but unlike Thoreau she is doing it for more than two years.

THE WEAVING

As is the case with many weavers, Elaine did not begin working at her craft until she was married and had a home of her own. She was always interested in rug-making, but her experiments with other rugs were not successful. "Most all types of rugs that I tried to make, they was slow to get them finished, and I had trouble too." The plaited rugs would not "lay down in the middle," and besides they "don't hold up." The crocheted rug was "a little better," but "you couldn't use worn clothing much in that. You'd have to have practically all new material." She made another type woven from rug yarn on a frame, but that was "pretty expensive," and it "took longer to make," and "probably you couldn't sell those." So a woven rug was best for her. It was easier, faster, and cheaper to make.

Elaine was soon convinced of the superiority of the woven rug. It "holds up better," because in the woven rug the warp "has a tendency to hold [the rags] together." The warp is "about twelve threads to the inch, so it's bound to be tighter and control better."[9] Elaine also liked woven rugs "for the simple reason that you could throw them in the washer and wash them, and . . . use them reversible, one side as well as the other." Because they were easy to maintain, woven rugs also sold well. "I have to furnish the warp and my work while they furnish their rags, the filler, and pay for the weaving of them. So that was a little income for your work rather than all output." Finally, the woven rug satisfied Elaine's need for beauty. "I can't hardly wait until I can get the rugs off the loom a lot of times to see how attractive they're going to be." She feels that most of the time, if the material is "done up neat," the rugs are "really beautiful."

Elaine can remember wall-to-wall woven carpet in her own childhood home. Her mother covered all the floors, except the kitchen, with the striped carpeting. The margins, which overlapped two inches, were either sewed together or tacked to the floor. Then "if they wanted rugs for on top of this carpet . . . they either crocheted them or they plaited them or they whipped them to a sack" and put them "in front of the couch and in front of the big chair." Every year this woven wall-to-wall carpet had to be washed, and "we'd just tear them apart in the spring and put them in the washer and wash one strip at a time." Modern carpet or, as she labels it, "this other kind of carpet" is not as easy to clean.

Elaine remembers helping her mother "get the rug rags ready" when she was a little girl. "I used to sit and help my mother cut them there rug rags of a night and on Saturday when I was home from school and help sew them together and everything. And we'd take them down to Greens' and have them wove." Her mother "cut that there round and around way of doing them," so they did not need much sewing. What stitching they did do on the rug rags was done by hand. Her mother's rounded corners were neat, of course, "the same width as her strip that she cut." Elaine still feels that preparing the rags is "what got me interested when I got older to make rugs. . . . I just loved it."

Elaine finally got a rug loom in 1946 shortly after she and her husband moved to their own farm. She bought it secondhand for ten dollars from "an elderly woman that was retired from making rugs." It is a Union Custom Loom and the one she still uses; newer looms are not "built as well as this old kind." She once bought a second loom with a fly shuttle, but she did not like it and quickly sold it. "It wasn't all there," and they had to add parts to it; and it was "one that you could sit down by." Elaine never sits while she weaves, so she found the newer loom "a size that wasn't becoming to me."

Her older Union Loom was also modified in several ways to make her weaving easier and her rugs tighter. Her husband drilled holes into the rug beam, and she uses leather shoelaces to tie the rug warp directly to the beam. In the past the rug warp was tied to a piece of canvas that was attached to the beam. The canvas would slip and stretch, thus loosening the warp. Now the shoelaces threaded directly through the rug beam and tied to the warp hold it more securely. Elaine's husband also added nails to the back of the loom to keep the warp from tangling when she is winding it onto the warp beam. In addition, she replaced a smaller bolt with a heavier one to secure the rug beam lever to the supporting frame so that it will not slip when she is tightening the rugs. Finally, her husband made extra shuttles for her which allow her to wrap the rags on a total of thirty-eight shuttles, enough "to make one whole rug at least two yards long."

Learning to weave was not easy. The woman who sold her the loom "couldn't seem to remember anything about making rugs," so she had to pick it up on her own. She read two books that came with the loom, both published by the Union Loom Company. The books "didn't tell you how to weave rugs. [They] just told you how to thread the rug loom up and get ready to weave." Her brother-in-law also helped her figure out how to put the loom together. Finally, she threaded it up and made a small rug for herself. Elaine adamantly claims that she learned how to weave on her own. "It's a thing that I didn't learn by somebody teaching me, and I had to learn it on my own, and when I made a mistake back there, whenever I been corrected, I remembered that mistake and didn't make that same mistake again." The whole process of Elaine's learning to weave, then, appears to be a result of individual experimentation, written instruction, and advice from relatives and friends.

After she had made a few rugs for herself, "friends came in and wanted to know if I wouldn't start making them rugs, and I said, well, I hadn't figured on making any for anyone else." But she did make rugs for another lady who was "well pleased" with them so she had me to make her some more." Soon she was making rugs for all her neighbors: "I collected a little money to get me some warp to get started, and one would tell another one that I made rugs. So I experimented really on all of them until I got on to it better and better. But they seemed to like them, and so I kept right on."

One particular customer helped to spread the word about Elaine's rug-making ability.

> There was a lady that used to travel around with McNess Products, and her husband had arthritis, and he'd cut the rags for several years, and she had as high as a hundred rugs a year made by me. . . . She took them around and really got me advertised. She sold those rugs to her customers where she sold her McNess Products.

Over a period of five years, Elaine made over five hundred rugs for that one buyer.

Today Elaine weaves four hundred or five hundred rugs a year for her customers, many of whom have twenty-five or thirty-five rugs made at a time. Church groups prepare their own filler and have her weave the rugs for them to sell. One customer recently had thirty-five rugs made to sell at a local flea market. Some of the rugs Elaine weaves for herself to sell at the gas station and at local gift shops. She is a small but important part of a thriving marketing enterprise.

One of Elaine's early experiments led to a rug she considers uniquely hers, although other weavers do make it. "I don't see very many, or hardly any I must say, that twists their rags in like I do mine." She calls this rug the variegated or twisted rug, for in it two pieces of filler, cut relatively thin, about one inch wide, are combined to make one shot through the width of the rug. She usually combines "a plain color with a figured color. It brightens it up better." She also finds the variegated rug a useful way to use up white rags, which she says are impractical in a rug by themselves. In a twisted rug, however, the white "makes the rug so it isn't neither too dark nor too light." Later she "decided to put a plain border on the end in the twisted rug, and it looked very nice." She tries to select bright colors for this purpose because they show up better. She will choose a "bright border, something like red or yellow or something that blends in well with the colors that's in the rug."

Elaine started experimenting with the variegated rug when a neighbor told her "about some people that she had seen that had gotten rugs that were two colors blended together and were twisted."

> So we seemed to think that it was a spinning wheel that they had twisted these on. . . . There was a preacher came to our place, and he said he had a spinning wheel, and if I could use it, why I could have it. So I said, well, I'd really appreciate it to try twisting my rug rags on because it made them a variegated color and really looked neat.

She experimented with the spinning wheel, and it worked. Later the minister passed away, "and the spinning wheel became mine. That was free. Gratis. So I've been using it ever since." Thus Elaine's most unique rug type developed through conversations with her customers, contributions from a neighbor, and her own desire to experiment.

Later Elaine began to weave striped rugs. "There's some people had their rags cut pretty heavy. I decided to just run those in single and stripe them in, which was very nice." Today she weaves few variegated rugs, but many plain and striped ones. The time involved is probably an important factor; it takes twice as long to prepare the filler for a variegated rug as it does for a plain or striped one. Another favorite hybrid of Elaine's is the "hit and miss" rug striped in on the ends but hit and miss in the middle. That too is a practical adaptation allowing her to use up odds and ends of materials.

Elaine's greatest achievement so far is the wall-to-wall carpeting she made for a customer several years ago. The four or five lengths of carpet were striped, and each stripe had to match. "It was hard to do. You just had to count every shot and your stripes. I had to stripe them so that they'd come just right too." The customer helped with the project. "She got her own filler ready. She had them all cut the same

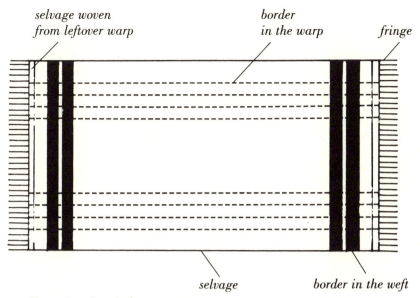

selvage woven
from leftover warp

border
in the warp

fringe

selvage

border in the weft

Figure 2. A typical woven rag rug

width, so therefore they came in neat." Still Elaine says, "It took a lot of planning to do that."

Before she begins to weave any piece of carpet or rug, Elaine has her loom threaded with warp, which she buys from the Oriental Rug Company in Lima, Ohio. She used to buy the boilproof warp, but "it was more expensive" and "I couldn't see where it was any better than just the colored warp." It takes thirty-five pounds of warp to thread up the loom, and from that she can make approximately forty-eight rugs. The loom has 12 strands of warp per inch, a total of 360 across for a thirty-inch rug. Elaine has a warping comb with thirty holes in it, one for each strand of warp; the comb is attached to the back of her loom, and she puts "twelve of those bunches on like that across."

A unique warp pattern gives Elaine's rugs a special trademark, which she values highly. "I have a way of putting my warp on that nobody else puts their warp on like I do. I stripe my warp in. I have bright colors . . . and my background is black and red. That's the way I can tell my pattern of warping." Thus in this secret way she can distinguish her rugs from those of any other weaver, and so could anyone else. "If they've had a lot made by me, they can tell my rugs."

The unusual aspect of her trademark is the black and red stripes, which she calls background, that run down each side and the middle of her rug. She puts a variety of pastel colors between the stripes, but as she says, "I try and keep that black and red background pattern even though I change the variegated stripes in between."

She chose the black and red colors in the warp for several reasons. First, they are colors that are "becoming to most any kind of material that people brings in." Red too "is a bright color, and the black gives it a neat-looking border along the edge of your rug." She also considers black and red to be "bright colors that hold your colors well after they're washed and laundered a lot." The variegated stripes, or "pastel shades in between, they don't hold it quite as good." She illustrated this principle by pointing to a well-worn rug on the floor. "See," she said, "[the pastel colors are] dying off and getting dull, but your black and red holds up."

Elaine claims that she changes "the variegated colors in between once in a while." She likes some variety herself, not "the same old story." She tries "to plan the variegated part to match [the customer's] material while I've got theirs to work up." I have never seen her plan the warp in this way, however. Once, in fact, I heard her chide herself for being too lazy to put in a color that would have matched the rug better.

Her warp pattern also has a practical aspect. When the rug is "cut down" and she is tying the warp in knots, it helps to have bunches of eight all one color for each knot. "You know that you have black and red, [eight] bunches of them all the time, and you don't have to be thinking about whether you're going to get the wrong thread tied on the wrong color." The warp colors, then, actually help in the final process of rug-making.

White warp is not popular with Elaine or her customers. Weavers use the white warp, she believes, because "it's cheaper. It costs more to dye the warp, and a lot of them has a tendency to think, 'Well, that's more money in my pocket.' " Primarily, though, she opposes white warp because it does not hold up well. "The white gets dingy looking, and it never comes clean if it gets tracked on enough. It just seems as though the soil will not come out of the white."

She likes to tell the story about "a couple ladies when I first started to weaving" who specifically asked for dark warp on all their rugs. They said, "I hate that white. In just a little while, it looks all dingy and dirty looking." That, she claims, "turned me against that white warp until I didn't want any of it on my own thinking." She assured the customers that she would always use colored warp. They in turn told her that the warp was one of the nicest features of her rugs: "You have the warp attractive and all colors, and it blends in with anything I bring in to have my rugs made up."

Elaine is an unusual weaver in her steadfast refusal ever to change her warp colors or patterns. She has, on occasion, used blue in place of black in her background, but that was only when the company sent her the wrong shade of blue for her variegated warp. Other weavers are quite willing to negotiate the color of warp, and they will thread the loom especially for one customer, but Elaine's trademark always remains the same.

The most tedious part of rug-making, but also one of the most important parts, is preparing the rags. Elaine does this at the gas station sitting in front of her Singer sewing machine or next to her small kitchen table. It takes her all day to prepare the rags for an average-size rug, one to one-and-a-half yards long. Because this part of the process can influence the rug's appearance, Elaine is fussy about how the rags are "worked up." Frequently the customer prepares the filler herself, which makes rug-weaving a truly collaborative craft.[10] Sometimes, however, Elaine prepares her own rags for rugs she will sell in the store.

She makes filler from "most any kind of material": old, new, cotton, or plastic. New fabrics "make beautiful rugs, and they hold their color brighter for a long time." Old fabrics, on the other hand, are "all right." They should not be put in, though, "if they're worn too much," and the badly worn pieces should be cut out. Elaine does not dye her fabrics. They "would be brighter just for a little while, while they're new, but after they're washed for a while, that has a tendency to wash out."

She tries to keep the materials separate if possible because some fabrics may "have a tendency to draw in" more than others when they are laundered, and the rug will not "lay good." This is especially true of wool and knitwear, although Elaine does violate this rule when the customer includes knitwear in her filler. Sometimes, too, Elaine will try to twist the knitwear with pieces of cotton and "make a border out of it for another cotton rug, and that seems to hold it from, after it's laundered, from stretching out of shape."

Rug rags should be either torn or cut into even strips. "Now the material that doesn't ravel too much, why it's better to tear it. You can make a neater, straighter job of it." A torn strip is automatically more even in width than a cut one. "The material that doesn't tear, of course you'll have to use the scissors and try to cut it as near to the same width all the time." Knitwear and silk frequently have to be cut, sometimes with a cutter, while cotton, most popular in rugs, can be torn.

The rule to be followed in cutting rags is, according to Elaine, "the heavier the material, the more narrow you cut the material. If I'm making a plain rug and striping it in, I cut the cotton material about an inch and a half wide. The heavier material shouldn't be cut over an inch to an inch and a fourth wide."

Elaine has a separate technique for preparing each item of clothing she encounters. Fabrics should never be cut on the bias, but "once in a while if there isn't too many seams in it, well you can cut those full skirts around the bias about an inch and a half wide." She approaches each item this way, as a separate project with its own special demands. She can discuss in great detail how to tear or cut rug rags from each piece of raw material—shirts, dresses, pants, knitwear, sweatshirts, nylon stockings, and plastic bread wrappers.[11]

Elaine's favorite technique for cutting the material is what she calls the "round and around" method. When she has help in cutting the rags, she uses this technique. With a plain pair of shears, she cuts along the length of the fabric to within one-quarter inch of the far edge; then she starts at that edge and cuts back parallel to her first cut until she is one-quarter inch from the other end. When the material has been entirely cut in this way, the square ends of each corner are then neatly rounded so that when stretched out a moderately flat strip of fabric is the result. Elaine considers this one of the oldest methods of preparing rags. Her mother did it this way and "the Amish people still do that."

Cutting around the corners is the tiresome and difficult part of this procedure. If the end is too narrow, it might tear when it is put into the rug; if it is too wide, it will not lie neatly in the rug. As Elaine says, "If you're going to round your corners, you don't dare to cut them too wide. They'll round easier if you cut them narrow because it makes [the rags] too wide at that place where they wind [or twist] them around."

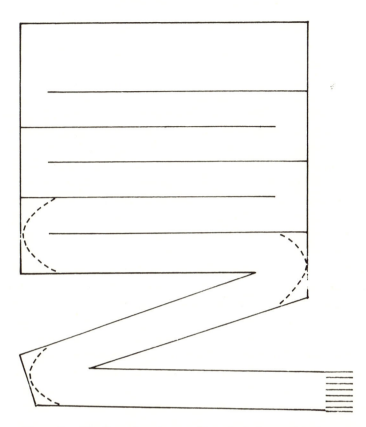

Figure 3.   The "round-and-around" method of preparing the rags

Elaine uses part of this technique when she cuts her own rags. She cuts from one end to the other, but she does not round the corners. "That there's a good bit of bother rounding them, so I don't bother to round them. I do it the quicker, easier way myself." She nevertheless manages to justify this violation of her own standards. "The square corners don't look too bad to leave them on. That's the reason I leave them on." Then she adds, "It makes a neater job if you round the corners, but I don't round them all the time."

After the rags are cut, Elaine joins them together in one of two ways: looping or machine-stitching. Looping is particularly useful when she does not feel like using the sewing machine; then she cuts "a large buttonhole" in each strip and loops one rag through the other. Rags are stitched in a variety of ways, but Elaine prefers to fold the strip of material lengthwise, "one piece over another, and sew a seam as near the edge as possible, and then turn it inside out." The result is a piece of filler folded in half with a small seam on the inside.

Rug makers constantly complain about the way customers prepare rags, and Elaine is no exception. She is distressed by those who think "any old happy way will do" in cutting and sewing rags. The worst mistake is to cut them unevenly. A customer may cut one part of the strip "three inches wide and then come down here to half-inch wide. That's no good." Some women "cut across the seams, leaving all these here deep seams a-hanging on. Well, that looks terrible." She always tells her customers "to cut all seams off [or to cut] lengthwise of the material." Some customers do not round the corners neatly; they leave "too much a-hanging on there," and others leave too many ravelings on the material.

Elaine's constant admonition to customers is that "the warp doesn't hide anything." Ravelings, seams, and poorly cut rags all show up in the rug. And the pressure of business keeps her from redoing the rags. "If the customers have fixed those rags all mixed up, why I'm not about to take them apart because it's too much extra trouble for me. I try to tell them to have them put together neat."

But as much as she tries to get her customers to bring in neat-looking rags, the fact that many of them do not compromises her efforts as a rug maker and dampens some of her enthusiasm. "I like to look at my rugs and take them off and see what they look like. Sorta makes me feel kinda bad if some of them don't look too good. . . . I tell them that it really upsets me to try to make a rug out of filler that's not done up neat." But she feels she cannot take time to redo the rags people bring her, nor can she prepare all of them herself. "I have to turn down a lot of them that I can't work the material up. That's all there is to it. I can't help it they don't like it."

Once Elaine has enough rags prepared (whether by herself or by a customer), the planning process begins. As she says, "I get [them] ready to weave in by the shuttles-full and plan about how I want the rugs made right here before I start weaving them in." The customers bring their rags to the station wound into large balls, which Elaine unwinds one at a time and measures out in lengths which will fill a shuttle. "I wrap about twenty wraps on my hand, and it makes a shuttle-full on my shuttles." No one else's hand will do; only hers is geared to her shuttles. She also knows that a shuttle-full will make "three inches across the rug" and that it takes thirty-eight to forty shuttles for a two-yard rug. Now, while still at the gas station, she has the rags sorted and wound into "shuttle-balls" and can begin to plan each individual rug.

At this point, too, Elaine begins to plan the overall color patterns for the rugs. She determines whether the rug will be plain, striped, hit-and-miss, or variegated. These decisions depend on the rags that are available. If she has many rags of one color, she will often make a plain rug; however, a few odds and ends mean a hit-and-miss rug. She also selects the rags for the border, which she likes to be made out of "something different," usually a fabric of solid bright colors such as yellow, red, lavender, or bright blue.

If necessary, Elaine telephones her customer to ask her the length she prefers for each rug. Then she tries to "plan out of her material the lengths that [the customer] wants her rugs and make them up." Elaine claims that her customers do not request particular types of rugs such as variegated or striped. "They leave that up to me to plan the rug." Sometimes they prefer a certain fabric in a certain room. "They might prefer that they want the cotton rugs for the kitchen and the length they want them, so I'll plan that out of the cotton material."

Elaine will not change the width of her rugs to suit a customer. Her loom is threaded for thirty-inch rugs, and depending on how heavy the material is, the width will be from twenty-eight to thirty inches. She believes that because she threads her loom for four dozen rugs at a time she cannot change the width. Besides, she adds, "if I started to changing the width with my customers, why they'd bother you so much with the different widths that you couldn't keep up with it."

She will make rugs any length though. She has made them from fifteen inches long to twelve feet long. Most of her rugs are a yard or a yard and a half, however, and the runners are two and four yards long. An important consideration for her in planning the length of the rug is remembering to allow for shrinkage—on most rugs three inches to the yard, but on her extra-tight rugs it is four inches to the yard. Sometimes "different material shrinks back more than others. Kinda hard to get them just exact."

When the rags have been wound on shuttles, Elaine piles them into cardboard boxes, carefully separating the rags for individual rugs with newspapers. She loads the boxes into her turquoise 1965 Ford pickup truck and heads for the rug room at the farm.

This, then, is the first part of the process of rug-weaving. It is important to note that the process is divided into two distinct parts, each with its separate work area, separate tools, and sometimes separate crafters. Like so much else that women do, rug-weaving activities are often interrupted and fragmented, and the interruption is not always brief. Preparing the rags at the station is an activity meshed with other tasks—selling winter butter, having a leaky roof repaired, visiting with a neighbor. It may take days, weeks, or months to get the prepared and planned rags ready to travel that quarter mile to the rug room. A good deal of concentration is lost during the delay.

Elaine's rug room is really one-third of a long cement-block building formerly used as a chicken house.[12] The building itself is in good condition with its cement floor, solid walls, and rafters covered with insulation. Heavy canvas tarps divide the building into three unevenly sized rooms. The first room, through which one enters, is a coal storage area. The second, slightly larger, room houses the rug loom. And the third and largest room contains the laundry. Sometimes, Elaine says, she weaves while she does the laundry for her rental trailers.

I spent two nights, from six-thirty to eleven o'clock, with Elaine in the rug room. The first night she wove two matching rugs, one-and-a-half yards each, and planned a four-yard runner. The second night she wove the runner and, finding that she had enough filler left for another small rug, planned and wove that too. It is the runner and the small rug whose creation I will describe.

Elaine was eager to weave the runner. Although she claims it takes her only a week to ten days to fill an order, these rags had been sitting at the station for two months. She had measured and wound them into shuttle-balls right after the customer brought them in, and thus had begun the planning process. Because of the garden, however, she had not been able to get any weaving done. She considers a runner "easier" to weave than a rug because "there are fewer selvages and ends to tie off."[13]

She started planning the runner as soon as she finished the two matching rugs on the first night of weaving. She wanted to "get some done on it, then it ain't so tiresome. I can get more done." This second phase of the planning process took about ten minutes. First she looked for the matching balls of rags and lined them up two by two on the old dining room table. "I lay them down on the table for the whole rug that I'm going to make." All the single balls of rags were set aside to be woven into the middle of the rug.

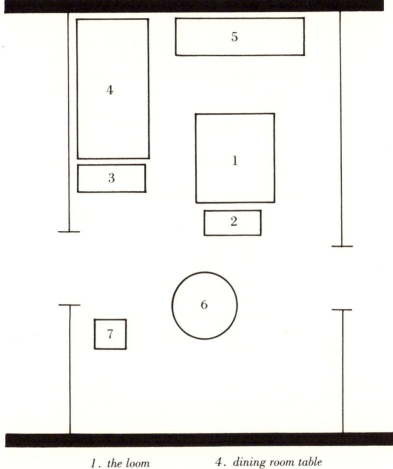

feet

1. the loom
2. foot pad
3. grocery cart filled
   with warp

4. dining room table
5. spinning wheel
6. stove
7. small table for tools

Figure 4.   Floor plan of the rug room in a former chicken house

She then began to arrange the matching pairs of balls into a color scheme that suited her. She decided to start with black filler on the end of the rug because it would help "brighten up" the beige border she planned to use. The two halves of the double border would not be the same color; because she did not have enough solid beige material, the second half of the border would have to be light green. Then she chose the rest of the colors. Green would look "pretty next to orange," and pink would "be nice next to green," but the tans were "a little too close together." She added some yellow—"Ain't got much yellow streaks yet." And she put a few streaks of red throughout the rug "so it shows up." She explained that "pretty near everybody likes quite a bit of red used in their rugs." Finally, as she began to run out of pairs, she placed the single balls at the top of the two double rows of rags.

Certain aesthetic principles emerged as Elaine planned the "striped-in hit-and-miss runner."[14] Because it is "a hit-and-miss affair," the rags come to her in a variety of combinations. "Some of them keeps their colors to theirselves in the balls and other ones don't." The balls made up of rags of similar colors may include a variety of fabrics—some plain, some figured, and some plaid—but they all "blend" together. Obviously Elaine can weave a clearly defined stripe from such materials. On the other hand, "some of them will put a little bit of this and a little bit of that" in the balls of rags. "That makes it complicated to plan," because a stripe may start out one color and end up another. In fact, that is exactly what happened with the runner; a black piece of filler at the beginning suddenly turned beige, and Elaine was left with a shade that not only didn't "brighten" the border, but actually smothered it. Thus the stripes in this particular kind of runner are only predominantly of one color. Sometimes they might be difficult to isolate.

The most important principle evident in planning the runner was symmetry, as Elaine clearly explained herself: "I try to have one end of the rug [as similar to] the other as possible. Go down to the center and reverse the pattern to the other end of the rug. Otherwise after you get this off of the roll it wouldn't look right." Every other aspect of planning was secondary to making one half match the other. Thus Elaine decided to weave an unmatched border—very unusual in a rug—because she didn't have enough fabric for a double border on both sides of the rug. "So I just put in what I have . . . so I'd have some for the other side of the rug." She adjusted the amount of filler on the shuttles to assure symmetry. If she had an "extra big ball" of filler whose size did not match its mate's, she would cut the excess off and put it at the center. One large unmatched stripe in the runner "might spoil it," she said. On the other hand, two oversized matched balls of filler would be all right, just "so they don't get out of hand too much." She also wove in filler that was not quite a shuttle-full because she had already halved it to make one side of the runner "near the same as the other side." Thus, even though the stripes were not perfectly matched she was careful to match the two sides of the runner as closely as she could. The result was near-symmetry, an interesting tension between order and confusion, but certainly satisfying to her.

Elaine frequently mentions two aspects of color that interest her—brightness and blending. She prefers colors she considers bright, especially yellow and red, and she spreads them throughout her rugs. Bright is most often a positive adjective for her. For example, she was sure the runner would be "pretty"; it had the "bright colors" in it. She uses the term "blend" in two ways: colors that match closely within the stripe are said to blend well; it does not matter if they are figured or plaid, just so the background "blends." The warp, too, blended well with the runner. It was not as variegated as it usually is, but it still matched many of the fabrics she wove into the runner. In between the black and red, she only had four colors—orange, green, blue, and yellow. She chided herself for getting "in a hurry" and not including more variegated colors that would "blend in" even more with the "bright rags" in the runner.

"Blend" is also used to refer to those colors that set up a pleasing contrast within the rug, often in terms of dark and light. Thus the black filler would blend with the beige border. If she had had a dark border, she would have started with a light filler. As she says of her planning in general, "I try to put colors that I think will blend well together if they have them available to use." For Elaine, "blending" means both contrast and similarity.

After seventy-two balls of filler were arranged neatly on the dining room table, Elaine chose the warp for the selvage or binding on the end of the runner. In this case she chose black for two reasons. First, it matched her beginning piece of filler, and second, she had many extra pieces of black warp, which she frequently tries to use with dark colors. Then she began to wind the filler onto the shuttles, grabbing only one of the balls in the first pair and moving quickly from the front to the back of her two double rows. She filled each shuttle and placed it in order in the former chicken-brooder tray. By then it was getting late, but Elaine had the runner planned, the selvage selected, and half the filler on the shuttles in the tray. She was ready to start weaving the following night.

At about seven o'clock the next evening Elaine started weaving the runner. She first put her "yardstick in [through the warp, which was already on the loom] to hold the selvage straight." Then she opened up the shed with her right foot and began to weave the selvage or binding of the rug, using spare pieces of leftover warp, which she slid through the shed from right to left by hand. Although she usually makes the selvage one-quarter inch wide, she made this selvage one-half inch, "a good bit," to keep the filler tight. In order to have enough warp to weave this selvage, she knotted the extra pieces together. The knots showed, but she did not seem to mind.

After she had placed the eight to ten rows of selvage in the runner, she took the first shuttle from the brooder tray, unwound some of the filler, and pushed the shuttle through the shed from right to left. To hide the loose end of the filler, she pulled out about two inches, which she trimmed "so that it's a little bit narrower." Then she folded it back under the first row to make a neat beginning. At the same time she cut the loose end of the filler with the snippers, she also clipped off the dangling piece of selvage, and the runner was started.

From this point on, Elaine's actions were largely repetitious. As she described it, "You open up the shed with your right foot for the first row . . . starting the rug, and then you open up with your left foot . . . and put [the filler] back this way." Then, "you pull back [the beater] for every shot when the material goes through. You pull back the beaters [at the] same time you open up the shed with your foot." At all times, "you have the shed open wide enough to take care of the shuttle . . . and you open the shed and close it with your foot treadles."

Elaine's actions were even more complex than her explanation indicates. She unwound some of the filler from the shuttle, slid the shuttle through the shed, and placed it on the unfinished rug in front of her. She quickly glanced at each edge of the runner and adjusted the filler with her finger and thumb to keep the sides of the runner straight. "It just comes natural to you," she said, "after you do enough of them." She straightened out the filler in the shed, leaving some slack so that it would not tighten up too much. Then she pulled back the beater at least twice with her right hand and stepped on the treadle.

Most of the time, Elaine uses the shuttle to push the filler through the shed. When the shuttle is almost empty, however, she takes the filler off the shuttle and pulls it through the shed by hand.

Because these are medium-weight rags, Elaine also had to stop after almost every shuttle-full and let out the warp. If she had not done so, the shed would have become too narrow, and she would have found it difficult to push the shuttle through it. She moved to the rear of the loom each time and released the warp beam slightly. Then she returned to the front of the loom, cranked the rug roll even tighter, and was ready to continue. These two processes, along with hard beating, are extremely important in creating a tightly woven rug.

Elaine beat her rugs with such force that the loom soon began to creep across the floor at a skittish angle. She had to stop several times during the evening to straighten it out. I have seen it turn almost a forty-five-degree angle under the pounding of her beater.

As she was weaving, Elaine commented on the rags she was putting into the runner. She noticed their colors: "Ain't that a pretty shuttle-full," she would say, or "That's a pretty shade of green. It's right odd, but pretty." On the other hand, she also was concerned about the quality of the filler. The customer had included knitwear, and Elaine was concerned that the runner would not "lay good" because the knitwear would stretch differently from the cotton. "I don't like it too good," she said, "but she's got it in so I'll have to run it in." She tried to keep the right side out on the knitwear, because that was where the print and the colors were. The filler itself, which she at first had thought was prepared "pretty neat compared to some of them," turned out to be "kind of a sloppy deal," but she had to work it in anyway. Some of the rags were too wide in places and then narrowed down to "a little bit of a shoestring"; other pieces had knots in them, and both these problems kept the warp from holding the filler in evenly and tightly. There were also too many ravelings, which would show up in the runner. Again she repeated the maxim, "This warp doesn't hide a thing. Everything shows up in a rug." She concluded, as she usually does, "It's going in though. I ain't changing it."

The "bad places" in the filler did in fact cause Elaine extra concern and extra work. She had to be careful that a knot or a poor seam was not on the edge where it would be "bulky." When she came across a problem of this kind she solved it in one of three ways. First, she might "pull it back in" so it would not be on the edge and thus not so visible, or she would "pull it clear out" beyond the edge and into the next row, or as a last resort, she would take her scissors and "clip it off if it gets too bad." Some seams which were not sewed together well simply tore apart, in which case Elaine had "to fold it in" without restitching the seam. She commented on every "bad place" she came across: "I just hate for them to have them bad places in it. It discourages me to try to have a nice rug out of it. I like to have something looking nice when I take it off. I don't like to have to have them ones that don't look nice."

Elaine stopped after weaving in fourteen shuttles of filler to rewrap the shuttles and measure the length of the runner with her cloth tape measure. She had woven thirty-seven inches of runner and used a safety pin to mark that length. It had taken fourteen shuttles of filler to get to that point, less than she had expected, which made her feel that the runner was "going pretty fast." She still did not know whether or not she would have enough left over for a small rug.

As she got nearer the middle, Elaine got "pretty particular" about the length of the runner. She stopped to measure again. She moved the safety pin three more inches to the forty-inch mark, exactly one-fourth of the runner's future size. She next measured from the pin forward and found that she had woven an additional thirty-one inches. She had nine inches left to weave before the runner would be half done. At that point she began to measure each shuttle-full as she put it in. "I don't want to do the wrong thing. It's too late after you don't have it done right. You can't take that off of there—you're out."

Although she ran out of shuttles prepared with filler, Elaine would wrap only one more at a time until she was beyond the halfway mark. She carefully selected each ball of filler for the last nine inches— usually the single balls with no mates—and wrapped the filler onto each shuttle when she was ready to put it in. She chose the single balls because they "don't show up too much to have [them] right in the middle—them there ones that they don't have two of them alike for each end." She continued to measure each shuttle-full she put in, and each gave her approximately three inches of runner. Finally she put two shuttles of filler that matched—but not exactly—in the center of the runner. At that point she had forty inches plus one stripe beyond. It was then that she realized she would have enough for a small rug. She pushed the filler for that, primarily odds and ends, to one side and wound the remaining twenty-seven balls of filler for the runner onto the shuttles. She moved back through the remaining two rows of shuttle-balls on the table in reverse order. Now she could "really go to town on it better," because there was no need to plan the second half of the runner so carefully; the planning had already been done.

By nine-thirty the runner was almost finished. When she got to the last row of filler, Elaine found that she didn't have enough to fill in the row, so she added a matching piece of rag from the box of rags she keeps for that purpose. Then she began to weave in the black warp to form the selvage, and the runner was complete. She was anxious to see her creation, but it wastes too much warp to cut down one rug at a time. She had seventeen balls of rags left, enough to make a rug "just big enough to put my two feet on," and she felt obligated to weave that before she cut down the entire order.

To prepare for the second rug, Elaine cranked the runner onto the carpet roll until it was just past the breast beam. Then she tightened down the warp firmly, leaving approximately six to eight inches of warp between the runner and the small rug, enough for knotting and a three-inch fringe.

Elaine remarked that she "hates these little ones. They take up so much of your time putting in selvage and so forth." She decided to use orange warp to weave the selvage because she had a number of long strands left over, and not having to join together small spare pieces would make weaving the selvage go faster. Using her yardstick as before, she put six to eight rows of warp through the loom to make one-quarter inch of selvage.

The seventeen balls of filler eliminated from the runner were simply thrown together in a group. Elaine next took five minutes to plan this small rug by arranging and rearranging the filler into one double row. The solid pink knitwear, which she earlier had felt would "ruin the runner," would this time be the border. She selected two of the most similar balls of filler for the outside stripes and tried to match the other balls of fabric as closely as she could. The odds and ends, as usual, went to the middle of the rug. Once she had the fabric arranged, she stopped, looked at it again, and rearranged it when she discovered some bundles of filler with fabrics that matched more closely. In both decision-making processes, Elaine tried to make this collection of leftovers as symmetrical as possible.

Elaine began by weaving in eight rows of hit-and-miss filler, then the border. She divided the knitwear in half, weaving in six rows of it while keeping the rest of the shuttle in front of her. Next she put in eight rows of hit-and-miss filler and another six rows of pink border. The division of the knitwear was not quite exact, however, and the first half of the border turned out to be thinner than the second half. Elaine continued by weaving in one of each of the paired shuttle-balls and the balls of odds and ends until she got to the middle of the rug. Then she continued back down the row of shuttle-balls. Again she put in a double pink border: six rows of pink, eight of hit-and-miss, and six more of pink.

Elaine was pleased when she was finished with the "little feller" and "every inch of fabric" had been worked into the rug. "They don't always come out that close," she said. She had used all the fabric the customer had given her—including the detested knitwear.

Finally, at 10:25, Elaine was ready to cut down the rug. Normally she would have waited until "the beater hits the rug roll" and she had at least twelve rugs on it. Perhaps because I was there, or because she was anxious to see the runner herself, or because this was now a complete order ready to deliver, she decided to cut the rugs off the carpet roll.

She cut the warp color by color, looped it, and threw it over the harnesses. It is important to tie a loop in the warp so "you don't pull it out of your harnesses and out of your beam . . . because if you did you'd have to thread up the whole thing again." Next she cut the rugs apart. "You cut in between each rug and leave out about three or four inches of your warp that you had left there."

She unrolled the finished rugs from the carpet roll and responded to what she saw with enthusiasm. "Isn't that something," she said of the runner. "Ain't that a doozie" and "Oh boy, that's pretty!" are only some of the remarks she made as she examined it more closely. The fringe was a little too long, but that would be no problem; she would just have to cut it off later. The two rugs she had made the night before "ain't too bad looking for them there dull colors [the customer] had." She had tried to make them "near the same" as possible because the woman had ordered a pair of rugs. She had put single borders on those rugs because the customer "didn't have nothing to pick from hardly." She had tried to put red streaks in the middle of both rugs, but in one it only came out "near the middle," which did not seem to bother Elaine. She was practical in her evaluation of these rugs: "I didn't have as nice a rags to work with on this one here. So you have to think of that when you think that some of them aren't quite as pretty as others." Generally Elaine was pleased with the results of her two nights of work in the rug room.

Before she took these rugs to the gas station, she examined them closely looking for any mistakes. "As a rule, I don't make any," she said. "Once in a while I'll miss a knot. . . . Sometimes I tie a knot in the filler when I'm getting ready for the shuttle. Sometimes I miss seeing it . . . , and if I find it, why I just open up that knot and straighten it out and pull my warp up over it." Occasionally a piece of warp breaks. "If you happen to break a thread, and you hadn't noticed it for a little bit, you can take a darning needle and weave it in." She also checked to be sure the edges of the rugs were neat and even. She knew her rugs would be tight. "I keep my warp drug tight at all times so that the rug is woven tighter together. It doesn't leave the dust and sand through under them as much as the ones that's wove just loose."

After each rug was checked, Elaine folded it up to take back to the gas station, where she would tie the ends of the warp. This third part of the process takes half an hour for each rug; every eight pieces of warp are knotted across each end. Then, when the rugs are complete, the customers can pick them up, although some customers have taken up to two years to do so.

Before Elaine left the rug room, she wanted to be sure she was ready for the next evening of weaving. She tied the warp on by pulling the leather shoelace through the loop in the warp and knotting it together firmly. She believes that the warp firmly tied to the rug roll helps to make her rugs tight. Finally, she left the rug room at 10:45.

Elaine is proud of her rugs because they are visually appealing to her and to her customers. "My customers told me that [my rugs] were all so pretty that they didn't know which one to pick." She herself likes the brighter, glossier rugs. "That's what's really pretty about these plastic bread paper rugs; they really have the color and the gloss and the brightness to them." Silk rugs, too, have "more gloss to the material, and they really show up better. Brighter colors and things like that." But unfortunately, silk frays and "doesn't seem to hold up good, but it's really attractive in a rug. They have a tendency to not last as long as a cotton rug does."

Elaine also feels that a rug's attractiveness depends partly on its use. "Depends on where these rugs are going to be used . . . is what I think about the attractiveness of them." A wool rug "is most attractive in bedrooms where you don't have to launder them quite as much. In kitchens, why, I think that the cotton is more— is really better because it— I think it wears better, and it washes better than wool does."

It takes Elaine approximately one and a half days to make a rug from beginning to end. It takes "all day . . . to get a rug ready for weaving." After the rug is planned, she can "weave the rug in an hour," and it takes approximately one half-hour to tie it off. Most of her rug preparation time is spent at the station. "You have quite a bit, many hours in it. You count your time much, why you couldn't do them as reasonable as you do. But I have to be [at the station] anyhow, so I just don't count my time too much."

The night I spent with Elaine in the rug room from seven to eleven o'clock she earned $9.60, and she still had one more hour to put in on the rugs. She charges by the inch for her weaving. "If I have to complete everything, I been charging ten cents an inch plus thirty cents for the fringe. If they bring the filler all ready and prepared, I'll charge five cents an inch, thirty cents for the fringe."

Elaine works more steadily on her rugs than most weavers. As she says, "I get everything ready to weave in over here while I'm waiting on customers." Then, "in the evening, after work hours in here, I make the rugs." She usually weaves two hours a night, five nights a week, which is all she wants to work. Weaving is, after all, "tiresome," and she does not feel she could put any more time in on it. Sometimes, as she did the night I spent with her, she works "until midnight on the rugs." In the summertime, when she is canning, she does not weave. "I lay off it about, I say, about a month to six weeks. The rest of the time, I weave."

What motivates her? Why does she work so hard at her craft when other women have given up weaving to become maids in local motels? First, it keeps her busy—just busy enough. "I like to be busy though. I couldn't be sitting down doing nothing. I wouldn't know how I'd pass the time away if I didn't keep busy." Weaving also keeps her busy in a way that pays. Several times Elaine mentioned hobbies such as painting that "didn't pay." "What good are they," she concludes, "if they don't pay?" Weaving gives her an important role to play in her family and in the community. She feels needed to the point of harassment, but it apparently enhances her sense of self-esteem. "We had so many that passed away in our family, and they brought these rags to *me*. Well, I couldn't turn them down neither." Added to that is the sense of "waste not, want not." For those who have saved rubber bands, tinfoil, plastic bags, and string, Elaine's lament "Well, I hate to throw them away" strikes a familiar chord. So often her customers have "nice, clean rags." "Some of the material is so new and bright looking. So I take them. But after while, it's going to get to be a burden: I can't take them." Finally she summarizes her own motivation. "Well, even though I don't . . . say that you make too much money, I enjoy doing it, and that's one reason that I do it, and I hate to see things throwed away because I think it's a sin."

NOTES

1. Further discussion of rag, or list, carpet can be found in Roth (1967), Hummel (1976), Partridge (1976), and Little (1967).

2. Journals of Samuel Rowland Fisher, Historical Society of Pennsylvania, MS AM 0652-11. Microfilm M-296, Joseph Downs Manuscript and Microfilm Collection, The Henry Francis DuPont Winterthur Museum, Winterthur, Delaware.

3. To protect the privacy of my informants, pseudonyms will be used throughout this study. The interviews and field observations took place during the fall of 1975 and during the summers of 1976 and 1977. Most of the quoted materials are from the typewritten transcript dated September 27, 1975. Other quotations are from subsequent field observations and tape-recorded interviews.

4. Michael Owen Jones's (1975) informant, Charley, created a combination bookcase-rocking chair that is referred to as Charley's "bookcase masterpiece."

5. See also Vlach (1973b) and Jones (1975).

6. For the techniques of oral history, I drew on several sources, including Dixon and Mink (1967) and Olch and Pogue (1972). Ideas on the content of life history came from Gottschalk, Kluckhohn, and Angell (1945) and Langness (1965).

7. Jones's thesis (1975) is that Charley's grief contributed to the style of the strange bookcase-rocker masterpiece; therefore he explores the basis for Charley's distress. Elaine too is grieving for a lost daughter, and this may account for her tendency to close herself up and devote more time to weaving (see Jones 1975:99 and passim). Elaine's grief, however, is not evident in her rugs, and I choose not to expand on this aspect of her life.

8. See Jones's comments on Charley (1975:139).

9. According to the Union Loom handbook, the warp consists of "the threads which extend lengthwise in the loom, passing through the harnesses and reed."

10. Kalčik (1975:3) uses the term "collaborative" to refer to women's storytelling techniques.

11. When asked how she would go about starting a rug, Elaine discussed methods of tearing rags at great length:

> *Elaine:* Well, I just take the material and start working it up. On the shirts, I take off the collars and the cuffs and the buttons and the shirttail hem, and I tear that lengthwise. I take it apart at the seams, and I tear that all up lengthwise. If it's heavy material, I cut it about an inch wide, and if it's wide cotton material, I cut it wider, about an inch and a half. Then I sew those strips together on the sewing machine, or you can loop them, just so that they're put together neat in length. . . .
>
> *Author:* Okay. . . . what you do next is sew the strips of material together?
>
> *Elaine:* Yes. Yes. And then when I'm working up— that was the way I told you I worked up a shirt. When I work up a dress, if it's a two-piece dress, why I cut the skirt up lengthwise in the material, rip the seams all apart and the hem out and take the zipper out. And I just tear that up then lengthwise. And the top part, I take the collar and cuffs off like I do the shirt and your button stay, and all that, and rip them at the seams. I tear all my material, make it a point to tear it lengthwise. It seems to work better. And if I'm working up sheets, I just tear the hems off and just tear them lengthwise and sew them together. If you're working up knitwear, why you take off all the neckpieces and the bottom piece of those knitwear shirts, and you can go around and around of them if you're cutting with your scissors like you would a stocking. Start at the bottom and just go around on it because there's no seams in it. You don't need to put that together much until you get up under the arm, and then you just go back and forth across on the back of that and in on your sleeves and what have you. And put them few little pieces together on the knitwear. Sweatshirts or whatever you call those, you know.
>
> The nylon stockings, you just open the tops of those and cut down to where it starts to narrow off, and you just leave them all in one. You don't need to cut them at all, and you just darn the toe to the top on another stocking and keep doing that until you get enough for a rug.

12. The tools and materials in the rug room included the following: loom, spinning wheel, measuring tape, yardstick, scissors, snippers, rug scissors, two brooder trays, thirty-eight shuttles, crank for loom, darning needles, extra bolts and ties for loom, tape, small clamps, rug warp of three types (new warp in boxes, extra warp on spools to attach to the loom, pieces of warp for selvage), rug rags of two types (rags in shuttle-balls ready to weave, pieces of rags for the ends of rugs).

13. According to the Union Loom handbook, selvage is "the running edge of cloth or carpet; also refers to the binding of warp woven in at the beginning and end of a rug to prevent raveling." I use the term in both senses, as most weavers do, but I will try to clarify its meaning in the context of the discussion.

14. Jones (1971; 1975:229–235) discusses the problems of investigating the "folk aesthetic."

Elaine's "little business place." It serves as a combination gas station, grocery store, and rug outlet.

Preparing the filler. A neighbor cuts rags in the rug room half of the gas station.

Elaine's home "down there in the hollow."

Elaine using the cutter for knitwear.

Below left: Wall-to-wall carpeting made by Elaine in 1977.

Below right: Wrapping the shuttles. Elaine begins the weaving process by wrapping the rags onto the shuttles and placing them in the former chicken brooder tray.

The parts of Elaine's Union Custom Loom labeled by the manufacturer.

The interior of Elaine's rug room.

The chicken brooder tray filled with shuttles.

Elaine straightens out the filler in the shed. She leaves some slack so that the rug does not tighten up so much.

Elaine pulls back the beater at least twice with her right hand and steps on the treadle to create at least another quarter-inch of rug.

PART TWO

WOMEN IN PUBLIC

· 6 ·
WOMEN'S HANDLES AND THE PERFORMANCE OF IDENTITY IN THE CB COMMUNITY
Susan J. Kalčik

CITIZENS BAND (CB) radio is a two-way, short-distance radio communication system used for personal or business activities and limited by the Federal Communications Commission to certain radio frequency channels. CB is often associated with truck drivers, who began using it on the job, but in recent years CB has begun to enjoy more general popularity, perhaps in part because of attention given it by the media, for example, in movies like *Smokey and the Bandit* and in television programs like "The Dukes of Hazard."

The largest percentage of ordinary citizens who own CBs use them in their cars when traveling long distances to check on road conditions and the location of speed traps. Many people also use these *mobile units* for the daily trip to the office, again to check on travel conditions but also to relieve the boredom and frustrations of that journey. Stuck in a rush hour traffic jam, they are solaced by information about its cause and by the opportunity to commiserate with other drivers. A smaller percentage of CBers set up *base stations*, a CB unit run on a power pack and hooked up to an antenna in their homes. From the base stations they can talk any time of day or night.

Individuals who use their CBs often begin to feel they know other regular users fairly well and may make efforts to meet face-to-face with some of the people they have been talking to. Informal and formal groups and organizations may eventually grow out of these contacts. A feeling of group membership is fostered by the fact that CBers share a private language (CB slang), special CB names ("handles"), technical information, problems, and jokes and stories that set them apart from non-CBers. For some, regular CB use results in a sense of belonging to a community of fellow CBers.

The CB community I am describing and on which my conclusions are based is a large, amorphous group of people, almost entirely white, who use one or both of two citizens band radio channels, not only while traveling to work but also at other times for socializing. Most of these people live in the northern Virginia area that is part of metropolitan Washington, D.C. Since anyone who owns a CB and uses it on these two channels has access to the group and its social life, this group is widely diversified in terms of class, work, pay scale, geographical origin, education, religion, and so on. And individuals also differ in the type and intensity of their relationship to the CB community as a whole.

Some members participate in the community only by talking over their radios. Others participate in social events (called "breaks"), such as regular gatherings at a local country-and-western bar, or a puzzle party at someone's home, or bowling, biking, or swimming excursions. In the summer there are "jamborees" in which members of various groups meet at campgrounds to socialize and to compete in various contests, such as a tug-of-war, to earn trophies for their clubs. In addition, some members of the CB community I am describing join more official organizations such as VARO (Virginia Association of Radio Operators) and involve themselves in formally and informally organized service activities such as supplying free CB radios to schools or homes for the elderly. These social and club activities offer the opportunity for people to interact in more private settings and to get to know one another well.

The CB community is especially rich territory for the folklorist because it underscores the oral/aural process of interaction. CBer language and its development, the rituals, and the ways all these are learned and taught are subjects for exploration. But the concern of this chapter is the investigation of expressive behavior marking group and individual identity, for which CB lore provides particularly useful materials. I am going to focus on one genre of CB lore, the

"handle"—or the name a person chooses to identify himself or herself by over the air—and I am going to discuss various aspects of the
"handle" in the performance of identity, both group and individual.

A person using a CB radio legally must identify himself or herself
over the air by a "call sign" (the official letters and numbers assigned
to a licensed CB radio operator by the Federal Communications Commission, or "Uncle Charlie"). And people usually choose also to
identify themselves by a name, or handle, chosen specifically for CB
interaction. The opportunity to choose one's own name is so attractive
that many persons who do not have or use CBs have chosen handles
for themselves as a result of exposure to CB from family, friends, or
media.

In discussing name signs adopted by some deaf individuals,
Kathryn Meadow points out:

> Names are a key symbol and summary of personal identity, the first
> identifying marker used for specifying an individual. The form of
> address that is used . . . very quickly captures the symbolic essence
> of the relationship between two persons. . . . The assignment of a
> name sign can be seen as a kind of rite of passage, defining [the]
> entrance to the community through the bestowing of a name that is
> signed in the language of the subculture. (Meadow, 1977:237, 239)

Likewise, in addition to revealing something about the individual
CBer, the CB handle signals to insiders and outsiders membership
and acceptance in the CB subculture.

The handle is chosen, or said to be chosen, because it reflects
some part of a person's identity—an interest, job, or geographical
origin. Thus, Rusty Piton's hobby is rock-climbing, Ball Joint works
on the front ends of cars, and Maine Yankee comes from that New
England state. Because a member of the CB community need never
meet other members face-to-face, however, the option of choosing a
handle that reflects some desired quality or state and building a
fantasy identity and life around it is also available to the CBer. Erving
Goffman (1959:2) points out that in face-to-face interaction there are
two kinds of information people give about themselves: that which
they *give* and that which they *give off*. The second acts as a check on
the first. But in interaction that is not face-to-face there is only the
information *given*, in this case the handle and whatever else, fact or
fiction, the speaker chooses to reveal about himself or herself. This

situation offers people a chance to play with identity, and some take the opportunity. CB lore abounds with stories of the sultry temptress or the country Don Juan who turns out in "real" life to be aging, bald, or dumpy. Handles such as Lone Ranger, King Arthur, Gladiator, Midnight Gypsy, and Wonder Girl reflect this play with the fantasy identity. CBers frequently discuss the significance and appropriateness of one another's handles and exchange stories about how they chose their handles and what they are trying to communicate about themselves through them.

Another significant aspect of handles is their sexual connotations (which are also commented on regularly by CBers). Some people choose their handles with a sexual message as the main consideration (Limber Dick, Bionic Beaver); others merely suggest sexual prowess or sexual attributes (Midnight Plumber, the Polish Sausage, Satin Sheets). Some people find themselves in hilarious discussions with strangers or friends because they did not think of the sexual implications of their handles when they selected them (Two-Plus).

Reactions to handles and joking about them is affected by how well the persons involved know each other, and this depends on whether they have taken the option that the community offers to close the social distance between community members. The sense of closeness or distance to other CBers, like the sense of privacy in a performance arena, is complicated for the CB performer. The radio interactions are essentially public—anyone can listen in—but extremely intimate conversations take place over the air. In the social settings of breaks, parties, and jamborees, one finds some people presenting their public faces, and others various of their private faces. Just as at a cocktail party where one knows some people very well and others not at all, individuals in the various CB settings manipulate public and private, real and fantasy identities.

In discussing handles and identity, then, some significant aspects of the CB community include the choice between "on the air" and "in the flesh" (or face-to-face) interactions; the choice between distant and close relationships with the group and its members; the possibility of fantasy and real identities and their separation, or the maintenance of both side by side; the shifting public and private forums that affect the performance of group and individual identity.

The CB handles listed in Table 6.1 are some I heard on the two channels I monitored for about a year. Many of these are people I also met at breaks and club meetings. The list is not meant to include every handle I collected, but to give the reader an accurate sample of the kinds of handles I heard used. In the first group of handles (from couples, married and unmarried), I have listed the handles of both the women and their mates. It is interesting to note that some women take handles linked to their husbands' or boyfriends' handles, just as many women take their husbands' names when they marry. (Fox's Angel and North Star's Lady actually changed their handles to indicate their relationship to Desert Fox and North Star.)

Although some women's handles are neutral in terms of sexual connotations and stereotypes (Bookworm, Yogi Bear) and some suggest strong or even hostile images (Brunhilde, Samurai), the main point I want to make about this list is that the majority of women's handles fall into two groups and reflect a stereotypical duality of women—the virgin and the whore, the good and bad girls, the light and dark side of femininity, sexy versus sweet, the temptress versus Doris Day.

This dual image of womankind is a common one and a tradition of long-standing in Western culture, expressed, for example, in the way women are presented in our literature (Fiedler 1966; Martin 1971; Rogers 1966; Sullerot 1971). Marina Warner discusses one aspect of this stereotype in the popular Christian conception of the "two Eves," one the temptress in the Garden of Eden and the other Mary the Virgin, who by bearing Christ saves humankind.

> The economy and proportion of this Pauline idea gave it great power and appeal. To this day it is a specially graceful analogue, architectural in its harmoniousness, a great vault thrown over Western attitudes to women, the whole mighty span resting on Eve the temptress on one side, and Mary the paragon on the other. (Warner 1976:60)

This duality is codified as well in the "official" music of CBers, country music. D. K. Wilgus (1970) and Barbara Sims (1974) both point to an underlying polarization in the Southern culture in which country-and-western music developed, a polarization reinforced by the strain urban life has placed on that culture. Wilgus describes Hank Williams and his songs as typifying the dichotomy between the two themes of country-and-western music, the sinful life of the honky-tonks and the good life of family and religion. But nowhere

Table 6.1. CB Handles of Couples and Women

Couples

Women	Men
Virginia Duchess	Virginia Duke
Queen Bee	Bumble Bee
Lady Sundowner	Sundowner
North Star's Lady (formerly Short Court)	North Star
Fox's Angel (formerly Cherokee Squaw)	Desert Fox
Comanche's Angel	Colorado Comanche
Samurai	Two Plus
Cricket	C. C. Rider
C. B. Widow	Red Pony
Midnight Gypsy	Graduate
Mountain Melody	Red Rider
Tasti Cake	Lucky Duck
Bookworm	Arlington Bluebird
Yogi Bear	Floater
Midnight Delight	Cross Bow
Dream Maker	Three Dog
Punkin Seed	White Whale
Sugar Babe	Jolly Roger
Sweet Angel	Honest Injun
Vienna Stringbean	Teddy Bear
Straight Arrow	Rusty Piton
Sweet Sue	Magnum Force
Stargazer	Pathfinder
Cinderella	Country Squirrel
Lucky Louie	Tarheel
Ding-a-Ling	Golden Ram*

*This couple was married over CB and had a CB radio in their wedding cake.

is the dichotomy clearer than in the two roles allowed women, the good and bad girls, which Sims describes fully in a study of feminine masochism in American country music.

Handles like Midnight Angel and Satin Sheets evoke the temptress image of women, and handles like Sugar Cookie and Barbie Doll evoke the other—the cute, cuddly, little, edible, and, especially,

Table 6.1. *CB Handles of Couples and Women   (Continued)*

Women

Cottonseed	Hot Pants	Carrot-top
Lollipop	Brown Eyes	Bit-o-Honey
Sugar Cookie	Crazy Lady	China Doll
Afternoon Delight	Sugar Fox	Susie Q
Sweet Pea	French Bandit	Honey Bee
Foxy Fraulein	Bubble and Squeak	Dancing Lady
Midnight Angel	Bouncing Boobs	Kitty Cat
Lone Star	Popcorn	Miss-Direction
Wacky Witch	Cupcake	Miss-cellaneous
Blue Angel	Sunshine Lady	Miss-print
Satin Sheets	Honey Bun	Wrong Number
Morning Dove	Shining Angel	Shady Lady
Brunhilde	Barbie Doll	Lady Bug
Country Convert	Wonder Girl	Rambling Lady

Note: Spelling is approximate.

sweet—image of women. This duality is underlined in the debate CBers carry on over whether women-in-general should be referred to as "beavers" or "sweethearts." Both images are considered sexy, but in different ways and with a differing sense of respect for women.

However, there is a lack of fit between this simplified, dual picture of women and the image CB women project by their activities. Neither in the CB community and its formal and informal power structure, nor in their lives outside the community, do these women fall neatly into the categories of honky-tonk angel or "total woman." The wide range of people involved in the CB community means that there is a wide range of types of women; and there is a wide range of philosophies about, and behavior toward, women in the group. There are army wives, housewives of the traditional style, working women married and single, women with and without children, and women in jobs that pay well and carry prestige and power. And women exert power in the observable hierarchies of formal CB organizations; they hold offices, do much of the work, monitor traffic during rush hours, patrol in CB groups working on the streets with local police departments, and so on.

To understand the social uses of the stereotypes as expressed in women's handles, one must explore the nature of the CB community itself. It is a community built on a rural, communal mythos that reflects a picture of life as it was in some frontier, pre-television America when neighbors participated cheerfully in barn-raisings and gathered around quilting frames at the drop of a needle, a golden age for which many in our complex society long nostalgically, especially those of us transplanted from a rural to an urban setting (Abrahams 1978; Hughes 1979; Wilgus 1970). But CBers live out the dream: they help each other move; lend each other equipment, often expensive, to try out; help put up antennas; visit and call the sick; give blood for the open-heart surgery of a member's infant daughter. And they legitimize their group identity to the wider community by participating in service activities like singing Christmas carols for hospital patients and raising money for charities. The CB community is another example of the movement toward small-group identity, the "retribalization" of our urban, mass society. And in these activities CBers hearken back to a simpler and safer time when sex roles, like everything else, were clear and stable.

This model of community and the activities it fosters, as well as the sense of group identity it supports, is extremely useful because, like other urban communities, CBers face the problem of building and maintaining cohesion in the face of powerful forces operating to keep people separate, lonely, working against rather than with each other. The spaces that separate people, as well as the differences in class, backgrounds, and thinking (including sex role expectations), work against their notion of a homogenous community, as does the ease with which people may enter and leave the community by means of the radio and social participation. The fact that membership is voluntary, however, works as a strong motivation for playing down divisive differences. Unlike at the office or in the neighborhood, these people have chosen one another's company, and many chose to make the CB community the main part of their social lives. And the radio that allows so many people to "pass through" the community also *allows in* people with little or no access to other communities—the handicapped, the elderly, women at home all day, newcomers.

CB interactions, especially initial ones, are fraught with pitfalls because of the differences between members of the community and because the participants cannot see each other on the air. Tip Top may develop a radio friendship with the Green Hornet only to find when they meet in person that the Hornet is Black and resents Tip

Top's racial prejudice. Blue Rose may get along fine in her flirtatious radio talk with the Doctor until he learns that she is a lawyer in the firm she works for and not the clerk typist he expected. Hence, early radio contacts are characterized by attempts to present an agreeable or neutral, nonthreatening public face and to test out what the other person is like before revealing more private bits of identity. This is true of much initial social interaction, which Goffman describes as characterized by the attempt to establish a "working consensus," a mutually acceptable social definition of the situation (1959:9–11; 1967:11). This process is complicated for the CBers on the air, how-ever, because of the public setting, the lack of face-to-face contact, and the difficulties of hearing and being heard over the CB radio. And it is complicated in the social setting by the feeling that people know each other well from prior radio contact even though they are meeting face-to-face for the first time.

One way of dealing with such social tensions, and thus working toward group cohesion, is to find a common ground, a safe neutral topic to discuss. The major one, naturally, is the radio itself, since the machine is the link between community members. Thus much air and social time is spent talking about antennas, power mikes, signal strength, modulation, adjacent channel rejection, bleedover, and so on. Other bits of social small talk such as the weather and traffic and the joys of working for the federal government can carry members a long way in conversations. But probably the second largest topic of talk next to the radio is sex, especially in talk between men and women. Flirtatious behavior, serious and unserious, and sexual joking are common patterns of interaction in the CB community between persons who have just met on the air or at a break, and between old friends, who may, for example, arrange dates with each other that they do not intend to keep, while their mates listen and offer helpful suggestions. Much of this sort of talk revolves around the sexual implications of a person's handle, and the joking may be initiated by male or female.

Just as stereotypical or suggestive female handles might aid in this sort of byplay, they are useful in another common pattern of CB community behavior, that is, in courtship. Single as well as attached CBers of both sexes shop around for temporary or permanent mates, as in most communities. CB lore is full of stories about over-the-air sexual solicitation, amateur and professional. Since static, skip, distance, a poor mike, and other factors can adversely affect communication (it is especially difficult to differentiate young voices by sex over the air, leading to some embarrassing conversations), new CBers are cautioned to pick a clear, easily understood handle, one that alludes to something or someone familiar to most people. The recognizably "feminine" handle, thus, is an important part of the performance of identity to persons interested in playing the dating and mating game.

And such a handle not only provides a public face and identity especially useful in initial interactions, but it in effect offers a protective coloring for women who may threaten men or other women because of their power inside or outside the CB community. Wacky Witch is the president of one local club and an important figure in the informal social networks. She is a strong woman who performs in a fairly traditional and acceptable feminine style. The two parts of her handle symbolize the strategy she and other women choose to use in the community; her "wacky" feminine traits and mannerisms defuse the powerful and threatening "witch" part of her personality and activities.

The handle is the first, and on the air the only, besides the voice, piece of information a CBer gives about himself or herself. It is the first footstep taken in the dark, the first statement a person makes about identity. It must be one that is safe and comfortable for both speaker and listener, if the interaction is to continue. Thus a handle that evokes a neutral, joking, or familiar image is often chosen by CBers. It gives the bearer an opportunity to operate in an acceptable way in the community until he or she feels more comfortable about revealing aspects of identity that might appear threatening or destructive to the group or to other individuals. The handle and the public identity it communicates can neutralize conflict or rejection without affecting the possibility of acting outside the handle's stereotype when the individual chooses.

Thus the use by CBers of handles that evoke stereotyped images of women help ease entry into the CB community and social interaction within it by (1) making the sexual identity of the speaker clear, (2) making role expectations clear, even if only temporarily, (3) promoting sexual banter and serious flirtation, (4) providing a safe public identity that fits with the group's public identity, and (5) playing down forces that work against social cohesion until a safer time and arena for their presentation occurs.

BELLE GUNNESS, THE LADY BLUEBEARD: NARRATIVE USE OF A DEVIANT WOMAN

Janet L. Langlois

BELLE GUNNESS, born in the village of Selbu in western Norway in 1859, settled on a farm just outside the city limits of the northwestern Indiana community of La Porte in the fall of 1901. From that time until the spring of 1908, she apparently murdered at least one husband, several women and children, and numerous would-be suitors who had answered her matrimonial advertisements placed in Norwegian-language immigrant newspapers. She apparently dismembered her victims, poured quicklime over them, put them in gunnysacks, and buried them in her backyard. On the night of April 28, 1908, her farmhouse burned down. In the aftermath of the fire, the bodies were discovered, although the question remains whether Belle Gunness herself died in the flames.

Residents of La Porte have been talking about "the Lady Bluebeard" and her "Murder Farm" ever since. I have examined and treated as "cultural fictions" or "texts" all sorts of community narrative that refers to the image of the murderess: newspaper interviews,

This chapter was originally presented as a paper in the panel "Women In Between Categories: Deviance and Role Reversal" at the Women and Folklore Conference, Philadelphia, 1979. The author would like to thank Professor Nancy Armstrong for her suggestions after a presentation of an earlier formulation to her class on "Women's Lives," English Department, Wayne State University, Detroit, 1978.

testimonies at coroners' inquests and court trials in 1908, subsequent oral histories done by crime writers, fictional retellings, and data collected by folklorists (including my own fieldwork in 1975–1976). (See Langlois 1977 for the full corpus.) In an earlier article, I examined those narratives about the murderess's cruelty to next-door neighbors and to prospective husbands in order to test the power of narratives to structure concepts of community and kinship ties through their symbolic inversions (Langlois 1978). In the present chapter, I have selected for analysis narratives that cast the murderess most clearly as the woman between categories, in order to explore narrators' differential use of the image "turned upside down" to define or redefine sex roles in the community.[1]

For two community narrators, both considered specialists on the Gunness case when I did my fieldwork and both men, the murderess was literally the lady on the edge. Her farmhouse, situated on the town's northern boundary, had once been an elegant mansion owned by one of the founding fathers of La Porte. Gene MacDonald, a community elder whom I interviewed when he was eighty-five, saw the decline of the house delicately intertwined with the lives of the women who had successively lived in it. This decline charted for him the progressive breakdown of community. He told me: "The house. Well, that was built [in 1846] for Harriet Holcomb. . . , the daughter of one of the founders of La Porte, John Walker. And he built these four mansions. . . . All the Walker mansions was made out of brick. And they all had marble furnaces."[2] Gene commented on the Holcomb mansion in particular: "Ah, that was a wonderful house. It had five fireplaces with marble mantles and mirrors all over."[3] The four Walker mansions functioned for Gene as the cornerstones of the community. They were "foursquare." They were family and town solidarity.

The Holcombs, however, had "trouble in the Civil War" and moved to King's County, New York, in 1864 because they were "Southern sympathizers." Gene, a Civil War buff who still mourned the 1,500 men La Porte County had lost and whose father and four uncles had fought on the Union side, saw this move as disruptive on many levels. The chink out of family and community represented by the empty Holcomb house was widened for him by Mattie Altic's purchase in 1892. He told me that Mattie was a "madam" from Chicago whose "two big, biggest friends was Hinkydink and Bathhouse John" and that she turned the place into "a sporting house."

I can remember her as a kid, you know. . . . She had the fanciest driving horses. My uncle bought a couple. I was there once, and she give me a sack of candy. It was good candy. I'd never eaten it. It was too damn rich. It kinda made me sick afterwards. . . . But she used to drive these fancy horses on a— Well, it was a surrey that— You seen 'em with the fringe on top? Well, she used to drive it with them girls downtown, and she always had white lines. . . .

I say Mattie Altic had a barn to keep them horses, fancy barn too. They had— The stalls in there was all fixed up so-and-so. . . . Then she had a fancy hack that they met the trains. And that had curtains so they couldn't see who was going there.

But you know what I used to laugh about? When she come to town, she'd bring two or three of them girls, and she'd go into the stores like Davidson & Porter. . . . They [store clerks] would go out of the rule to fawn on her, to wait on them. 'Course they bought. But she had the biggest ostrich plume I ever seen! . . . I can remember. As a kid, you know, she was a great curiosity to us.

She had the most beautiful marble, in her parlor there or whatever you want to call it—entertaining room. And she had a bar in there too! . . . And across the road she had a kind of park and a boat landing where they went out on Fish Trap [Lake]. It was a swell place. Real swell. (March 10, 1976)

By turning the mansion into a house of ill-repute open to outside clientele, Mattie effectively modified its former symbolic value for Gene. In fact, she created a red-light symbol of chaos.

If Mattie had been bad (but elegant), Belle Gunness was worse. The mass murderess consistently took one more step beyond the pale as developed in Gene's narratives. After Mattie had "dropped dead," Belle bought the place in 1901 because "nobody wanted it" and "it was cheap." The house had been "in good shape yet when she got it," but she immediately insured the fancy carriage house and the boat pavilion and burnt them up for the insurance money, foreshadowing the burning of her own farmhouse seven years later. "Well, she didn't have no use for that. She just had a barn. She just had cows, work horses."

And Belle's clientele were not Mattie's Chicago demimonde, but hardy immigrant farmers. "She had quite a few Norwegians come from Minne-so-tay. . . . But most of them that she butchered were all Norwegians." Her relations with these men—not only outsiders but also foreigners—were not only illicit but also murderous, the ultimate severance of social bonds. Belle's relationship with store clerks was not as cordial as Mattie's had been either. "You know, Old Belle was kind of a keptomaniac [kleptomaniac]. . . . Everybody knew that. Hell, everybody was scared of her!" And in place of Mattie's elegant ostrich plume, Gene recalled Belle sporting her own full face "as red as a tomato." The disintegration of house and community through the agency of deviant women is completed.

Martin Barlag, age sixty-five when I interviewed him and a former president of the La Porte Historical Society known for his owning "the largest collection of Belle Gunness material in the world," depicted the house in Mattie Altic's day in a much more sinister light than Gene had done. Martin's narratives outlined a sense of community fragmentation that was pervasive rather than progressive. He told me:

> I have a little story about the place itself. Prior to Gunness living there, it was called "The Farm." A house of prostitution. The local blades visited there. Iron bars on the windows for a twofold purpose: to keep the unwilling inmates in and to keep the reckless ones out. (April 26, 1976)

At a later interview, Martin reiterated that the bars kept Mattie's girls, who had been "brought there as white slaves and kept there against their will, see," enclosed while they kept "these local gay blades" outside, as only wealthy Chicago gentlemen were allowed entrance. When he told me, "There were bars on the windows . . . when it was used as 'The Farm' and, of course, they remained there when Mrs. Gunness was there," Martin was using the prison metaphor to mark "The Farm's" connection with the Gunness "Murder Farm." He correlated Mattie's "man-trap," a contemporary figurative term for a house of prostitution, with Belle's literal "man-trap," and so separated the property from ordered family and community life. The liminal status of madam, murderess, and the house they lived in is summed up in Martin's report of community tradition:

> Well, this version I've heard from a number of people—that the house of prostitution, that it had been prior to Mrs. Gunness's buying the place, that the evil of those days persisted in that site . . . and that that site was so impregnated with evil that it brought all the other effects on Mrs. Gunness to being, see. (June 1, 1976)

No women narrators who were considered specialists in the Gunness tradition made this historical correlation, however, but connected Belle's farmhouse spatially instead to a small shack in the center of town. This hovel was the home of "Nigger Liz" Smith, a black woman who was one of a marginal community who had lived on "The Levee" at the south edge of Clear Lake at the turn of the century.[4] Maxine Ford, age sixty-three at the time of our interviews and a reporter for the La Porte *Herald-Argus*, drew from her family's oral traditions in her description of Liz and her house:

> But at one time apparently she was a very, very attractive young girl and the mistress of a number of professional men, very prominent professional men, in the town, and had, it was rumored, a daughter by a local attorney. . . . But as she became a bit— older she became very, very strange, and of course she had no means of livelihood except sort of odd jobs, as I remember. And then she got into that syndrome of stacking newspapers around the rooms, which is something that often a recluse will do. (April 3, 1976)

Liz's refuse-filled shack and her extralegal activities with La Porte's prominent men, police and lawyers included, place her as deviant woman at the town's center. Symbolically, her presence precludes familial and community order.

Liz's connection with the mass murderess operates on several levels within the narrative structures. In one of Maxine's favorite stories, Belle Gunness and Liz Smith employ the same lawyer, who might have learned the truth about the Gunness murders from Liz on her deathbed in 1916 had he not been out of town on a hunting trip. "And as a result the secret died with Nigger Liz, who undoubtedly could have told him exactly what happened because she claimed to have remembered and probably did. She was there all the time. She was frequently seen, at least, around the Gunness home." A second narrator, Almetta Hay, age seventy-six, shares this tradition: "Liz always used to go out to Belle Gunness's and help her. Work out there as a hired hand." (April 26, 1976)

A third narrator, Martha Alderfer, onetime neighbor of the murderess interviewed in 1952,[5] stated that the two women shared the sexual favors of the same mentally retarded handyman, who spent alternate nights at each woman's house. An Alderfer family narrative supports the tradition that Belle escaped her farmhouse fire in 1908 by hiding out in Liz's shack while the town authorities were searching for her. The two deviant women supported each other.

While the men's narratives, relating Belle Gunness to Harriet

Holcomb and Mattie Altic, kept disorder on the fringe of the community, the women's narratives, relating the murderess to Liz Smith, moved disorder to the fringe element in the heart of town. Within this matrix of external/internal social chaos, three narrative images of the murderess emerge—monster, trickster, and victimized heroine. All three images place the murderess as a liminal figure who inverted the normal social codes of the community, but in distinctly different ways with somewhat different results for different narrators.

MONSTER

In 1908, in reference to Belle Gunness, the noted criminologist Cesare Lombroso stated that "in general the moral physiognomy of the born female criminal approximates strongly to that of the male." He detailed the "virile characteristics" that produced the "Gunness monster":

> The female criminal is exceedingly weak in maternal feeling, inclined to dissipation, astute and audacious, and dominates weaker beings sometimes by suggestion, and at other times by muscular force; while her love of violent exercise, her vices and even her dress, increase her resemblance to the stronger sex. (As quoted in Wooldridge 1908:165–167)

Narratives shared by older community tellers about the murderess's relationship to her children, about her strength, and about her personal appearance and dress preference dramatize her blurring of the socially acceptable categories man/woman. For instance, neighbor women's stories about the birth in 1903 of Belle's youngest child, Philip—one of three children she presumably killed later—set up this sexual ambivalence in the women's world of midwives and childbirth. One woman, Mrs. Swan Nicholson, told her family that the door of the Gunness farmhouse was shut on her when she went up to help at the time of delivery. The family deduced from this act that Belle had not given birth at all but had shammed a birth.[6] Dora (Diesslin) Rosenow, age seventy-eight at the time of our interview, came to the same conclusion with the help of this narrative:

> And my mother went to call on her when this baby was supposed to have been born. And when she got down there (it was just a day or

so after), and she was out in the yard chasing pigs and running around. My mother says, "How can you do that, a new mother?" "Oh," she said, "the baby's in there in bed." She had him in a big bed, covered up, you know. And, really, he was an adopted child. (September 22, 1975)

Frances (Lapham) Dawson, interviewed in 1952,[7] recalled her mother's having had much the same experience. Her mother found Belle by the cistern at the back door of the farmhouse washing the baby's clothes and shouted, "You shouldn't be up!" and Belle responded, "Ah, in the old country they never go to bed after they get a baby!" Frances concluded that Belle had not delivered because she was indeed a man hiding in woman's clothing. This idea was shared by a midwife who found the baby dressed and bathed almost before she was sent for and who said thereafter that this incident gave her further evidence that Belle was "way too masculine to be a woman."[8] Narrative proof for the murderess's role reversal lies in the shared perceptions of birth as a communal women's act and of postpartum weakness.

Belle's disclaimer of "old country" strength contributed to those narratives in which the murderess's muscular powers place her in the men's world of the field and market. John Nepsha, Jr., told me how his father learned from one of her former handymen that the murderess "was a real husky woman. Could pick up two hogs weighing over a hundred pounds under each arm." When I asked Gene MacDonald if Belle was strong, he responded, "Oh, wonderful. Why she could pick up two-bushel-and-a-half bag of wheat and just throw it in the wagon and never think nothing of it." Louis Blake, age seventy-seven, told me, "They tell this story about her going to auction sales and maybe she'd buy a two-hundred-pound hog and would throw it up in her little cracky wagon that she had, that she drove with her horse," and went on to comment, "Fact, there's a lot of people doubted whether she was female or male." Narrative proof lies in the shared conceptions of strength of this sort as a male prerogative.

Mabel Carpenter, age seventy-five, specialist in the Gunness tradition, for her narratives are based on personal experience, used the strong-man motif shared with the tales told by men:

So, well, all at once she lifts up this great big basket of potatoes and puts it on her shoulder, and I said to Leona [her sister], "Look," I said, "that lady put a big basket of potatoes on her shoulders." And she marched right to the house. And as I said, the nice, polite girls that we were, we simply opened the door for them that was Mrs. Gunness.

Mrs. Carpenter's narrative, however, shifts to the theme of sexual ambiguity in dress which is characteristically shared by women narrators:

And that's when I said I looked her up and down. And that hat she wore with this plume. . . . And then she had this great big jacket on . . . and this enormous big skirt. And then I looked down and there was her shoes peeking out from underneath her skirt. And man's shoes. I thought, "Man's shoes. Now what's she doing with man's shoes on?" (April 12, 1976)

Lucia (Racher) Egle, age eighty-two, used the dress theme to authenticate the murderess's grotesque sexual fusion. Her personal experience narrative begins and ends with ambiguity:

I always said she was a man dressed up in a woman's clothing. . . . Because she'd— She would have a skirt that was one of these real *heavy* things, you know, that you'd, if you kicked at it, you couldn't even dent it, you know! Such a stiff black thing. . . . I can just still see her on that porch, and I always said afterward, I said, "You know," I said, "I believe she is more man than she is woman." (March 9, 1976)

Dorothy Rowley, La Porte County Oral Historian, recalled her grandparents talking about Belle's coming to their farm auctions wearing a sealskin cap and a man's fur coat. Dorothy said that the murderess would tramp around in the mud with the men looking at farm machinery while the rest of the women would stay up near the stove and look at household items. Narrative proof depends on the shared attitude that no woman would wear men's clothing and take on men's chores unless she were a man disguised.

The narratives quoted above are put to practical use by those residents trying to account for the murderess's ability to dismember victims' bodies and to escape undetected from her farmhouse fire. In their worldview, if she were a man, she would have the appropriate strength to wield an axe, and by resuming actual masculine identity she would have the perfect disguise, since all authorities would be looking for a woman.

The symbolic use of these narratives, however, is to place the murderess in between the categories of male and female for two complementary purposes: to focus on her "unnatural" acts and to highlight, through inversion, the necessity for clear sexual distinctions in a well-ordered community. The fact that no younger narrators share this tradition questioning Gunness's sexual identity suggests that its symbolic power is not relevant for groups who define order in ways other than the separation between men's and women's roles.

Narratives about the murderess's wearing a man's fur coat, however, are those shared most often among both men and women of all ages and at all times recorded since the event of the murders. The popularity of these narratives points to their symbolic significance on several levels. They are more than a sign of the male/female confusion discussed above, because almost all narrators qualify or explain that the coat worn had belonged to Belle's last victim, a South Dakota farmer named Andrew Helgelien, whose body was the first unearthed in Belle's backyard on May 5, 1908. Bob Coffeen, age sixty-eight, a longtime newspaper reporter and local radio announcer active in presenting community history, made a statement (April 21, 1976) that is representative: "She even put the coat on to go downtown, to go to the bank. And stuff like that. The coat of one of her victims. Andrew Helgelien. . . . Big heavy fur coat." These narratives become further signs of disorder, for the murderess blurs the socially acceptable categories of public/private through her indiscretion. For residents, she is unnatural not only in her multilations but also in her lack of decorum, for she presents, even parades, this indication of her murders in public.

Further conversation with Bob Coffeen and his wife, Ruth Andrew Coffeen, who has composed a popular local ballad entitled "The Lady Bluebeard," suggests another level of symbolic chaos embedded in the fur coat narratives. When I asked if it had been the style at the turn of the century for men to wear beaver coats, Ruth responded, "But I think this was different." "Coarser," Bob added. "Uhuh. More like *bear*," Ruth finished. The murderess, in wearing wild-animal furs, signals her awful mediation between human and animal. Like that of the ogre bridegroom in the Märchen (Type 425A, the Monster [Animal] as Bridegroom), her animal skin is removable, yet it marks her as a monster. It places her in Edmund R. Leach's (1964) category of Stranger,[9] with whom no social relations are possible. She becomes what James Fernandez has called "the primordial metaphor" (1974) connecting man and beast and in this liminal state foregrounds the narrators' adherence to the principles of rationality and logic defining the natural boundaries of humanity.

TRICKSTER

The narratives discussed in the preceding section capture the image "Monster" so that concepts of order are outlined differentially for a significant number of La Porte residents according to their sex and age; narratives about the murderess's possible escape from her farmhouse fire, however, cast her in the role of "Trickster," with subsequent realignments of the order/disorder problem. Although the county coroner officially determined that the body of the decapitated woman found in the ruins of the Gunness home was that of the murderess,[10] some official opinions and most unofficial opinions to the present day have it that Belle substituted another woman's body for her own, set the fire, and absconded with the wealth acquired from the unfortunate suitors she first bilked and then murdered.

The "Belle Gunness is alive and well" tradition ranges from simple belief statements, such as the terse "She got away," to detailed accounts of her flight which place the murderess in that legend category of famous or infamous characters who live on and on (motifs A570, Culture Hero Lives, and A580, Return of the Culture Hero). The number of La Porte residents' personal experience narratives about encounters with the murderess after her supposed death was great enough for a skeptical reporter to headline his newspaper article "The Mrs. Gunness Very Numerous." One such subtradition that I have labeled "Shamming Sickness in Flight" deserves attention, for it suggests that the narrators in the sample (both male) define "trickster" by correlating it with the stereotype of the woman who manipulates her own "complaints and disorders" so that her position of apparent powerlessness becomes one of power (see Ehrenreich and English 1973).

The first narrator, Jesse L. Hurst, was a cabman for a Decatur, Indiana, line in 1908. Hurst believed that he had seen the murderess bundled up and borne on a stretcher at the train station in Decatur the day after the fire. His account, extant only in the remaining copies of the chapbook *The Mrs. Gunness Mystery,* published in July 1908, outlines their meeting:

> On the Wednesday after the fire, while I was standing with my hack at the depot, a man came to me and wanted me to haul a sick woman from the Erie depot to the Grand Rapids & Indiana railway station. . . . The woman was on a stretcher. She was very large, weighing about 225 pounds. She was carried to the train on the cot. . . . During this the woman acted very strangely. I looked closely at her and saw that she was not sick but shamming. They hurried away on the southbound train for Berne, Indiana. (As quoted in Anonymous 1908:171–172.)

The second narrator, Louis Blake (already quoted above), told me of his encounter with the fugitive in 1917. He had been an ambulance driver for an undertaker, and his wife-to-be, Lydia Decker, had been a student nurse at what was then Epworth Hospital in South Bend. Lydia's father had had a farm neighboring on the Gunness farm in La Porte and had often bought eggs from the murderess prior to the events of 1908.

> And we [ambulance drivers] had gotten this call. We went down and got this old lady who claimed she had been hurt on the train. Well, we took her to Epworth Hospital, which now is Memorial Hospital in South Bend. And they examined her, could find no injury of any kind, could find nothing wrong with her, but they put her in a room.
>
> And, as I told you, Mrs. Blake, of course, at the time was a student nurse. . . . Mrs. Blake went into this room where she was that day, and this woman in there who had registered under a different name, of course, said, "Is your pappy still out on the farm?" (September 13, 1975)

Mr. Blake's story does not end there. The murderess continued her ingenious duping of authorities:

> That night South Bend police detectives (I assume [they] were detectives, maybe they were just officers) came up to the hospital and said they had traced her that far. But in the meantime she had evidently bribed this man who was a great big colored boy, probably weighed two ten, two twenty, and he had gotten a taxi for her and spirited her out of the hospital, unknowing to the authorities. She was gone.

These two structurally similar accounts reveal certain ambiguities in Belle Gunness's image and in the structure of law and order itself, with a resultant ambivalence toward both for narrators and audience. The murderess is no longer a monster, but a clever woman who inverts the proper role of the sick person in order to outwit representatives of institutionalized order. When townspeople in La Porte have labeled Gunness "that tricky Norwegian," and when they've said she was "too smart" to die in the fire and was able "to pull the wool over everybody's eyes," they are granting her the admiration that journalist Stewart H. Holbrook feels "that Americans have made and lovingly preserve for certain of their folk villains" (Holbrook 1941:240). She is given the sympathy that has been the due of the outlaw as underdog.

A corollary to this shift in the murderess's image has been the shift in residents' perception of "the law." Louis Blake's account of Belle's foiling the South Bend detectives reveals disorder in the structure of order brought about through official ineptness. His additional comment that the La Porte county sheriff had been "accused of being in cahoots" with the murderess (a tradition widespread at the time of my field research) suggests a widening of this disorder through official complicity in criminal acts. Narratives of the fugitive murderess dramatize the credibility gap between appearances of order in the executive branch and its underlying chaos. Residents of La Porte have used this image as evidence for their skepticism toward government on all levels.

The order/disorder problem intersects the reality/appearance problem so that appropriate rules for role behavior in certain relationships (e.g., citizen to governing body, child to parents, husband to wife) cannot be clearly defined. Narratives about the murderess's forever escaping are ambiguous; they are "to be continued." Like the open-endedness of the picaresque novel, they remind narrators and audience that "laws are man-made fictions" (Babcock 1978b:95–116). This reminder has ambivalent results: the possibility of redefinitions of role can be both terrifying and exhilarating.

VICTIMIZED HEROINE

The third possible image of the murderess, that of victimized heroine, does not appear in La Porte oral traditions, but it does appear in two plays[11] based on community narrative—Lillian De La Torre's 1954 *The Coffee Cup* and Harold W. Poe's 1963 *Gnista* (De La Torre 1954; Poe 1963). Each play grounds the murderess's acts in her understandable motivation to surmount economic and sexual domination. Poe's play, set back in the 1890s on a Swedish immigrant's farm in Indiana, presents just cause for the inarticulate farm woman Belle to kill her first husband Sven with a heavy cast-iron skillet in an unpremeditated act. Act I opens with the wife holding an interior monologue with her inner self (Idgo) while she responds submissively to her husband's ugly comments. When he demands, "When I talk, you listen. I got rights here. I'm to get respect in my home," she says nothing to him, but says to herself: "Ours, Sven. Not mine. Not yours. Ours." When he tells her, "We got no time for tea an' cakes," in response to her plea to invite church folk into the parlor, she remains silent but remembers:

> We had a fine proper wedding. In the church with friendly peo-ple. . . . But he took my money. *He took all of my money from my trunk.* He took it. "Your dowry," he said. "Your dowry for us," he said. And he took it and I did not see it again. (Poe 1963: Act I, Scene 1)

In De La Torre's play, set forward to the summer of 1913, similar motivation for killing husbands is presented in dialogue between Miss Palliser, a lady crime-writer interviewing townspeople about the mass murderess; Mrs. Bluet, a gossipy farm woman; and Mrs. Larson, a Norwegian immigrant who has Belle Gunness's implements of mur-der—a butcher knife and a flowered cup for poison—as grisly keep-sakes.

> *Mrs. Bluet [to Miss Palliser]:* Killed 'em for their money, Belle did.
> *Mrs. Larson:* Foolish talk.
> *Mrs. Bluet:* Foolish talk, is it? Then why did she kill 'em?
> *Mrs. Larson:* They got too bossy. Men! You gotta have men, and when you got 'em, they begin to get bossy.
> *Mrs. Bluet [mournfully]:* Ain't it the truth!
> *Miss Palliser [writing in her notebook]:* Oh, wonderful! This adds flavor! "You gotta have men, and when you got 'em, they begin to get bossy"!
> *Mrs. Bluet:* And then killing's too good for 'em!
> (De La Torre 1954:73)

But understandable motivation for wives to kill, given the socio-economic conditions of marriage at the time (see Hartman [1978] for sociological analysis), shifts to the incomprehensible amplification of murderous acts in the following exchange between Miss Palliser and Mrs. Larson.

> *Miss Palliser:* But that's no motive for murder, or they'd have to hang every woman in creation. She *must* have been crazy.
> *Mrs. Larson:* What's crazy about that? She done what she had to do. *[Dangerously.]* They had no call getting bossy with her.
> (De La Torre 1954:73)

It dawns on Miss Palliser, somewhat later than it does on the audience, that Mrs. Larson is the murderess and has been living under an alias during the years since her supposed death in the 1908 fire. The story turns to an event of real horror for the unfortunate detective writer, who becomes one more of Belle's victims by the play's conclusion.

The insanity of the murderess, guessed at in Miss Palliser's "She *must* have been crazy," emerges full-blown in the final act of Poe's play *Gnista*. Belle's second husband, Emil Bergstrom, remarks on their wedding day, "Now I can be my own employer working on my own farm." His statement, mirroring Belle's first husband Sven's, elicits her explosive "*Your* own farm?" while her inner self responds in the primal scream "*Mine!* Man takes *mine!*" The farm woman's just desire in Act I to share property equally with her husband has been replaced in Act II by a narcissism not socially sanctioned. It is only a short step to Emil's murder and to the emergence of Belle's Idgo triumphantly asocial at play's end (Poe 1963:8).

Both playwrights, in dramatizing the progressive madness of the murderess, have made the order/disorder problem intersect with developmental psychology and sociocultural patterns. The ordered mind of Belle Gunness (Act I of *Gnista*) fragments under the inequities in the marriage system, a social institution. Her disordered mind sees a logical way to beat the system through her murders of multiple husbands (Act II of *Gnista*, and *The Coffee Cup*). No longer is she simply against society as she is in her monster and trickster guises, but society is also against her, for she is portrayed as a woman victimized by the social structure. The irony of it is that the repressive aspects of marriage have created a victim who responds by becoming a monster.

The liminal figure of Belle Gunness as the victimized heroine might have been used in a revolutionary way in these dramas, that is, to demonstrate the need for a redefinition of conventional set roles. Neither playwright, however, consciously used the image of the deviant woman to reevaluate marriage relationships or to promote real changes in the marital sphere. Harold Poe states that *Gnista* "can easily support the idea of Belle as a victimized heroine. However, I did not and do not think of Belle as such. . . . In any event, I certainly did not intend any suggestion of a reevaluation of the marriage system or to invite a male-female revolution" (Personal communication, May 1, 1979). And Lillian De La Torre, speaking of *The Coffee Cup*, states that the writing process for her is "more a kind of impersonation" than a consciously devised frame for a message: "Belle said those lines in my head, and I wrote them down. When, creating the part, I said them, they rang true." De La Torre does suggest, however, that she might have been subconsciously influenced in her creation of the character Belle by the historical fact that the two persons the real Belle spared, her handymen Ray Lamphere and Joe Maxson, were "ineffectual little men" (Personal communication, May 14, 1979). Narrative tradition in La Porte corroborates the impression of the two survivors as being marginal characters themselves. Both men were considered mentally retarded or very slow at the least. Both men were bachelors and hired out to other farms rather than owning property themselves. One man was an alcoholic and the other was afraid of ghosts. Neither man was a representative of the system that might have been threatening to the "Lady Bluebeard."

The narratives considered above indicate that the image of the woman turned upside down has been used conservatively by La Porte narrators and audiences in order to confirm their worldview. The narrative tradition that presents the murderess as an unnatural monster reaffirms the community's acceptance of the inherent rightness of the way things are. Humanity is defined through the natural law of reason and the natural separation of men's and women's roles. The slightly less conservative narrative tradition that presents the murderess as trickster focuses on the community's ideal of human justice tempered with realization of human fallibility. Laws, though not natural, and therefore mutable and uncertain, are still necessary. The two plays that present the murderess as victimized wife present the greatest potential for criticism of the way things are, but even these accounts stop short of actually suggesting a weakness in the system.

In short, the Belle Gunness narratives communicate concern about the maintenance of traditional role behavior. But in their portrayal of a deviant woman, they function to reaffirm rather than to undermine traditional values.

NOTES

1. See Babcock (1978a:13–36) and Peacock (1969:167–177) for discussion of the structuring power of narrative.

2. Gene MacDonald to Janet Langlois, March 10, 1976. Subsequent reference to my own field research will be in parentheses after quotations.

3. Indiana University Folklore Archives. 68/42. Gene MacDonald to Janis Mellenthin, December 31, 1967.

4. Male narrators have discussed Elizabeth Smith, but narratives about her are not central. Few narrators under fifty years of age discuss the black woman at all.

5. Martha Alderfer to Lillian De La Torre, July–August 1952, for her book (De La Torre 1955). I would like to thank Mrs. De La Torre McCue for the use of unpublished transcripts of interviews.

6. Albert Nicholson to Lillian De La Torre, July–August 1952.

7. Frances (Lapham) Dawson to Lillian De La Torre, July–August 1952.

8. Mary Swenson, age eighty, to Janet Langlois, October 6, 1975.

9. Leach's linguistic category of verbal abuse in which I am placing the murderess is set up as this analogy: animal category—wild animals : food source—inedible :: kinship category—strangers : marriage potential—no social relations possible.

10. La Porte County Historical Society, Belle Gunness Inquest, April 29—May 13, 1908. Coroner's official statement signed and sealed May 20, 1908.

11. Mrs. De La Torre's play, based on her 1952 interviews (see note 5), has not been performed in La Porte and is not known by residents. Dr. Poe, recently retired from the University of Southwestern Louisiana at Lafayette, is a former La Porte resident and based the play on his recollections of community narrative. *Gnista* was performed in La Porte in 1966 and 1973. I would like to thank Dr. Poe for use of the unpublished script.

· 8 ·
THE MISUSES OF ENCHANTMENT: CONTROVERSIES ON THE SIGNIFICANCE OF FAIRY TALES
Kay F. Stone

LITTLE DID we realize while reading our childhood fairy tales how controversial these seemingly simple and amusing stories were. Adults were enthusiastically engaged in determining whether such tales were damaging because of their violence or irrationality, or whether they instead furnished powerful fantasies good for developing psyches. The battle over the significance of fairy tales has been raging in various forms for some time. As early as the 1700s we find a writer of children's stories referring to fairy tales as "frolicks of a distempered mind," a sentiment still very much alive today (Kiefer 1948:87).[1]

In recent times the battle has spread to a new front, where opposing forces clash over the issue of sexual stereotyping. There are those who feel that fairy tales are unsuitable because they reinforce sexist stereotyping for both boys and girls, others who feel that fairy tales challenge such stereotyping, and still others who insist that these stories have neither a negative nor a positive impact in terms of gender. Because a major premise of folklorists studying women's folklore has been that gender is indeed significant in terms of interaction between people and material, I would like to examine the arguments in this controversy and describe actual rather than theoretical connections between fairy tales and their readers, both male and female.

I have found no clear statements on sexism in fairy tales from the suffragist movement of past decades, probably because feminist efforts then were devoted to legal and economic problems. Writers from more recent decades, however, have expressed themselves clearly on the issue of sexual stereotyping in all forms of literature. Simone de Beauvoir complains that "everything still encourages the young girl to expect fortune and happiness from some Prince Charming rather than to attempt by herself their difficult and uncertain conquest" (Beauvoir 1953:126). She mentions "Cinderella," "Snow White," and "Sleeping Beauty" as the stories most widely read and therefore most pervasive in their influence. Bullough and Bullough, in *The Subordinate Sex*, provides a scenario for a modern heroine who has read the stories carefully:

> The most obvious example of this today is the beautiful girl with the right measurements who catches the attention of a rich sponsor and simply by being female in a male-dominated society can advance far beyond her own social origins. Men, on the other hand, are more likely to have to earn their status through hard work. (Bullough and Bullough 1973:53)

These observations cited from Beauvoir and from the Bulloughs appear in the context of much longer works dealing with the broader problem of male-female roles. In 1972, however, we find a lengthy article devoted to the impact of fairy tales in sexual stereotyping. After examining tales in a number of Andrew Lang's fairy-tale books, Marcia Lieberman states:

> Millions of women must surely have formed their psycho-sexual self-concepts, and their ideas of what they could or could not accomplish, what sort of behavior would be rewarded, and of the nature of the reward itself, in part from their favorite fairy tales. These stories have been made the repositories of the dreams, hopes and fantasies of generations of girls. (1972:385)

Lieberman's pointed remarks are a reaction to the positive comments of Alison Lurie, who writes that "the traditional folktale . . . is one of the few sorts of classic children's literature of which a radical feminist would approve" (1970:42), emphasizing that the bulk of the tales portray strong and positive women:

> These stories suggest a society in which women are as competent and active as men, at every age and in every class. . . . The contrast is greatest in maturity, where women are often more powerful than men. Real help for the hero or heroine comes most frequently from a fairy godmother or wise woman; and real trouble from a witch or wicked stepmother. (Lurie 1970:42)

A professional folklorist, Stith Thompson, also seems to define märchen (or fairy tales) in terms of heroines when he states (about various translations of the term), "What they are all trying to describe such tales as 'Cinderella,' 'Snow White,' or 'Hansel and Gretel' " (Thompson 1946:8). Similarly, another folktale scholar, Max Lüthi, reminds us that a great many of the Grimms' fairy tales have heroines, that fairy tales are most often told by women, and that "today children learn fairy tales mainly from their mothers, grandmothers, aunts, and female kindergarten and grade school teachers" (Lüthi 1970:136).[2] He concludes from this:

> The woman is assigned a privileged position, not only by social custom; in art and literature, as well, she has occupied a central position since the time of the troubadours and the Mariology of the late Middle Ages. In painting and in the novel, she has been the subject of persistent interest and loving concern. (Lüthi 1970:136)

Lurie, Lüthi, and Thompson all emphasize that fairy tales demonstrate the power of women simply because these stories are dominated by women, both as protagonists and as narrators. None of them mentions that most of the heroines are pretty and passive rather than powerful. Thompson and Lüthi almost immediately move on to describe tales with male protagonists only, and Lurie apologetically observes: "Even in the favorite fairy tales of the Victorians it is only the young girls who are passive and helpless. In the older generation, women often have more power and are more active than the men" (Lurie 1971:6). More power, yes—and most often it is of a kind destructive to both heroines and heroes, because the older women are often wicked stepmothers or witches.

The favorable reactions noted above make an interesting contrast to the reaction of a young mother who did not want her daughter to read fairy tales precisely because they are so dominated by women and because the so-called "privileged position" emphasized by Lüthi is really a very restricted one (Minard 1975:vii). Her comment inspired Rosemary Minard to compile a collection of traditional tales with active heroines, because she felt these stories were too valuable to give up. In contrast to Lüthi and Lurie, Minard observes:

> Many of us . . . are . . . concerned today that *woman* be recognized as a full-fledged member of the human race. In the past she has not often been accepted as such, and her role in traditional literature reflects her second-rate position. Fairy tales abound with bold, courageous, and clever heroes. But for the most part female characters, if they are not witches or fairies or wicked stepmothers, are insipid beauties waiting for Prince Charming. (1975:viii)

Minard's relatively modest statement was sharply attacked by Susan Cooper, who objected both to "that uncomfortable title" (*Womenfolk and Fairy Tales*) and to "the motive behind the collecting" (1975:8):

> It's a false premise: an adult neurosis foisted upon children. I don't believe little Jane give a damn that Jack the Giant Killer is a boy. Lost in the story, she identifies with him as a *character*, just as little John shares Red Riding Hood's terror of the wolf without reflecting that, of course, she's only a girl. (Cooper 1975:8)

Cooper, a writer of science fiction fantasy rather than an expert on either fairy tales or neuroses, expresses an opinion shared by many scholars who are interested in the psychological interpretation of fairy tales.[3]

N. J. Girardot, for example, presents a detailed study of "Snow White" in support of his view that fairy tales are essentially nonsexist. He suggests that many fairy tales echo the general outlines of *rites de passage*, thus offering listeners the possibility of a religious experience during which they can recognize "that life itself is a story, a story told by God or the gods, to accomplish the happy passage of men and women through a dark and dangerous world" (Girardot 1977:300). He feels that the difference between male and female acts in fairy tales is superficial and deceptive: "Heroes and heroines in fairy tales, more so than in epic and saga, do not ordinarily succeed because they act, but because they allow themselves to be acted upon—helped, protected, saved, or transformed—by the magic of the fairy world" (1977:284).[4] In Girardot's opinion, fairy tales reflect the struggle for maturity and enlightenment, and both hero and heroine are engaged equally in this struggle. The manner in which they "allow themselves to be acted upon" might be different in degree, but not in its basic essence. Both seek an awakening rather than a mate.

Bruno Bettelheim makes an even more forceful statement in his lengthy and detailed comment on fairy tales, *The Uses of Enchantment*. I reproduce the following passage in full to avoid possible misrepresentation:

> Recently it has been claimed that the struggle against childhood dependency and for becoming oneself in fairy tales is frequently described differently for the girl than for the boy, and that this is the result of sexual stereotyping. Fairy tales do not render such one-sided pictures. Even when a girl is depicted as turning inward in her struggle to become herself, and a boy as aggressively dealing with the external world, these two *together* symbolize the two ways in which one has to gain selfhood: through learning to understand and master the inner as well as the outer world. In this sense the male and the female heroes are again projections onto two different figures of two (artificially) separated aspects of one and the same process which *everybody* has to undergo in growing up. While some literal-minded parents do not realize it, children know that, whatever the sex of the hero, the story pertains to their own problems. (Bettelheim 1976:226)

Like Girardot, Bettelheim feels that gender is irrelevant in the tales' ultimate significance for young readers, and he suggests that only misguided adults fail to see beneath the surface. Children, he maintains, react unconsciously and positively, regardless of any possible surface stereotyping of the characters.

We can assume from the intensity of the statements both attacking and supporting fairy tales that these stories are regarded as meaningful for both children and adults rather than as merely quaint and amusing. Moreover, fairy tales apparently have the power to affect readers deeply, either negatively or positively, in ways that other forms of children's literature generally do not. The fact that these multilevel stories are usually read early in life when a child is struggling to find a place in the world, and a sexual identity, can be used to support the arguments of both proponents and opponents of fairy tales.

In Thompson, Lüthi, and Lurie seem to feel that fairy tales offer strongly positive images for both boys and girls; Girardot and Bettelheim suggest that gender differences are less important than the psychological significance of the tales; Beauvoir, Lieberman, and Minard insist that significant differences in heroes and heroines exist and that these are important because they contribute to differential socializing of boys and girls in contemporary Western society.

While the authors discussed here argue that fairy tales are negatively or positively significant, none has given the readers themselves much of a voice. Even the mother concerned about sexism described in Rosemary Minard's book speaks *for* her daughter, not from her daughter. Bettelheim does occasionally refer to some of his patients, but only to support his own views. The others speak only in general terms about the effects and the meanings of fairy tales for a hypothetical and therefore silent audience. In the following section I will draw on the reactions of readers of various ages and backgrounds, both male and female. Their varied responses demonstrate that there is no single truth about either the meaning or the impact of fairy tales that is applicable to all readers, but there are some definite patterns.

For several years I have questioned people informally and formally about their memories of and reactions to fairy tales. Formal interviews were conducted with forty-four people individually and in small groups.[5] Of these forty-four, twenty-three were girls between the ages of seven and seventeen. Only six of the total number were males, ranging in age from nine to sixty-eight. This small number of male respondents is a result of the inability of male informants *of any age* to recall fairy tales at all. Many males, questioned informally, could not even remember if they had ever read fairy tales. With females, on the other hand, I found that all could remember clearly having read and reacted to fairy tales, and several in different age groups accurately recalled specific stories—even when they had disliked and rejected them. At first I assumed that boys simply did not read these stories, but parents, teachers, and librarians have assured me that they did. The mother of a nine-year-old boy who had just claimed he had no favorite fairy tales told me she had read him "Jack and the Beanstalk" only the night before. She suggested that he was embarrassed to admit that he read "those girls' stories." Another nine-year-old boy was willing to admit that he had read such stories but had since rejected them:

> I like that one ["Jack and the Beanstalk"] a lot better than those other stories, like "Snow White" and "Cinderella." Those are all girls' stories. They're about girls and not boys. I like the ones with boys a lot better because they're not boring, like the girls' ones. The only one I like with a girl in it is "Molly Whuppee,"[6] because she does things, sort of like Jack.

A male student-teacher of a fifth-grade class described the same pattern of boys' rejecting and girls' accepting fairy tales, at least in part because of the dominance of heroine tales in popular collections. But his description of boys' and girls' reactions indicates that the situation is more complex than boys' rejecting and girls' identifying with protagonists because they are female, for the boys seem to have forgotten the tales altogether.

> In the winter of 1978, while discussing fairy tales with a group of grades five and six students, an interesting phenomenon arose. When the discussion centered on the subject of "Cinderella," it became apparent from student remarks that there was a definite difference between boys' and girls' attitudes to the story. The boys' remarks, "It's boring," or "It's a kids' story," reflected a definite lack of interest. The girls, however, said it was one of their favorites. In fact, the majority of girls seemed to feel that someday their prince would come and they too would live happily ever after. From this difference in attitudes I am theorizing that fairy tales like "Cinderella," while being enchanting and entertaining in their own right, also serve another purpose entirely. (Spiller 1979)

Apparently the female-dominated tales extolled by Lurie and Lüthi fail to retain the interest of male readers as they mature. We cannot know for sure whether boys consciously reject them because they are viewed as girls' stories, or whether choices were made on the basis of the passivity or aggressiveness of protagonists rather than strictly on the basis of gender. We cannot even be certain whether this was a conscious decision, or whether boys did work through childhood problems in the way that Bettelheim suggests, thus leaving enchantment with no further uses for them. In any case, the pattern for girls and for boys here is clearly different.

A few girls and women seemed to agree with males in their rejection of heroines who were too passive to be interesting, but these readers did not give up fairy tales. They attempted to compensate for disappointing heroines in other ways. A nine-year-old, for example, decided that she preferred heroes to heroines:

> My favorite people now are boys named Jack. I remember "Cinderella" too, but I didn't like it as much as some others. The ones with boys in them are more exciting. They usually go out and do things. "Cinderella" doesn't have that.

A twelve-year-old reported that she had usually identified with the older sisters "who never got anything and made stupid mistakes like not giving bread to the birds in the woods." Negative as such characters were, they were more interesting to her than "the ones who just sit by the fireside and never do anything, and then one day blossom into beautiful girls." Similarly, a thirty-one-year-old woman observed:

> I certainly identified with the women in the stories, but the ones I remember are the ones where the woman was dominant—like in "The Snow Queen," where the woman is sort of all-powerful. She may be meant to be a negative figure, but I didn't see her that way. But looking back, I suppose it was the boys who had the action and did things in most of the stories.

While choosing the active but negative women in fairy tales provided these readers with a less passive model, it did not free them from the knowledge that these women were punished in the end for their aggressiveness. The woman just quoted, for example, stated later in the interview:

> I wanted to be beautiful like in the stories but I didn't think I was or would be. It just seemed ridiculous. So I was more inclined to the stories where ghastly things would happen to bad little girls. I hated them but I would read them over and over.

The twelve-year-old admitted that, as an older sister herself, she was frustratingly aware that in her life, as in fairy tales, it was the younger sister "who got all the goodies."

These sentiments are more clearly expressed by a twenty-nine-year-old mother who said:

> I remember a feeling of being left out in the fairy stories. Whatever the story was about, it wasn't about me. But this feeling didn't make me not interested in them. I knew there was something I was supposed to do or be to fit in there, but I couldn't do it, and it bothered me.

Others were more definite about why they felt left out, and clearly resented the apparent fact that boys "went out and did things" and girls did not. Said one fifteen-year-old:

> I don't think it's really fair that in all the fairy tales, it's usually the princess who's locked away. Or someone's bartering her off. In the ones with boys—I only remember "Jack and the Beanstalk"—Jack being a boy meant that he had more curiosity. I don't think I could imagine a girl being Jack, in that kind of story.

Some echoed the sentiments of the thirteen-year-old who was annoyed by the disparity between heroines and heroes ("Big Joe Tough") and insisted, "You know, there are some girls who can cope better with things than boys can!"

Not all females felt restricted by the seemingly narrow choice of models offered by fairy tale heroines. I would like to examine one especially popular story in greater depth to see how both the acceptance and the rejection of fairy tales on the basis of gender relates to the observations of the writers quoted in the first section of this chapter. The issues raised here revolve around the possibilities of fairy tales as either problem-solving stories, as Bettelheim and Girardot suggest, or as problem-creating stories, as feminist writers insist.

While the Cinderella story is found orally in all parts of the world, most North American readers will be familiar with only two versions, from printed sources. The first of these, and by far the most popular, is Perrault's 1697 reworking, complete with fairy godmother, pumpkin coach, and glass slipper. The less popular but more dynamic Grimm version has a more resourceful heroine who does without fairy godmothers and coaches and who makes her own curfew. She does not reward her sisters at the end, as does the Perrault heroine, but neither is she responsible for their mutilation, which occurs first at their own hands (cutting off pieces of their feet to force them into the slipper) and then from them as punishment from the vengeful doves, who blind them for their treachery. Apparently this popular story expresses an entire range of hopes, fears, and possibilities for both narrators and audiences.[7] Significantly, it is the more passive variant (Type 510A rather than Type 510B) that is strongly favored in the books and unanimously chosen by those I interviewed.

Like most good folktales, "Cinderella" functions on a number of levels of meaning and has several possible interpretations even at surface level.[8] In the Grimm version, Cinderella's stepsisters equal her in beauty but are "vile and black of heart" (Grimm and Grimm, 1974:121). More significant, they are interested in getting ahead and hope to do so by marrying the prince. They do not consider their stepsister a serious competitor—although their mother is more perceptive on this score. Cinderella herself is not primarily interested in meeting the prince or in gaining any material benefits—her handsome clothing cannot be purchased at any price—but wishes to escape the confines of her painfully narrow existence. She is rewarded with magic objects because she follows precisely the instructions of her dying mother. She wins the prince at least in part because she is *not* a man-chaser, as are her stepsisters. One interpreter of the tale insists that the prince is merely a symbol for Cinderella's well-deserved freedom and that marriage is not at all the point of the story (Kavablum 1973). In any case, her marriage signifies that she has managed to reject her subservient position and to take action in getting herself to the outside world, and that she has demonstrated her acceptance of maturity by entering into marriage.

Among those interviewed, only three theorized about the possible psychoanalytic significance of the "Cinderella" story. A sixty-eight-year-old male said:

> I liked all these stories because in that time of life [childhood] you feel you can't accomplish anything by yourself. And if you're the youngest and trampled on, like Cinderella, you really need to have impossible dreams and read impossible fairy tales.

A seventeen-year-old female adds, "You can take the stories like 'Cinderella' from two points of view, for the very serious aspect or for the face value. It depends on what you want at the time. That's what you get out of it." Similarly, a fifteen-year-old girl noted that she didn't expect to see fairy godmothers, witches, dragons, or giants walking on the street, but knew people who took similar roles in real life. For these readers, gender is of little importance, because they are reacting to the tales on an abstract level. The sixty-eight-year-old male, for example, identified Cinderella as an early favorite of his because as a child he identified with her feeling of powerlessness—though his later preferences were for heroic fairy tales, epics, and myths. The two girls likewise did not feel that the sex of the protagonist was significant to them, though they all noted in their interviews that there was a definite difference between heroes and heroines.

For other readers, however, the story of Cinderella was interpreted more literally as a model for feminine behavior as well as a depiction of the rewards to be gained. A ten-year-old girl, for example, stated:

> "Cinderella" is my favorite. She's a happy person, when she gets away from her family. People could live like that, like Cinderella. I guess I'd like to live like that, like the happy part. Not in a castle, though. And I wouldn't want to marry a prince, but maybe somebody *like* a prince.

The emphasis here is not on the unpleasant aspects of Cinderella's ordeal, but on her rewards—and on the fact that she "gets away from her family." Here we meet a modern Cinderella, a model for the maturing girl who dreams of escaping with her boyfriend from her restrictive family situation, acquiring a fine wardrobe, a steady income (from her "prince," not from her own efforts), and a suburban castle, all of which will presumably allow her to live happily ever after with glamour and material comfort. An eleven-year-old said, "I really liked 'Cinderella.' Yeah, when I was about five I guess I wanted to grow up and be a princess, or something like that." Her friend added: "I used to like 'Cinderella' too, like, it should be *my* story. She starts off very poor and then she gets rich and very successful, and I used to think of myself that way. I thought I'd just sit around and get all this money."

The eleven- and twelve-year-old girls described by the fifth-grade student-teacher quoted above were less cynical (or perhaps just less defensive about romantic fantasies), for they had not yet rejected the happily-ever-after ending promised by "Cinderella." But in contrast to the ten-year-old who still expects to marry "someone *like* a prince," the eleven-year-olds seem to be more realistic. However, the eleven-year-olds' responses reflect the fact that they have only recently stopped reading fairy tales (few children read them beyond the age of ten, if my sampling is any indication) and are on the defensive about "childish" things. More significant, older women who might have expressed the same somewhat cynical tone at eleven years of age were not so certain upon reconsidering their reactions. For example, a twenty-six-year-old mother of two, now divorced, said:

> I figured Cinderella was pretty lucky. First I felt sorry for her, and then she went to the dance and got the guy, and I thought this was going to apply to my life. I really figured you just sit around and wait, and something fantastic is going to happen. You go to the right dance and you've got it made! It was definitely "Cinderella" I liked best. She was gorgeous. I was homely, and I kept thinking it would happen to me too—I'd bloom one day. But it's never happened. I'm still waiting!

Those readers who identify with Cinderella are definitely interested in the dance and in the prince. A university student comments:

> My favorite fairy tales were the romantic ones, like "Cinderella," "Snow White," and "Sleeping Beauty." The romantic, "prince and princess live happily ever after" ones. I easily put myself in the princess' role, waiting for Prince Charming.

Thus the message of the Cinderella story that seems most relevant for modern girls and women concerns the rewards one is supposed to receive for being pretty, polite, and passive; the primary reward, of course, is marriage, and marriage to not just anyone but to a "prince," someone who can provide status and the material benefits of the beautiful life.[9] As Simone de Beauvoir asks, "How, indeed, could the myth of Cinderella not keep all its vitality?" (1953:126). Thus for this group the message of the tale shifts from Cinderella's growing independence and maturity to the rewards she receives and how she receives them. In this kind of narrow interpretation, success for the female comes from being beautiful and from sitting around and waiting. It is ironic that Cinderella, the ultimate in humility and selflessness, becomes for such readers a woman who uses her beauty and personality to gain material success—and at the expense of other women. In this interpretation, there is little difference between Cinderella and her stepsisters, except that she is more "feminine": unlike her openly ambitious sisters, she masks her real hopes for the future by just "sitting and waiting" for everything to turn out happily ever after for all eternity. In *Transformations*, a poetic reworking of several Grimm tales, Anne Sexton captures this frighteningly static aspect of the tale in her poem "Cinderella," which concludes:

> Cinderella and the prince
> lived, they say, happily ever after,
> like two dolls in a museum case
> never bothered by diapers and dust,
> never arguing over the timing of an egg,
> never telling the same story twice,
> never getting a middle-aged spread,
> their darling smiles pasted on for eternity.
> Regular Bobbsey Twins.
> That story.
>
> (Sexton 1971:56–57)

Another aspect of the story commented on by readers was the competition between the women, a competition our society seems to accept as natural. Sisters in particular reacted to this conflict, which they reluctantly accepted as inevitable. One thirty-two-year-old still recalls her sibling relations clearly:

> I always felt my sister was making it more than I was. She was blond, blue-eyed, and as a child this was always commented upon. She was the sweet baby girl. I suppose those fairy tales with elder sisters are the ones I have identified with most.

A twelve-year-old (quoted earlier) agrees: "You know, being the oldest daughter like me is sort of . . . well, I didn't want to be a princess, or anything, but I didn't want to be the bad one, either." This supposed inevitability of female competition is commented on by a junior high school guidance counselor:

> It's just amazing! The conflicts that occur between girls at this stage are even much greater than the conflicts between the boys. . . . I don't know why, for sure, but I guess they're preparing to compete for male attention even when they don't know it.

It would be simplistic to blame fairy tales for encouraging females to see their lives primarily in terms of competing for and winning male attentions, when many other aspects of North American culture reinforce this same ideal. The popular interpretation of the Cinderella story can be identified in disguised form in popular magazines and books, in films, and on television. Psychologist Eric Berne has suggested that one's favorite fairy tale, reinforced by other aspects of culture, could set a lifelong pattern of behavior. "The story will then be his script and he will spend the rest of his life trying to make it come to pass" (Berne 1973:95). Despite the masculine pronoun intended to encompass all humanity, Berne provides only female examples when it comes to fairy tales. He describes two "scripts" in detail, one of which is Cinderella, to whom he devotes an entire chapter. Her story, he says, is adopted by women who feel themselves to be unjustly treated or generally unrecognized for their better qualities. They learn to put on a sweet outer personality to improve their chances of getting more recognition and may, when they succeed, taunt other women whom they have bested. Such women, according to Berne, might be unable to give up the exciting game of "Try and Catch Me," first played with the prince and later continued with various adulterous lovers (Berne 1973:238).

Berne might be exaggerating in suggesting such a firm connection between stories like "Cinderella" and later behavior, but it would be a mistake to pass fairy tales off as "child's play." If one agrees that childhood is a critically impressionable time of life, especially in terms of forming sexual identity, and if popular fairy tales consistently present an image of heroines that emphasize their beauty, patience, and passivity, then the potential impact of such tales cannot be ignored. Certainly some who once favored Cinderella will later find her irrelevant, but many others will continue unconsciously or consciously to strive for her ideal femininity—or will be annoyed with themselves for failing to attain her position. The remarks of a twenty-nine-year-old woman indicate that the fairy tale model undermined her desire for independence:

> I couldn't really say whether the impact of stories is stronger when you're an adolescent or when you're younger; but the impact in both cases was harmful to me, I think, because instead of making me feel confident or able to develop my strengths or anything, they made me feel there was something in me I had to stamp out.

A thirty-six-year-old mother of four felt that fairy tales were good stimulation for the imagination but also encouraged impossible expectations, especially for girls:

> I never felt I would ever fit in, but I wanted to. There was a nice romantic thing about fairy tales that was misleading, just like Sunday school was misleading. I identified with them very much. Now I know they didn't relate much to people I knew then . . . well, on the other hand, the men seemed to be able to handle themselves, but the women didn't. Lots of things came together to prevent them. Outside forces controlled their lives, so the only way they could solve it was with some kind of magic. It doesn't say anywhere in the fairy tales I remember that if they just got off their ass and thought about their situation they could maybe do something—except for the ones who were already aggressive and mean.

Several others of various ages mentioned the emphasis on beauty and expressed disappointment in their own inability to measure up, and one astutely observed: "I was troubled by the fact that these women were, first of all, very beautiful, and second, virtuous enough not to care about it. So it was sort of a double insult to those of us who worried about our appearance."

Does it all matter? It would be simplistic, as noted earlier, to credit fairy tales with full power as a socializing force, when everything from early nursery rhymes, school texts and other books, television and movies, and personal contacts contribute to our particular system of differential socialization for girls and boys. Still, many adult female informants felt that fairy tales in particular had definitely affected their lives to some degree, and "Cinderella" in particular was the story remembered best. Why "Cinderella," and why such a materialistic interpretation of a story in which the main point is that Cinderella is *not* materialistic or even man-hungry? Judging by the comments of these respondents, Cinderella seems to present the clearest image of our idealized perfect woman—beautiful, sweet, patient, submissive, and an excellent housekeeper and wife. She also represents the female version of the popular rags-to-riches story that can be found at all levels of North American culture, one which assures us that the small can become the great and that we all have a chance to do so. For only one example, here is a *Newsweek* article describing the "Cinderella Story" of the British model, Twiggy:

> Once upon a time, back in the 1960's a wisp of a Cockney lass named Lesley Hornby parlayed her bean-stalk figure and wide-eyed air into fame and fortune as Twiggy, one of the world's most photographed fashion models. She became an international celebrity and a movie star. There haven't been many real-life Cinderella stories to match it—and if the slipper fits that well, why not wear it? The Twig is turning into Cinderella in her stage debut, when she will play the fairy-tale heroine in pantomime. (Anonymous 1974:72)

Certainly, if the slipper fits, it is likely to be worn, but it should not be forced. Julius E. Heuscher emphasizes this aspect of the story in his study of myths and fairy tales: "Finally, Cinderella is the individual who is able willingly to restrict her enjoyment of the prince's palace and feast, until she has grown sufficiently, until the slipper fits perfectly" (1974:55).

But for many women it does not fit, though they try to wear it anyway. And that is why it *does* matter how and why readers, male and female, interpret and reinterpret fairy tales that they feel were significant to them as children. The few males who mentioned "Cinderella" concentrated solely on the fact that she was a mistreated and powerless person who later obtained position and power. Women, however, concentrated on Cinderella's innate goodness, on her mistreatment at the hands of her own family (a familiar complaint for adolescents of both sexes), her initial lack of beauty and proper clothing followed by her "blooming," and finally the rewards she received for at last being recognized as the ideal female, in contrast to her ambitious stepsisters. [10] Many of the women who remembered her story recognized, either early or late, that the shoe did not fit. For example, a twenty-eight-year-old divorced mother of three complained:

> I remember "Cinderella" and "Snow White." Now I don't think they show the ideal woman—at least not for me, or for my daughter, but I liked them at her age [nine]. It's too glamorous. A man is supposed to solve all your problems. I thought this would be the answer to what I'd been growing up and waiting for. What a bunch of bullshit! Fantasy is okay, but not if it puts patterns into kids' heads about what to expect from life.

This woman's statement, made in response to a simple query concerning what she remembered about fairy tales in general, returns us to the issues raised in the first section of this chapter. She responded as a girl, and continues to respond as a woman, to heroines rather than heroes in fairy tales. Furthermore, she now views her initial positive response to these tales as problem-creating rather than as problem-solving.

Perhaps her response reflects only the surface level of meaning and neglects the psychoanalytic level emphasized first by Bettelheim and then by Girardot, who insist that the "real" meaning of the tales cannot be taken from the surface story alone. Perhaps as a young child she, like other children, unconsciously reacted to this deeper meaning but was later distracted from it by other aspects of socialization and her responses to them. In any case, emphasis on the surface level of these stories by this reader and others has been carried into later life, even though fairy tales may no longer be read or even clearly remembered. Furthermore, it is females and not males who continue to be troubled by the view of women presented in fairy tales. It would seem, then, that gender is indeed significant, both in the protagonists of fairy tales and in the readers. Still, the question of the importance of gender is not a simple one.

Bettelheim's observation that fairy tales help certain children work through certain problems at certain times of their lives is undoubtedly correct, though it is difficult to demonstrate this precisely because the working-out process is an unconscious one. For males, fairy tales apparently cease to function at an early age, but for many females these stories continue to function on some level well past childhood. Whatever positive functions the tales have for girls in their early lives apparently become less positive for them in later life. The fact that all the adult females I questioned easily recalled fairy tales both generally and specifically seems to indicate this. That a girl at the age of seven, perhaps, may react to fairy tales as initiatory rites, as Girardot suggests, or as psychoanalytically valid, as Bettelheim suggests, does not prevent them from later interpreting the same tales as literal models for ideal female behavior in later years.

The emphasis on ideal female beauty, passivity, and dependence on outside forces suggested in the fairy tales is supported by Western culture in general. The women and girls who felt uncomfortable with this model, or even those who challenged it, were not fully certain that they had the right to do so. Even when they felt they did not fit in, they did not give up the tales that on the surface suggested they *should* fit in. Similarly, even those who claim to have accepted the ideal feminine model at some time in their lives were defensive. The women often claimed that they had envied and admired Cinderella at an early age, leading one to assume that this was no longer so—but these readers generally did not clearly admit that they had indeed rejected their earlier model of behavior. Often women who said they still felt that the fairy tales projected a positive model for women expressed some doubts about the universal truth of such a model— especially with regard to their own real or hypothetical daughters. A thirty-one-year-old mother of two sons and one daughter, for example, told me:

> I guess I would say that the image of stories like "Snow White" and "Cinderella" would be good for a little girl. I gave my daughter a fairy tale book for Christmas once, I think. But then when you get down to it, maybe Cinderella and Snow White were too goody-goody. Everyone's doing things to them and they never say anything. Not exactly like real life!

I am not suggesting that men cease to be concerned with the problem of ideal masculine roles, but simply that they cease to use fairy tales as a model, while women who have not read these stories since they were children have not left them completely behind. Even when they think they have done so, as did the mother above, they are still struggling with the problem of female roles as they are presented in fairy tales, if not for themselves then projected onto their daughters (or onto other females). The surface message of popular tales like "Cinderella," "Snow White," and "Sleeping Beauty" is that nice and pretty girls have the problems of life worked out once they have attracted and held Prince Charming. Girls and women who have felt that in some way they cannot or will not fit themselves into this idealized role, into an image that does not suit their individual characters and needs, still cannot free themselves fully from the fairy tale princess. Her power is indeed strong.

Thus fairy tales, as they are presented through popular collections in which passive heroines outnumber more active heroines or heroes, do not continue to function in the problem-solving manner ideally suggested by Girardot and Bettelheim. For many females they become instead problem-creating as "purveyors of the romantic myth" (as discussed by Rowe n.d.). In this myth love conquers all, and one who is not loved is incomplete. While there are certainly male versions of this "myth," fairy tales generally do not figure in them. Thus gender does indeed seem significant in terms of readers' reactions to fairy tales. Males and females at some stage of their lives (and not only as the "literal minded adults" conjured up by Bettelheim) clearly view fairy tale heroines and heroes as providing different kinds of idealized behavior, and both males and females react to these differences in different ways. Most important, females continue to react to them even when they consciously feel that the problem was left behind in child-hood. For women, the problem-creating aspect of the tales is the attempted identification with the ideal woman, or the guilt if one fails to identify with her, and the expectation that one's life will be trans-formed dramatically and all one's problems solved with the arrival of a man. Females who once reacted strongly to the problem-creating aspect might continue to reinterpret their responses at various ages, but often without solving the problem. Life is not a "happily ever after" affair for either males or females, nor can anyone else make it so, regardless of how princely they might be. Certainly women under-stand this as well as males, but they are still held back rather than released, disturbed by the stagnant "museum case" image created by Anne Sexton's poem.

But if women remember fairy tales, consciously or unconsciously, they can reinterpret them as well. It is the possibility of such reinter-pretation that gives hope that women can eventually free themselves from the bonds of fairy tale magic, magic that transforms positively at one age and negatively at another. Such reinterpretation, conscious or unconscious, can occur at any age, of course. I offer here a sponta-neous and conscious reworking of "Cinderella" by the nine-year-old girl who earlier claimed that she preferred Jack to Cinderella. Despite her rejection, she did not give up "Cinderella," but came back to the story later in the interview and re-created it in a more pleasing man-ner for herself.

I like "Cinderella," but I think it should be more exciting. Well, Cinderella goes to the dance, finally, and then she loses her slipper and the prince gets it. Then the prince comes with the slipper but her mother won't let him try it on her. Cinderella comes in and sees that it's her slipper, but she doesn't say anything. So that night she sneaks out and she goes to the prince's palace when he's sleeping, and she gets the slipper back. And maybe she doesn't marry him, but she gets a lot of money anyway, and she gets a job. It would be more fun that way, if she had to work for it, wouldn't it?

This girl is coming to grips with a problem. She revises for herself a story she dislikes but cannot abandon. Such personal reworkings, whether conscious or unconscious, are bound to have more impact than those imposed by well-meaning adaptors.[11] As Heuscher reminds us, echoing the observations of other scholars, the dynamic possibilities of such stories in meaning and impact, understanding and response, are richly varied: "The fairy tale is not static, is not a rigid image of an immutable situation. It is subject to all kinds of modifications which depend on the psychological makeup of the narrator [and audience] as well as on his [their] cultural environment" (Heuscher 1974:389).

Thus, while fairy tales are not inherently sexist, many readers receive them as such. This study indicates that many females find in fairy tales an echo of their own struggles to become human beings. Gender of both reader and protagonist is indeed significant in this struggle.

NOTES

1. The early controversy on fairy tales is discussed by Elizabeth Stone (n.d.). A more contemporary opponent of fairy tales is Lucy Sprague Mitchell, who feels that their irrational fantasy might "delay a child's rationalizing of the world and leave him longer than desirable without the beginnings of scientific standards" (1948:24). The most eloquent proponent of fairy tales thus far is Bruno Bettelheim, who suggests, "Nothing can be as enriching and satisfying to child and adult alike as the folk fairy tale" (1976:5).

2. Not all scholars agree that tale narration is female-dominated. For example, folktale specialist Linda Dégh observes that the reverse is true in Hungary (1969:92–93), and this seems to be the case in North America as well, judging by material in Anglo-American collections.

3. Marie-Louise von Franz deals with the Jungian *animus/anima* (male/female) concept in *Problems of the Feminine in Fairytales* and proposes that the real function of the fairy tale for both females and males is gaining "individuation—the attainment of that subtle rightness which is the far-away goal of the fairy tale put before us" (1972:194).

4. Here he also chides me for overemphasizing female passivity in Stone (1975): "In this way Kay Stone's comments on what she considers to be the insipid and uninspiring 'passivity' of female characters in the Grimm tales, while not entirely unfounded, do seem to miss the point that ultimately initiation is the fortuitous work of the gods (however they are disguised)." See also the exchange of letters between Steven Jones (1979) and Girardot (1979).

5. I conducted interviews (in Winnipeg, Minneapolis, and Miami, during 1972–1973) with adults and children of both sexes and of differing backgrounds. Twenty-five people were interviewed individually, and nineteen were interviewed in groups sharing the same age. In addition to forty-four formal interviews, countless other children and adults have informally responded to the basic question: "Do you remember anything about fairy tales, and do you feel they have affected you in any way?" I have also received material from students and colleagues. Most notably, Linda Dégh showed me the responses to a similar question she asked students in her course in European folktales, taught at the University of California at Berkeley in the spring of 1978. Karen Rowe, of U.C.L.A., recently sent me a detailed questionnaire on fairy tales now being handed out to students in a number of classes. Michael Taft also shared student responses from his classes at the University of Saskatchewan.

6. The Scottish tale "Molly Whuppee," in which the heroine saves herself and her two sisters from the giant and then steals his treasures, is reprinted in one of the third-grade reader series in Canada.

7. Michael Taft, now at the University of Saskatchewan, recently sent me twenty-seven versions of "Cinderella" written by students of his folklore class in Newfoundland: "They had no prior warning of the assignment and I gave them half an hour to complete this in-class assignment." Not a single student failed to re-create the story in detail—although Taft unfortunately does not indicate the gender of the respondents. The success of Taft's experiment is not surprising to me, because almost all my informants, including some of the males, named this story either as one they definitely remembered or as their favorite story.

8. For a discussion of different narrative levels, see Jason (1977:99–139).

9. In a recent interview in Winnipeg, Anne Bowden, who is preparing a book on the history of marriage in Manitoba, observed that the wedding as the high point in a girl's life seems to be a post–World War II phenomenon. She agreed that girls easily identified with the "happily ever after" conclusion of many fairy tales that end in marriage and suggested that many girls have never thought beyond the wedding ceremony.

10. In my current folklore class I asked students to describe in one sentence what they considered to be the main point of the "Cinderella" story. The men overwhelmingly responded that it was a "rags-to-riches" story, emphasizing the heroine's positive actions and her reward. The women characterized it as a "good-over-evil" story, concentrating on the heroine's inherent and unchanging nature and her need to find outside recognition of her goodness.

11. In an attempt to make the Cinderella story more rational, one concerned psychologist has his "Cinderelma" reject the prince and palace life, set up her own dress shop, and fall for the nextdoor printer. However, his ending is even more romantic than the original: "They never seemed to get bored with one another. They never seemed to get tired of doing things together. In time, they married and had children and lived together until the end of their days" (Gardner 1974:96).

PART THREE

TWO WORLDS/
ONE WORLD

"WOOF!" A WORD ON WOMEN'S ROLES IN FAMILY STORYTELLING
Karen Baldwin

LIKE OTHER folk groups, family folks have well-developed, traditionally persistent, and artistically recreative bodies of oral narration.[1] They generate and transmit jokes and anecdotes, homiletic tales, and hero legends about themselves, their historic and current circumstances, the famous or infamous among them, the youngest members, and those who have "gone before." Indeed, the entire life cycle of the family is framed in narrative performance.

Families will mark funeral and reunion gatherings with traded and "topped" reminiscences about a deceased member. All the while storytelling turns on the lamentable drunkenness or the remarkable cheerfulness or the uncompromising honesty of the dead kinsman, he is "remembered alive" by the surviving family. "His very words" are part of the dramatically performed dialogues that carry the action of the tales. He is, in these circumstances, still counted a member of the group, at the same time that the tales about him serve to reintegrate, entertain, and console his remaining relatives.

This article is the offspring of two papers. One, dealing with team telling, was read at the 1977 meetings of the American Folklore Society. The other, a typology of family narrations, was a 1979 visiting scholar lecture given at Western Carolina University and Appalachian State University. I am grateful to colleagues in all three forums for their criticisms and their own kin-traditional corroborations.

Parents and other family adults mark the recognition of group membership for the children among them with prideful or chiding accounts of the youngsters' earliest achievements or embarrassing exploits. These "infant tales" are first formed and transmitted by the adults ("outsiders" to the children's family experience), and they live in the continually reenacted circumstances of, for instance, weekend visits from out-of-town relatives. At some point, though, the child begins to take over the tale-telling, perhaps only in self-defense, and reforms the narration to suit his or her own tastes. And when the child actor in such tales begins to narrate them as well, we see the first stages of competency in the genres of personal-experience-telling and memorates.

My kin and almost everyone else's have various types of tales as well as a mélange of the usually recognized genres of traditional expression and life. They have their own proverb forms and folk speech, rhymes and rituals, folk poetry, music, and song. Much of what is kin-traditional, though, is also likely to be obscure to outsiders and apt to be heard only in social circumstances whose place and purpose are recognized as "family." It is, then, within the private contexts of family life and folk tradition that the following consideration of women's roles in storytelling takes place.

The body of narratives common and private to any community of kin is a composite and dynamic whole. Its constituent elements—the tellings of family history and news and all the sorts of tales, jokes, and anecdotes a family is heir to—are both changing and interchangeable. No one person in the family is the ultimate source of the group's oral history, its poems, tales, and proverbs. Many people must be heard to tell their "two bits" before the whole begins to make sense. And the performance of this whole body of narratives has as many social centers as there are kitchens and parlors, side yards, and front stoops for hearing out the family yarn spinners and oral historians. The family draws its narratives from many sources and tells its story with many voices, and the ways in which family tellers change and interchange their portions of the whole are importantly collaborative.

Among my mother's people, the Solleys of Clearfield County in central Pennsylvania, the image for the process of the family narrative is a crafty one. My maternal great- and great-grand kin talk of "knittin' " and "piecin' " when what they are doing is remembering child-naming stories, reckoning a particularly remote in-law relationship, and recalling the circumstances of a family poem composition. The knitting and piecing is not aimlessly or haphazardly done, either. There is a discernible structure for both sequential and simultaneous telling among my various aunts, uncles, and a countryside of cousins. This structure underlies the din of "visiting" which fills the Greenville Brethren Church basement throughout the sit-down dinner at the annual homecoming. It patterns the exchange of "lies" and "Now, that's the *truth*" tales told out between the parked cars that are a buffer between the pacifist church and the old schoolhouse-turned-gun-club next door and that block a clear view of the preacher pitching horseshoes on a Sunday. And those same patterns are the rules for order in a husband and wife argument of detail about a story held in common. "Hush up, now, and let *me* tell it." "No! Get it *right!*" Understanding these rules for collaboration aids our appreciation of the differences in telling by women and by men in the family and gives us some notion of how the family maintains the privateness, the esoteric quality, of its traditions.

Generally, it is the Solley women who remember and tell the family genealogy, keep the family photographs and letters, and swap information about the "doin's" of various family members and of neighbors who are "just like family." As a result, they can provide with good authority their own descriptive narrative asides about the family and can interject "correct" detail when "the truth of the matter" has gone astray in the stories told by Solley men. "Now one thing about your Grandad Lee," I have been reminded often, "he never lied. He just told stories." It is usually the men who, like my grandfather, tell the marked and linear family narratives, those dramatized, actioned accounts in which Great-Grandfather George Washington Solley saves his home and children from an early morning fire by dousing the flames on an upstairs curtain-wall with the night's accumulation in the chamber pot. So it is that when Solleys and their other-surnamed kin gather around in a family place and time to talk and tell, a narrative balance is struck between descriptive detail and dialogued action by the sequential or simultaneous telling of the women and the men. When both sides are heard, the family story is complete.

The "sides" are, first, a complement of content and of narrative style. The following account represents an illustration of that complement in the different ways apple-butter-making is remembered by

Great-Uncle Roscoe Solley and his wife of then fifty-two years, Great-Aunt Rheva Rowles Solley.

We sat around the kitchen table one summer afternoon several years ago and talked away the hours between dinner and supper. The tape-recorder microphone picked up our voices from its place beside the sugar bowl and the translucent plastic strawberries that were the newest additions to Aunt Rheva's already considerable collection of souvenir salt and pepper shakers. At one point, the subject was "socials"—play parties, moonlight picnics, cornhuskings, and apple-peelings. Uncle Roscoe had just finished remembering the courting at a cornhusking:[2]

"And then you'd pair off and a fella and a girl would get to huskin' corn, and every time you got a *red* corn ear, you had to kiss your girl." He nodded a wink to Aunt Rheva with his punch line. "That's why I always said Mom saved the red ears and *took* 'em to the cornhuskin'."

Aunt Rheva, who is "Mom" in most of Uncle Roscoe's stories, deadpanned her husband's gentle gibe and let him start again without the rise he wanted from her.

"Then the apple-peelin's," he remembered. "We had 'em here at home. The whole gang sat around in the evening and had the apple peeler goin'. Oh . . . one time we's out there, and I'll never forget it as long as I live. Aunt Annie had a big copper kettle for to boil apple butter in. It don't work right in any kind but a copper kettle. And you had a great big paddle on the end of a long stick and the paddle had holes through it so the apple butter could run through. And you stood off at the end of that stick and kept stirrin' that apple butter so it wouldn't burn. And you just kept goin' and goin'. . . .

"Well, anyhow, we'd go over to Aunt Annie's, and she'd make two big kettles of apple butter. And it was huntin' season, and Cliff and Currier and I'd went huntin', and when we come home them two huntin' dogs got to playin' around. Aunt Annie had her apple butter all cooked and was settin' there coolin', and them damn dogs come after each other, and one run down over the hill, a lickerty-hellin' . . . went right *in* that apple butter kettle, that boilin' apple butter. And just his hind end, his hind legs and his belly went down in it. Didn't jump clean over the kettle. He just jumped far enough his front legs went out one side and his hind legs went down in. And he . . . 'YOWUP!' . . . and oh, Jesus . . . Aunt Annie! I think if she'da had a rifle, she'da killed every dog in sight. She had to dump the whole kettle out. And that's the first time, only time, I ever heard Aunt Annie swear. 'God damn the goddamn dog,' she said. And she told Fritz to get the gun and shoot them dogs! I imagine if Uncle Will'd been there, he *woulda* shot 'em. I can still see the old apple butter flyin' when ol' Dewey jumped in the kettle."

Without a pause, Aunt Rheva followed with her family's version of an apple-peeling. Her telling frames Uncle Roscoe's story of Dewey in the kettle and indirectly comments on his omissions of detail:

"We gathered the night before at our house, and we pared all our apples by hand. We didn't have an apple-paring convenience. So there'd be Grammy, and whoever was goin' to get part of the apple butter, and mostly Aunt Pearl. And we'd pare. Oh, I's pretty good. But I did my share of corin' apples and slicin' them too. And they would pare, oh . . . I forget how many bushels. And we only had one bushel of sour apples. The rest of our apples were sweet Catawbas, that we cooked. We had to go buy the apples. Or sometimes a neighbor man would give us the apples. Once or twice he gave us the sweet Catawbas. And that made delicious apple butter. And whenever you was almost done stirrin' your apple butter then you put in your cloves and a few sprinkles of cinnamon . . . and that's to flavor your apples. Then you'd git up in the morning and cook it."

Aunt Rheva's recipe for an apple butter social is not a "story" by the standards set in Uncle Roscoe's tale of the disastrous day at Aunt Annie's, but it is a story nonetheless. Features of her narrative style contrast with his in several ways and characterize the telling other Solley women usually do in the company of Solley men. Hers is a story whose artful purpose is to organize for my benefit all the necessary details he neglected. Therefore, she mentions *only* those ingredients of the apple butter recipe and the evening of communal preparation which he did not. Her story is entirely open-ended. It bears no familiar marks to guide the listener from start to finish. It also has no plotted line of action, nor would it ever likely have. Rather, it tells of textures and tastes and the social relationships among those who gathered to pare. Its artistry is importantly achronological and needs no dialogue or dramatization. Her story casts a *general* description of the *usual* performance of an apple-peeling from the vantage point of one who remembers doing all the various tasks of preparation at one time or another. With Aunt Rheva's telling, then, the afternoon's talk of socials is brought into narrative balance.

The formal contrasts in these styles of storytelling, and their collaborative presence in an otherwise informal conversation, seem to spring naturally from the interdependent and different concerns and expectations in the lives of Solley men and women.

Solley women center their concerns almost exclusively in the homes they keep, the gardens they tend, the foods they shop for, put up, and cook. They are the ones who bear and then care for the family's children on a daily, immediate basis. Women spend most of their time where they can see and must cope with conditions and behaviors that are private and discretely individual. It is not surprising, then, that women are also the ones who can best name the family members and discuss their idiosyncrasies, and that it is they who take prideful responsibility for keeping order in the memory and memorabilia of the family's background. Much of the purpose for women's telling is to survey the range of details and descriptions of family people, family places, and things in order to maintain currency and accuracy for those descriptions. Women place such purposes in their lives when they "set a spell" and "visit."

"Visiting" is a social and narrative occasion that can happen anywhere for brief or extended periods of time. In the gathering and telling of family information, which are the core performances of visiting, the exchanges are several and concurrent and reflect a pattern of the daily lives of women in their homes. A visit can be easily engaged and just as easily interrupted for the doing of other things. Like cross-stitch embroidery, or pieced-top quilting, or corn shuck rug-weaving, the artistry of visiting can be put down at any time a diaper needs changing, a quarrel needs unsnarling, or a batch of chicken needs turning in the oven. A visit can be picked up again after interruption without any loss of coherence, or it can be accomplished right along with the washing of dishes after a meal.

Solley men are responsible for the financial support, long-term survival, and public leadership of the family group. In their wage-earning, leadership capacities, the men spend much of their time in public situations away from the daily, private centers of family life. The perspectives men have of the family can be informed with a distance not usually possible for the women, and their storytelling artfully demonstrates that distancing. Men's family stories may be born at home, but they are reared at the edges of mines and slate quarries and at the doors of the state barns where road-building equipment is stored. The patterns of hierarchy and skill specialties by which the Solley men order most of their working lives are reflected in their storytelling styles. Solley men tell as much for entertainment value and dramatic impact as they do for validating the experiences of family life. Consequently, men are less concerned with accuracy of details of texture, aroma, social relationship, color, and chronology. When a "few twists and turns here and there" might make a better, funnier, more dramatic presentation, details are changed to form a story "with a point worth tellin'." Such stories have a stated beginning and end, and the listener is obliged to hear them through, see the action, laugh at the humor, and get the point. Stories with a point are not organized with the expectation of interruption. The teller must be allowed to "speak his piece" entirely or he will invariably lose his point and have to begin again in order to find it. Women's narratives do not have the same aesthetic stricture. There is usually no "point" in women's telling. Their storytelling roles are played out differently.

In the process of knitting and piecing the Solley family's narratives, then, the men's and women's performance modes are equally important. The two styles and purposes for telling are brought together in the same social time by changing patterns of collaboration. Understanding the differences between men's and women's complementary conditions of life and narrative styles helps place the dynamic, changing frames of family storytelling in their best perspectives. In public, at the supermarket and the bank, the priority of men's performance is recognized, and after greetings are exchanged with neighbors and kin, the pattern of sequential and solo telling of jokes and personal experiences is most often appropriate. At home, the women's sphere of simultaneous, cooperative telling usually frames the occasions for men's marked narratives and when necessary serves the men's performance with correction and with no apology for interruption.

The transfer of porch talk to the printed page is difficult at best. But in order to illustrate the dynamic patterns of collaboration which organize Solley storytelling, I offer the following excerpt from a tape-recorded afternoon's "set" in the out-kitchen of Ross and Rheva's home in Grampian. My translator's voice is the same one used in any family circumstance where outsiders are listening in and need a bit more explanation to understand what is going on.

Roscoe's older sister, Great-Aunt Lois Solley Thompson, and I were telling of our recent visit to the old house at Harmony Crossroads where Great-Great-Grandfather Isaac Solley went to farming when he set up housekeeping with his first wife, Hannah. The man who now owns the farm makes his living as a miner in a coal operation farther east in the state, and he keeps a pack of dogs to guard the house and forage for themselves when he is not there. We had a terrifying run-in with the dogs, which Aunt Lois began to narrate in the style of story-telling that seeks corroboration and exchange. Her purposes for engaging my collaboration were mixed though, and as a result our story formation was neither smooth nor successful. She wanted to tell *with* me our shared experience at the house. She wanted to tell *on* me as well. I had been scared silly by the snapping, close-circling pack, and she had rescued me by growling at the dogs and knocking them out of the way with her cane. I was chagrined and unwilling to let her capitalize on my city-bred fear of guard dogs.

"We was up at Ted's yesterday, and then we come across and down to Westover. And I said to Karen, 'There's the road back into where we used to live.' Well, she wanted to go in. And I didn't have any idea who was in there. But we went in, and when we got out of the car there was *six* dogs in there . . . wasn't there?" Aunt Lois directed her question with a nod to me, and without much pause or practice in the storytelling style, I changed the subject. "Oh, my! I never got so scared in my life!"

Less daunted than piqued at my lack of cooperation, she continued. "Well, I *know'd* there was six. And there was this black one there . . . I forget what you call them. . . . " Less openly, without a glance or gesture, she offered me another chance to help the telling. I declined with silence. "And this black one just barked and barked. And it just seemed to want to go for Karen. And he didn't seem mean . . . just 'roo, roo, roo.' "

By this time Aunt Lois and I were more in competition for the story's telling than in agreement on any of its details. I thought the dog had indeed looked mean, and I attempted to "correct" her statement of what happened. "Well, he looked like he was pullin' his lip back on me and . . . " The mention of the dogs had already "cued" Uncle Roscoe, and before I could finish he mandated a change in the entire sorry proceeding with a joke.

"Well, whenever you see a dog doing that, make up your mind he's not going to bite you. Yeah . . . that's a little bit like when we was out here one night taking the boys over to the baseball game. Young Zigger said, 'Carnigan, get off and go in there and ask that fellow which way you get out of here, and when you get out of here how you get to Madera.' Carnigan jumped off of the truck and started to go in around the house, and there was a great *big* bulldog come out of the house with a face about this wide." He gestured the size of the dog's head with both hands, then put his own face in the space and "became" the bulldog with the deep, gravelly voice. "Oh . . . 'R-ROW, R-ROW, R-ROW.' "

"Carnigan, he jumped back on the truck and Howard Spencer, he was the manager of the ball team . . . and Howard said, 'Oh, what's the matter with you? Go on in there. A barking dog never bites!' 'Well,' Carnigan said, 'he might quit *barkin*'!' "

I laughed when I got the point, and Aunt Lois picked up her story again, undeterred. The dogs had never concerned her much. At the house she had butted them out of the way with her cane and, once her brother butted in here with his joke, they were out of the way of her story as well. She continued:

"Well, when somebody didn't come out of this house, I was going around to the back door to tell them we was in there. Finally Karen said, 'There's some machinery moving back behind the house.' And then he come into the house. And I don't know whether he heard the dogs barking or not, if that's why he come in. But he stopped then, and he talked to us. And he said we's welcome to look all around, he said . . . and, 'Any time, just go around,' he said . . . and I don't know whether he has a wife or not." Hers was a roundabout, "storied" way of asking who now owned what used to be her grandfather's farm.

Uncle Roscoe remembered, "Well, there was some Polish people living in there the last time . . . " Aunt Rheva interrupted to agree. "Yes, that's him. Lavinsky or Lachinsky . . . Oh, he has some lovely children. They're just grand. They have boys, and they have girls . . . and part of the boys is married, and part of the girls is married."

Aunt Rheva's mention of the "Lavinsky or Lachinsky" children somehow triggered Uncle Roscoe's thinking about their own family of five, some boys and some girls, all of them married. But the clue was neither verbal nor visible. He simply started in on a family story about Jay Blaine, their oldest son, who fought in the Pacific during World War II. The tale of "How's the Milk Situation?" can never be told within Aunt Rheva's earshot without her interruption. She figures importantly in the action of the narrative, and he *never* gets her part "right." They perform here as a team.

"Jay wrote us a letter one time. He was out there in the islands, and he couldn't . . . They didn't dare tell where they was. Come in here and read the letter and . . . right, just at the back end of the letter, he said, 'How's the milk situation at home?' And Mom said, 'Now what did he ask that for?' So we's all settin' around here and wonderin'. That was a funny question to ask, how the milk situation was. And then, all at once . . . we was settin' there at the supper table . . . and Mom jumped up and let out a scream. 'Oh! I know!' And she run and grabbed the letter and stuck it over the lamp here . . . " While his back was turned to point at the place where they used to hang their kitchen coal oil lamp, Aunt Rheva made her move into the storytelling:

"No! I throwed it in the *oven!*"

"Let me finish it!"

"No! Get it right!"

"That don't make any difference. . . . Butt out. Anyhow, she went and roasted the dang thing . . . whether she roasted it in the oven or over the lamp . . . and there, right between the lines, he'd wrote in milk, 'I'm in Goodenough Island.' And told all about what he was doin'. And that didn't show up, you know, 'til you'd heat it and it turned brown."

I didn't understand. "How'd you know to heat it?"

Aunt Rheva was the first to explain. "You write it in milk and then let that dry . . . your letter . . . and then that don't show up. You have to put it in the *oven* and brown it before it'll show up."

Uncle Roscoe reiterated his contention that the "correction" was unnecessary. "You can just hold it over the chimney of a *coal oil light* and it'll do just the same . . . it'll come right up. And the kids had been at that here at home . . . playin' 'detective' and one thing and another . . . and all at once she let out a scream at the supper table and jumped up . . . "

As Uncle Roscoe began again where the point of his story had been lost to the argument of detail, Aunt Rheva claimed her right to the first of two "tags" with which they traditionally end a telling of "How's the Milk Situation?"

"I was always the head of the detective agency, when we was playin'. And the kids would hide, and they always would write notes in milk and tell me where they was and give directions. We had an old dog, and so they made me bring the dog into the house, because if any of the rest of the neighborhood kids that was playin' would say,

'Hey, Ditchy. Go and find Jay or go and Find Lou or Flora Mae' . . . he'd take you right to them. Oh . . . he was a traitor."

Uncle Roscoe always gets the last word in any performance of this oft-told tale. His "tag" comes right on the heels of Ditchy, the traitor.

"I told Bill Edmundson . . . up town, here . . . about Jay writing that in between the lines. And Bill looked that way, you know . . . " Uncle Roscoe cocked his head, puckered his face into Bill Edmundson's frown and pout, and growled Bill's comment about his own son, Fritz: "That goddamn Fritz! He's too dumb to ever think of anything like that!"

This interchange among the four of us is as exemplary as it is commonplace. First of all, the patterns for performance quite naturally shift, when necessary, from simultaneous to solo storytelling. Next the range of possibilities for simultaneous collaboration is represented. At one end is the disjointed and conflicting array of statements meant to tell the story of experience shared by Aunt Lois and me. At the other end is the practiced and polished team performance of a marriage pair whose life and storytelling experience together is golden. Rehearsals for such performances as Ross and Rheva's telling of "How's the Milk Situation?" are staged in private, when just the two of them talk about a shared experience and cue correction in each other's recollection of what happened. When the experience was not shared or when Aunt Rheva will not be bothered to monitor what she calls Uncle Roscoe's "monkeyin' around" with a narrative, the license to "storify" is given freely for a larger audience. "None of them was there, Roscoe. You can go ahead and tell it any way you want to."

There are psychological implications in the wrangling, rankling pattern of exchanges exhibited by any family pair whose lives together have made their knowledge of each other's commissions and excesses all too familiar. More to the point in this discussion, though, is one pair's artful resolution of their conflicts into complement.

Aunt Rheva puts up with very little of Uncle Roscoe's storytelling monkeyshines. He is always "butting out" her butting in. The narrative interplay between these two is so well established that they have a long-standing joke to frame their team performances and help disarm whatever arguments ensue. The prize is an imaginary "golden-handled chamber pot" or "pee pot" or "piss pot," depending on the decorum required by the circumstance in which the prize is offered, and the contest is constant to see which of them will be awarded the "golden handle" by the other in their storytelling spats. The following brief tale of "The Indian Washbaskets" comes from one of my aunt's and uncle's many vacation rambles down the Blue Ridge Parkway. Even though there is here resonance of many "rehearsals" when they were alone, when I was present for this telling of the tale, the golden handle of correction went from Ross to Rheva one more time.

"And you know, down there at Cherokee, we were trying to buy clothes baskets. We thought we'd get some Indian-made clothes baskets. A little, stinkin' basket about that big around . . . an Indian relic that the Indians made . . . they wanted *five* bucks for!" Whether Uncle Ross's gesture of a six-inch basket was exaggerated, Aunt Rheva silently nodded her corroboration. "So she decided she didn't want any big baskets. So comin' up through Virginia, she let out a war whoop . . . and I was goin' along about sixty-five mile an hour . . . *'There's* my baskets!' And I started to stop . . . I was a thousand feet apast it . . . "

"Half mile."

"We . . . well, I'll give you the handle on that one. So, we back up, anyway. I wasn't so far ahead that I couldn't back up. We backed up . . . "

"You turned around."

"No. I did *not* turn around. We *backed up* there aside the road and got two, nice big clothes baskets for five bucks . . . five and a half."

"No. Just one."

"No . . . " His disagreement changed in mid-sentence. "No, now I'm gettin' ahead of my story. We got the *other* one the next year."

"That's right."

The real-life "chamber" has a black wooden bail grip and a station all night long in the hall beside the bedrooms. Trekking it to the outdoor toilet for cleaning in the morning is nobody's prize chore. Vying for the golden handle, then, is a metaphoric test not lightly undertaken. The arguments may be stylized, but the interruptions that give rise to them are never idle. They bespeak an understanding of the flow of family storytelling which needs to check the course of creativity and change each time an old person forgets or a young person misunderstands. The roles of Solley men and women, with their sometimes unselfconscious, often purposeful reactions to each other's tales, are played to differentiate the "truth" from out the "telling." The Solleys conscientiously uphold a balance in their conversations, a mean between an entertaining, storied formulation of experience and a "That's *not* the way it happened!" sense of history.

Then too there are some women in the family who "storify" as well as Solley men, and to "set a spell and visit" with some men will profit genealogy and gossip. But in recognizing the differences between their traditional spheres of interest and styles of storytelling, Uncle Roscoe laughingly admits, "Mom, she usually wins. She gets the last word in." The last word is very often *woof,* and calls up another private joke in tandem to the golden handle. The traitorous dog, Ditchy, long since dead but still remembered, had a territorial yard bark that occasionally got the best of those inside the house. Someone would holler out, "Ditchy! Shut up!" Ditchy would always obey the command when it came, but not without one more contrary "woof" directed at his humans in the house. So in any Solley family argument where the competition for the golden handle is a draw, getting the last word is done with a "woof" from one contender or the other.

Uncle Roscoe has a "perverted" proverbial expression that he uses after one of Aunt Rheva's "woofs" or when he's had to "give Mom the handle on that one." It is an entertaining quip which serves as well to release whatever tension remains over the question of who is right.

"You know, before I's married, life was just one damn thing after another. After I's married, it was two damn things after each other!"

Her reply to this is downright, doggone predictable:
"Woof!"

NOTES

1. Family folklore, family oral history and genealogy, family photographs, documents, and collected memorabilia are the materials of interest to a wide range of scholars. The literature dealing with such subjects is written by historians, sociologists, and family members themselves, as well as by folklorists. Zeitlin, Kotkin, and Cutting-Baker (1982) present family narratives from the Smithsonian Collection and five essay treatments of other traditions from individual families. Useful bibliographies for family folk tradition also appear in Cutting-Baker et al. (1976), and in Kotkin and Cutting-Baker (1977).

There are several folkloristic treatments of family narrative in particular. Boatright (1958) casts a literary-historical view of the process of oral transmission and change in Texans' family stories, including his own family. Morgan (1973) is in many ways a direct ancestor of this piece on the women tellers in my family. Morgan's participant perspective of the generations of tellings about the wily, witty Caddy informs her analysis of the heroine legends with an important subjectivity. Other analytical discussions of family traditional narratives include Garrett (1961) and Brandes (1975).

There are two book-length discussions of the folk traditions within single families. Leonard Roberts (1974) presents a rich and revealing collection of the various verbal and musical arts of the Couch family of Harlan and Leslie counties. Jean Ritchie's book (1955) is a fine example of autobiographical and family reminiscence. In the process of telling her own storied search for the roots of the family's ballad and folk-song tradition, Ritchie describes family tale-tellings, family customs, and rituals. My own study of the Solleys, *Down on Bugger Run: Family Roots and Folk Tradition,* is in final preparation.

Finally, the Solleys have a considerable tradition of versifying as well as story-telling. There are five family poets among my grandfather's ten siblings, and the stylistic and performance differences discussed here are borne out again in the poem preferences of the women and men rhymers. See Baldwin (1976).

2. The quotations that follow have intentionally not been set off as long quotations normally are. The speeches are slightly edited, but the ellipses only indicate the speakers' pauses and are used to pace the reader's eye as he or she would "hear." The speeches are important illustrations of the argument, of course, but they do require context glossing throughout. The final reason for the format is that I have a reformed opposition to the specimen display of "folks' speech" as something different from my own.

Jay (L) and Roscoe Solley "sizing things up" at a family Fourth of July picnic, Curwensville Dam, Pennsylvania.

Lois Solley Thompson (R) with her granddaughter and namesake at a family Church of the Brethren reunion, Greenville, Pennsylvania.

Vesta Thomas Mahlon (L) and Mary Place Thomas "visiting" at a family reunion. Mary Thomas holds her prize for being the oldest person at the celebration.

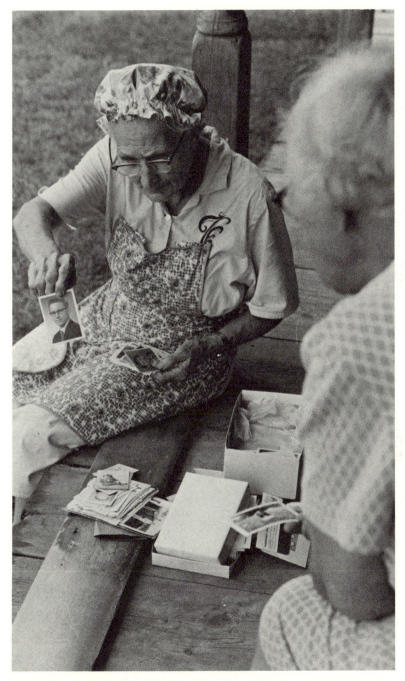

Vesta Thomas Mahlon "telling" her shoebox of family photographs to Lois Solley Thompson out on the back porch near Bilger's Run, Clearfield County, Pennsylvania.

Aunt Rheva Rowles Solley getting the "last word" in a conversation with her husband, Roscoe Solley, at a family wedding rehearsal party in Niagara Falls, New York.

· 10 ·
SOME DIFFERENCES IN MALE
AND FEMALE JOKE-TELLING
Carol Mitchell

Τ HIS STUDY was undertaken in order to discover and delineate the differences in male and female joke-telling in a single community as a first step in addressing the larger question of whether there are any real differences between the joke-telling patterns of men and women.

The fundamental hypothesis was that men and women have basically different attitudes toward joke-telling and that these different attitudes should affect the kinds of jokes told by men and by women, the situations in which they told jokes, and the audiences to whom they told the jokes. It seemed probable that neither sex was really aware that there were two separate but interrelated traditions of joke-telling, precisely because those traditions were so interrelated and so similar. In order to test these hypotheses, it seemed necessary to begin by collecting a large sample of jokes from many different individuals in one community and, as often as it was feasible, to collect them in situations that were natural joke-telling situations. In addition, to further substantiate the relevance of whatever findings might be suggested by statistical analysis, additional questionnaires and a number of in-depth interviews with expert joke tellers (both males and females) were also conducted.

COLLECTION PROCEDURES

A collection of jokes was therefore begun during the winter of 1972 at Colorado State University in Fort Collins, Colorado, and completed in the fall of 1975. A total of 1,507 jokes were collected, 1,194 (79.2%) from students, 66 (4.4%) from faculty and staff, and 241 (16.4%) from nonuniversity acquaintances and family. Of these, 988 (65.6%) were collected by folklore students and 519 (34.4%) were collected by me.

In addition to the joke texts, the name, age, sex, ethnic origin or race, religion, and occupation (i.e., student, faculty, staff, or other occupation) of the informant were collected, and the name, sex, age, ethnic origin or race of the collector were noted as well. A description of the setting in which the text was collected was also included for each joke. Almost two-thirds of the texts were collected in situations in which jokes were told spontaneously or in situations set up by the collectors approximating spontaneous joke-telling situations. However, the other one-third were collected when the collectors simply asked other people to tell them jokes.

For this collection, anything that was told as a joke during a joke-telling session or anything that an informant called a joke was considered a joke. It became clear that the informants did not consider all kinds of humor to be jokes; for instance, spontaneous puns and witticisms were not classified as jokes. Limericks, on the other hand, seemed to be thought of as a subcategory of jokes. When limericks were collected, it was always during joke-telling sessions, and sometimes the teller would say, "I have a limerick," but sometimes the limerick was told without setting it off from the other jokes. When asked, informants always knew that their rhymes were called limericks, but felt that limericks were a specialized form of the joke and that the collector was quibbling if she did not accept the limerick as a kind of joke. A similar attitude seemed to be held for humorous graffiti, although fewer items of graffiti were collected than limericks. Both limericks and graffiti were told after jokes on a comparable subject had already been told, suggesting the importance for the informants of context in establishing the limits of what might appropriately be considered a joke.

While the majority of jokes collected were narratives, some of these were quite short. For example:

> Mary Jane was taking a bath one night when a man jumped in through the window. Mary Jane wasn't worried though. She knew she had the soap.

Well over one-third of the jokes were question-and-answer jokes, which Brunvand (1968:54, 113) calls riddle jokes. Although some folklorists consider riddle jokes a subcategory of the riddle, clearly nonfolklorists consider riddle jokes to be jokes.[1] While the large majority of the jokes classified as absurd or silly jokes or as Polack jokes used the form of the question-and-answer joke, practically every category included some riddle or question-and-answer jokes.

In this collection 51.1 percent of the jokes were narratives, 39.55 percent were question-and-answer jokes, and the other 9.35 percent included limericks, graffiti, pictorial jokes, knock-knock jokes, "Mommy, Mommy" jokes, and one-liners such as, "She was only the stableman's daughter, but all the horsemen knew her."

CODING OF JOKES

In order to allow detailed analysis, the jokes were coded for the SPSS (Statistical Package for the Social Sciences) computer programs (Nie 1975).[2] Each joke was coded for the sex, age, race or ethnic group, religious affiliation, and occupation of the informant; for the sex and age of the collector; and for whatever theme(s), character(s), and form the joke utilized. This system of coding made it possible to count quickly the various kinds of jokes that were told and to see what kind of teller told them to what kind of audience.

Jokes can be classified according to form, plot, character, theme, and sometimes setting (although for this study plot and setting were not coded), and each of these groups can be subdivided into various categories. For the purposes of this investigation, form was divided into Narrative Jokes, Question-and-Answer Jokes, and Other Forms of Jokes. Character was divided into the categories of Children, Fools, Animals, Women, Religious Figures, Political Figures, Polacks, Negroes, Members of Ethnic Groups (excluding Polacks and Negroes because jokes with characters from these groups were numerous enough to be considered separately), Authority Figures, Deformed Characters, Military Personnel, Female Professionals, and Male Professionals. Theme was divided into categories of Death, Drinking, Sports, Filth, Male Approach, Sadism, Premarital Sex, Marriage, Adultery, Homosexuality, Prostitution, Disease, Castration, Euphemism, and Scatology.[3] In addition, the jokes were coded to indicate the presence of the following elements: Word Play, Obscenity, Non-Obscenity, the Absurd, and the Morbid. Classified as obscene were those jokes with any mention whatsoever of sex or scatology. Absurd jokes were almost entirely of the question-and-answer form and included the very silly jokes about elephants, five-hundred-pound canaries, and so forth. Morbid jokes included those about Helen Keller, dead babies, and the like.[4]

Since jokes usually involve several themes and characters at the same time, all jokes were coded for any themes and characters mentioned, rather than for one primary theme. Therefore correlations could be made between the various themes and characters and other variables. For instance, it was possible to learn how many jokes about fools were also obscene jokes, or how many ethnic jokes also involved the theme of death. It was also possible to correlate forms, characters, and themes with the sex of the performer and the sex of the audience.

THE MALE AND FEMALE JOKE-TELLING TRADITIONS

The differences in the male and female joke-telling traditions are similar to and derive from the different roles that men and women have been expected to play in our society. And in turn the joke-telling traditions continue to help in the maintenance of those separate roles. As a rule, our society has expected men to be considerably more aggressive than women. This expectation is reflected in the kinds of jokes men and women tell, in the stereotypes within the jokes, and in the ways in which the jokes are performed. In general, men told more of the openly aggressive kinds of jokes than women told; and usually males indicated that they appreciated these jokes more than women did, for women were more likely than men to be offended by open hostility in jokes. Thus, men told more obscene jokes, more racial, ethnic, and religious jokes, and more jokes about death than women told. On the other hand, the only openly hostile categories of jokes in which women exceeded men were morbid jokes and jokes about authority. Nevertheless, on the whole, men told a considerably higher percentage than women of the openly hostile and aggressive jokes.

Furthermore, a number of students and faculty commented that they thought male jokes were often more openly hostile and aggressive than female jokes. In order to check these opinions more objectively, 60 jokes told by males and 60 jokes told by females were presented to 28 female and 22 male undergraduates and to 5 female and 5 male faculty members, who were then asked to rate each joke on its degree of hostility. They were told only that the jokes had been collected from students; they were not informed of the sex of the informants. Both sexes agreed that the male jokes were more hostile than the female jokes.

The male and female characters in jokes also reflect the fact that aggressiveness is more acceptable for males than it is for females. While there are exceptions, aggressive females in jokes are usually pictured negatively, as in the stereotypes of the nagging wife, the bitch, and the promiscuous and insatiable female. And often these women are punished in some way by a male character in the joke. On the other hand, male aggressiveness in jokes is usually acceptable, except sometimes for extremely aggressive behavior. And a male who is not as aggressive as he should be is often pictured as a fool. Thus the behavior of males and females in their aggressive and passive roles is further reinforced by the joke stereotypes.

The acceptance and expectation of male aggressiveness are further apparent in the performances of jokes. Men often seem to enjoy competitive joke-telling sessions where each man attempts to tell a joke funnier than the last. Women very rarely participate in these competitive joke-telling sessions, even if they are members of the audience. Not only do women refuse to tell jokes in these sessions, but they are much more likely than men to feel uncomfortable during the joking, for they seem to fear that the competitive nature of the event will lead to hurt feelings and hostility. Women are much more comfortable in joke-telling that seems to conciliate opposing views. And finally, male tellers are more likely to use jokes sometimes to deride someone whom they dislike, while women rarely do this; and men are more likely than women to tell jokes that they think might be offensive to some members of the audience. Thus, we see that both the content and the performance of jokes reinforce the social expectation of male aggressiveness.

Operative in conjunction with the social assumption that males should be more aggressive than females is the idea that men should participate in public life while women should participate primarily in the private life of the home. This idea has several consequences for male and female styles of joke-telling. Since men are expected to be active in the public sector, they become accustomed to dealing with large groups, while women who remain primarily in the home tend not to feel as confident as men in participating in large groups. Thus men enjoy telling their jokes to larger audiences than do women, and men are more willing than women to tell jokes to casual acquaintances. Women prefer telling their jokes to very small groups of close friends. Furthermore, men tell many more jokes in public places, such as bars and places of business, than do women, who tell most of their jokes in their homes. Women also indicate that they often prefer telling and listening to humorous anecdotes about personal happenings rather than to jokes (Green 1977). And while men gain prestige for being good joke tellers, women seem to gain more prestige by being good tellers of humorous personal anecdotes.

In general, men's estimates of the number of jokes in their repertoires and of the frequency with which they told jokes were greater than women's estimates of their own repertoire size and joke-telling frequency. However, women averaged more jokes per person than men on one of my questionnaires, on which they wrote down examples of jokes they knew of various kinds; and when jokes were collected in natural settings, the ratio between jokes collected from men and jokes collected from women corresponds almost exactly to the ratio of males to females on campus. Thus, it is difficult to tell whether men really tell more jokes than women or whether, perhaps because they value joke-telling more than women do, men believe they do more of it. And since women value humorous personal anecdotes more than they value jokes, they believe they tell more anecdotes than jokes.

Finally, probably because men must learn to participate in competitive public life, they seem to develop a sense of camaraderie with their fellow men rather than very intimate friendships, for a strong sense of competition seems to be detrimental to intimacy. But women are not encouraged to be competitive because they are expected to participate primarily in the private lives of their families, and therefore they seem to prefer intimate relationships rather than the more distant camaraderie of men. The effect of these attitudes on joke-telling is that men use jokes more aggressively than women do, and in such a way as to keep friendships from becoming too intimate, while women tend to use jokes as a way of sharing pleasure, and they attempt to make even formal jokes seem like intimate communications.

FACTORS INFLUENCING PERFORMANCE, ACQUISITION OF SKILLS, AND REPERTOIRE SIZE

The audiences preferred by men and by women are also different. Table 10.1 shows the sex of the joke teller and the sex of the audiences for 1,078 jokes that were collected in natural settings. Men told the largest number of their jokes to men, and of the remainder about the same number to mixed groups of men and women as to women; women told a large majority of their jokes to women, a smaller number to men, and the smallest number to mixed groups of men and women.

Another difference in audience preference that is relevant to these figures is that male tellers prefer to tell jokes to larger audiences than female tellers do. Most of the jokes collected from males were collected when there was an audience of two or more; quite often there were four or more in the audience. Females, on the other hand, much preferred an audience of one or two, and most of the time no more than three. The preference for a small audience is one of the reasons that women tell so few jokes in mixed groups. The collectors found that women who were asked for jokes were very reticent about telling them in large groups, whether all female, all male, or mixed. Some-

Table 10.1. Percentages and Numbers of Jokes Told in Natural Settings

	Male Audience	Female Audience	Mixed Audience	Totals
Male Teller	38.76% (238)	30.45% (187)	30.78% (189)	614
Female Teller	21.76% (101)	61.63% (286)	16.59% (77)	464

times the informants would agree to tell the jokes they knew in private, but they would flatly refuse to tell jokes in groups of four or more. Men, on the other hand, almost never refused. Furthermore, men were much more likely than women to tell jokes in the presence of casual acquaintances and even strangers.

One of the factors influencing women to tell their jokes in smaller groups seems to be that women place a lower value on joke-telling as a form of social interaction than men do. Frequently if one man tells a joke in a group of men, a series of jokes will follow from the other men who are present. This situation rarely occurs among women. If one joke is told, the women will laugh appreciatively and then continue the conversation. Later another joke may be told, whereupon the audience will respond, and again continue their conversation. Among women the telling of a joke is more likely to stimulate the telling of personal humorous narratives than other jokes, one of the few exceptions being that when one woman tells an elephant joke or another short absurd joke of that kind, four or five more may follow. Jokes in women's groups usually become a part of the general conversation, and a very minor part at that, rather than becoming an end in themselves, as they sometimes do in men's groups.

Because of this lesser value placed on joke-telling in women's groups, women tend to gain little prestige for being good joke tellers. Prestige is much more likely to be given to the woman who can speak amusingly or wittily about herself or others in an informal way rather than using the formal conventions of the joke. Furthermore, while men give prestige to men who display joke-telling skills, they do not often give women prestige for being good joke tellers. Many men feel that joke-telling is inappropriate behavior for a woman, especially if she includes "dirty" jokes in her repertoire. Thus, since the female joke teller gains little prestige from women or from men for her joke-telling ability, women often simply do not learn to tell jokes well, which further contributes to their reluctance to tell jokes in public situations. This does not mean that women do not know or enjoy jokes; they do, but they tell their jokes in very small groups of close friends in the privacy of their homes where they feel secure about their relationships with the members of the audience.

Because males give greater value to joke-telling than do females, they tend to learn to be better performers. They do not necessarily have to have a large repertoire of jokes, but they are expected to be

CAROL MITCHELL

able to tell well whatever jokes they do tell; and in order to participate in this form of social interaction they must know at least a few. Another indication of the greater value that men place on joke-telling as a form of social interaction is the greater number of males who are known as outstanding joke tellers. Most outstanding joke tellers are in fact older men, who have had more time in which to learn and practice their repertoires. But young men do gain reputations among their own acquaintances as being good joke tellers, and there is a certain prestige attached to this ability.

Since men and women differ in their attitudes toward joke-telling as a form of social interaction, sex is also a factor in determining who become active and who become passive bearers of joke lore. As would be expected, men tend to be the more active bearers of joke lore and women the more passive bearers; that is, although both men and women *know* jokes, men are more apt to *tell* them. A survey made of joke-telling habits of 38 males and 37 females supports this conclusion. As can be seen in Table 10.2, the men's estimates of how often they told jokes were considerably higher than women's estimates of their own joke-telling frequency, and the men rated themselves as better joke tellers than the women rated themselves. Women's and men's estimates of the number of jokes known to them are less radically different, although the numbers women mentioned were still lower than the numbers men listed.

Table 10.2. Joke-Telling Habits

How Often Jokes Are Told	Almost Daily	Weekly	Rarely	Special Occasions	Never
Males (N = 38)	5	10	15	7	1
Females (N = 37)	1	2	28	5	1

Skill of Joke Teller (Self-Rated)	Good		Average		Poor
Males	3		22		12
Females	0		19		17

How Many Jokes Known	50–100	20–50	10–20	1–10	None
Males	2	6	9	20	1
Females	1	2	6	27	1

It is interesting to note that the one woman who tells jokes almost daily and estimates her repertoire to include 50 to 100 jokes still sees herself as an average joke teller, while the men who told jokes daily and also had repertoires of 50 to 100 jokes considered themselves good joke tellers. This woman is in fact a good teller of jokes, but like many other women she tends to underrate herself even though she is an active bearer.

That women are bearers of joke lore, even though passive, is borne out by responses to another part of the questionnaire, where the students were asked to write down jokes that they knew. In this part, female students averaged 5.6 jokes per student while male students averaged 4.7 jokes per student. This finding probably does not indicate that women on the average know more jokes than men, since, as psychologists have shown, female students often try harder than male students to please the teacher, especially where there is no grade involved. It does, however, reinforce the evidence that women know jokes that they could tell but that they just do not tell them often; in other words, women are passive bearers and, should the attitudes toward the value of joke-telling as a form of social interaction change, potential active bearers of joke lore.

INCIDENCE OF TENDENTIOUS AND OBSCENE JOKES

While men and women tell many of the same jokes, each sex shows certain preferences in the kinds of jokes it tells. Table 10.3 shows the percentages of men's jokes and women's jokes which fit each category when the jokes are classified by form, and the percentages of jokes dealing with particular themes or characters, so that comparisons between the jokes men told and the jokes women told could be made and so that trends in men's and women's joke choices would become apparent. Thus, although the differences in percentage in any one category may be fairly low, when looking at Table 10.3 as a whole we see a very real difference in the kinds of jokes men and women tell, in the themes, in the characters, and in the forms of the jokes.

Men told more narrative jokes than women told, while women told more of the short question-and-answer jokes. Men told higher percentages of obscene jokes, religious jokes, ethnic and racial jokes,

jokes about death, and jokes about drinking; women told higher percentages of absurd jokes, morbid jokes, Polack jokes, jokes about authority figures, and jokes based on plays on words; men and women told the same percentages of political jokes and jokes about the military; and while men told a higher percentage of obscene jokes in general than women told, in the obscene categories of jokes about premarital sex, marriage, and scatology, men and women told the same percentages.

It has been assumed by Legman and Freud and many of the experimental psychologists that obscene jokes are primarily male humor. This is true to the extent that 5 percent more of men's jokes than women's jokes are obscene. However, women do participate in the telling of obscene jokes, even if to a lesser extent than men. Male scholars simply have not realized the extent of the joke-telling tradition among women, since women do most of their joke-telling privately to other women and not to men.

In general, men tend to tell more openly aggressive and hostile jokes than women do. It is difficult to say exactly why this is so. Since our society encourages males to be more aggressive than females, perhaps men have a greater need to relieve their aggressive and hostile feelings through joking, and perhaps women really do not feel those same tensions. But it may also be that since society does not approve these feelings in women, they are forced to disguise their hostilities and aggressions more than men in the joking they do. Whatever the reason, women tell a lower percentage of openly tendentious jokes than do men.[5]

In the survey mentioned above, women considered the content of most jokes to be more hostile than men did. But while both males and females considered the content of male-told jokes to be more hostile than the content of female-told jokes, nevertheless, females considered the content of their own jokes to be as hostile as males considered the content of their (male-told) jokes to be.[6] There seems to be, then, a certain level of hostility which both males and females display in their jokes, but since women considered all jokes to be more hostile than men did, women actually tell more jokes from the less tendentious categories of jokes. In other words, women, taught that they should not be openly aggressive and hostile, express hostility in a somewhat more disguised form than males do.

Table 10.3. Percentage of Joke Forms and of Themes and Characters in Jokes Told by Males and Females in Natural Settings

	Narrative	Question-Answer	Other Forms	Word Play	Obscene	Non-obscene	Absurd
Male Teller (614)	57.9%	31.0%	11.1%	17.9%	45.2%	54.8%	5.6%
Female Teller (464)	44.3%	48.1%	7.6%	18.8%	40.2%	59.8%	5.8%

	Morbid	Death	Drinking	Sports	Filth	Male Approach	Sadism
Male Teller (614)	4.4%	12.1%	6.1%	2.6%	6.9%	5.6%	5.7%
Female Teller (464)	7.7%	8.8%	2.2%	4.6%	11.7%	4.9%	4.6%

	Premarital Sex	Marriage	Adultery	Homosexuality	Prostitution	Disease
Male Teller (614)	3.6%	7.4%	4.4%	4.6%	5.6%	0.8%
Female Teller (464)	3.8%	7.5%	3.5%	2.2%	3.3%	0.4%

SEX OF THE AUDIENCE AS A DETERMINANT OF JOKE CHOICE

While men, like women, tell most of their jokes to audiences of the same sex, men are much more likely than women to tell jokes to members of the opposite sex and to mixed audiences. Table 10.4 shows the differences in percentages of jokes utilizing various subjects, characters, and forms when jokes are told to audiences of the same sex, to audiences of the opposite sex, and to mixed audiences. For example, in the first category of jokes, Nonobscene, 52.53 percent of the jokes that males tell male audiences are nonobscene, while 73.27 percent of the jokes females tell male audiences are nonobscene. And 52.41 percent of the jokes that males tell female audiences are nonobscene, while 53.5 percent of the jokes females tell

Table 10.3. Percentage of Joke Forms and of Themes and Characters in Jokes Told by Males and Females in Natural Settings (Continued)

	Castra-tion	Euphe-mism	Scatol-ogy	Children	Fools	Animals	Women
Male Teller (614)	5.6%	5.1%	6.2%	6.1%	21.3%	9.2%	6.4%
Female Teller (464)	4.6%	3.5%	6.2%	4.9%	24.7%	3.8%	10.6%

	Religious Figures	Political Figures	Polacks	Negroes	Ethnics
Male Teller (614)	11.3%	3.4%	14.8%	9.3%	16.9%
Female Teller (464)	9.1%	3.1%	26.9%	4.0%	11.5%

	Authority Figures	Deformed Characters	Military Personnel	Female Professional	Male Professional
Male Teller (614)	5.9%	3.0%	2.1%	4.6%	13.1%
Female Teller (464)	7.1%	6.0%	2.2%	3.1%	11.3%

Note: Percentages are of the total number of jokes collected from males, 614, and of the total number of jokes collected from females, 464.

female audiences are nonobscene. Finally, 60.85 percent of the jokes males tell mixed-sex audiences are nonobscene, while 71.43 percent of the jokes females tell mixed-sex audiences are nonobscene. The fifth column shown for each category of jokes shows the level of statistical significance as determined by chi-square tests. The majority of these categories show very high levels of significance, which indicates that sex is indeed a factor in determining who tells obscene jokes to whom.

Male to Male

The kinds of jokes that men are most likely to tell men are those jokes that they consider to be most openly hostile and aggressive. Thus, the

Table 10.4. Percentages and Numbers of Various Categories of Jokes Told by Males and Females to All-Male Audiences, All-Female Audiences, and Mixed-Sex Audiences.

	Male Audience	Female Audience	Mixed Audience	Signifi-cance*
NONOBSCENE				
Male	52.53%	52.41%	60.85%	
Teller	(125)	(98)	(115)	.0000
Female	73.27%	53.5%	71.43%	
Teller	(74)	(153)	(55)	
OBSCENE				
Male	47.47%	47.49%	39.15%	
Teller	(113)	(89)	(74)	.0000
Female	26.73%	46.5%	28.57%	
Teller	(27)	(133)	(22)	
ABSURD				
Male	2.94%	4.81%	9.52%	
Teller	(7)	(9)	(18)	.0254
Female	0.99%	5.24%	12.98%	
Teller	(1)	(15)	(10)	
MORBID				
Male	5.46%	2.67%	4.76%	
Teller	(13)	(5)	(9)	.0000
Female	4.92%	9.79%	2.59%	
Teller	(5)	(28)	·(2)	
DEATH				
Male	12.18%	11.22%	12.69%	
Teller	(29)	(21)	(24)	.0245
Female	12.87%	7.34%	7.79%	
Teller	(13)	(21)	(6)	
DRINKING				
Male	11.76%	2.13%	2.64%	
Teller	(28)	(4)	(5)	.0000
Female		3.49%		
Teller	(0)	(10)	(0)	
SPORTS				
Male	2.94%	1.6%	3.17%	
Teller	(7)	(3)	(6)	.2484
Female	4.95%	3.14%	9.09%	
Teller	(5)	(9)	(7)	
FILTH				
Male	5.88%	7.48%	7.4%	
Teller	(14)	(14)	(14)	.3569
Female	22.77%	6.64%	14.28%	
Teller	(23)	(19)	(11)	
MALE APPROACH				
Male	6.3%	5.88%	4.23%	
Teller	(15)	(11)	(8)	.0033
Female	1.98%	5.94%	3.89%	
Teller	(2)	(17)	(3)	

*Level of significance as determined by chi-square.

Table 10.4. Percentages and Numbers of Various Categories of Jokes.
(Continued)

	Male Audience	Female Audience	Mixed Audience	Signifi-cance*
SADISM				
Male	6.3%	4.27%	6.34%	
Teller	(15)	(8)	(12)	.0136
Female	3.96%	4.54%	5.19%	
Teller	(4)	(13)	(4)	
PREMARITAL SEX				
Male	4.2%	2.13%	4.23%	
Teller	(10)	(4)	(8)	.0003
Female	0.99%	4.89%	2.59%	
Teller	(1)	(14)	(2)	
MARRIAGE				
Male	7.98%	6.41%	4.76%	
Teller	(19)	(12)	(9)	.0031
Female	5.94%	8.04%	5.19%	
Teller	(6)	(23)	(4)	
ADULTERY				
Male	2.1%	8.02%	3.7%	
Teller	(5)	(15)	(7)	.4288
Female	1.98%	4.19%	2.59%	
Teller	(2)	(12)	(2)	
HOMOSEXUALITY				
Male	5.04%	5.34%	3.17%	
Teller	(12)	(10)	(6)	.0442
Female	1.98%	2.79%		
Teller	(2)	(8)	(0)	
PROSTITUTION				
Male	7.14%	4.81%	4.23%	
Teller	(17)	(9)	(8)	.0086
Female	2.97%	3.84%	1.29%	
Teller	(3)	(11)	(1)	
DISEASE				
Male	2.1%			
Teller	(5)	(0)	(0)	.0302
Female		0.34%	1.29%	
Teller	(0)	(1)	(1)	
CASTRATION				
Male	6.3%	5.34%	4.76%	
Teller	(15)	(10)	(9)	.0028
Female	3.96%	5.59%	1.29%	
Teller	(4)	(16)	(1)	
EUPHEMISM				
Male	5.46%	5.34%	4.23%	
Teller	(13)	(10)	(8)	.0476
Female	3.96%	3.84%	1.2%	
Teller	(4)	(11)	(1)	

Table 10.4. Percentages and Numbers of Various Categories of Jokes.
(Continued)

	Male Audience	Female Audience	Mixed Audience	Signifi-cance*
SCATOLOGY				
Male	5.88%	6.95%	5.82%	
Teller	(14)	(13)	(11)	.0016
Female	3.96%	7.69%	2.59%	
Teller	(4)	(22)	(2)	
CHILDREN				
Male	5.46%	6.95%	5.82%	
Teller	(13)	(13)	(11)	.0002
Female	0.99%	6.99%	1.29%	
Teller	(1)	(20)	(1)	
FOOLS				
Male	24.36%	23.5%	15.87%	
Teller	(58)	(44)	(30)	.0002
Female	30.69%	23.42%	18.18%	
Teller	(31)	(67)	(14)	
ANIMALS				
Male	11.76%	9.09%	5.82%	
Teller	(28)	(17)	(11)	.0112
Female	3.97%	4.19%	2.59%	
Teller	(3)	(12)	(2)	
WOMEN				
Male	7.98%	5.34%	5.29%	
Teller	(19)	(10)	(10)	.0051
Female	11.88%	10.13%	9.09%	
Teller	(12)	(29)	(7)	
RELIGIOUS				
Male	10.92%	11.76%	11.11%	
Teller	(26)	(22)	(21)	.0055
Female	7.92%	9.09%	9.09%	
Teller	(8)	(26)	(7)	
POLITICAL				
Male	3.36%	4.27%	2.64%	
Teller	(8)	(8)	(5)	.3605
Female	4.95%	2.79%	1.29%	
Teller	(5)	(8)	(1)	
POLACK				
Male	11.76%	20.85%	12.16%	
Teller	(28)	(39)	(23)	.0185
Female	52.47%	19.23%	18.18%	
Teller	(53)	(55)	(14)	
NEGRO				
Male	11.34%	7.48%	8.46%	
Teller	(27)	(14)	(16)	.0000
Female	2.97%	5.24%		
Teller	(3)	(15)	(0)	

Table 10.4. Percentages and Numbers of Various Categories of Jokes.
(Continued)

	Male Audience	Female Audience	Mixed Audience	Signifi-cance*
ETHNIC				
Male	11.76%	14.97%	15.87%	
Teller	(34)	(35)	(34)	.0001
Female	1.98%	11.87%	20.77%	
Teller	(2)	(34)	(16)	
AUTHORITY				
Male	7.14%	5.34%	4.76%	
Teller	(17)	(10)	(9)	.0000
Female	4.95%	9.09%	1.29%	
Teller	(5)	(26)	(1)	
DEFORMED				
Male	3.78%	2.67%	2.11%	
Teller	(9)	(5)	(4)	.0009
Female	1.98%	7.69%	3.89%	
Teller	(2)	(22)	(3)	
MILITARY				
Male	2.1%	3.2%	1.05%	
Teller	(5)	(6)	(2)	.9409
Female	3.96%	1.39%	2.59%	
Teller	(4)	(4)	(2)	
FEMALE PROFESSIONAL				
Male	3.78%	6.41%	3.7%	
Teller	(9)	(12)	(7)	.1396
Female	2.97%	5.59%	5.19%	
Teller	(3)	(16)	(4)	
MALE PROFESSIONAL				
Male	16.8%	12.83%	8.46%	
Teller	(40)	(24)	(16)	.0000
Female	4.95%	13.28%	10.38%	
Teller	(5)	(38)	(8)	
NARRATIVE				
Male	68.4%	55.3%	50.0%	
Teller	(163)	(103)	(64)	.0000
Female	35.4%	52.2%	45.2%	
Teller	(36)	(149)	(35)	
QUESTION-ANSWER				
Male	21.5%	32.9%	38.7%	
Teller	(51)	(62)	(73)	.0000
Female	50.0%	39.6%	54.7%	
Teller	(51)	(113)	(42)	
OTHER FORMS				
Male	10.1%	11.8%	11.3%	
Teller	(24)	(22)	(21)	.001
Female	14.6%	8.2%	0.1%	
Teller	(15)	(23)	(1)	

Table 10.4. Percentages and Numbers of Various Categories of Jokes.
(Continued)

	Male Audience	Female Audience	Mixed Audience	Signifi-cance*
WORDPLAY				
Male	13.86%	18.18%	22.22%	
Teller	(33)	(34)	(42)	.0000
Female	14.85%	20.27%	15.58%	
Teller	(15)	(58)	(12)	

largest numbers of obscene jokes, morbid jokes, Negro jokes, jokes about drinking, jokes about deformity, and jokes about authority figures are told by males to all-male audiences. In each of these cases, the percentages of the jokes are higher when told by males to males than the percentages of the same kinds of jokes in the general male collection. Thus, while Negro jokes made up 9.3 percent of all the jokes collected from men, Negro jokes made up 11.34 percent of the jokes males told to males.

The fact that men tell their most openly hostile and aggressive jokes to other men does not necessarily mean that they are showing hostility toward each other, but may rather mean that their hostilities can be most openly relieved in joke-telling with other males, who also share the tension released by these hostile jokes. Eastman (1936:252) comments that some of these jokes act as a "frank release from the demands of aggression as a cultural ideal." So while the jokes may express aggression and hostility openly, they may also be a way of laughing at the aggressive ideals of bravery and courage, sexual aggressiveness and prowess, drinking capability, and so on.[7] And since these aggressive ideals are primarily for men and not women, men can laugh together about the ideals that sometimes seem oppressive to them.

Male to Female

While men tell women slightly higher percentages of jokes about adultery, children, scatology, and female professionals than they tell to other audiences, the only category of jokes that is unmistakably more popular for telling to women is Polack jokes, probably because female audiences seem to enjoy Polack jokes more than male audiences do, and successful joke tellers soon learn what jokes get the best responses from different kinds of audiences. Also, the fact that women tell men more Polack jokes than any other kind demonstrates that women like these jokes. Furthermore, Polack jokes are considered appropriate for telling to women because the level of hostility they express is relatively low or well disguised.

While the *number* of obscene jokes men told to men was higher than the number of obscene jokes they told to women, the *percentage* of obscene jokes they told to women was almost exactly the same as the percentage of obscene jokes they told to men. Undoubtedly Freud is right, at least sometimes, in considering these jokes to be a form of sexual aggression to women (1963:97–98). Since men are taught that they should take the lead in sexual matters, they are put in the position of being openly rejected. Women are sexually rejected too, mainly in not being approached by males, but the male must openly make his sexual approach to a woman and risk her rejection. Thus, to protect his ego a male may begin his approach by various subtle means, which can be denied if the female seems uninterested. Since men and women sometimes tell each other sexual jokes today when they are not making sexual advances, a man can act as if his joke was not intended as a sexual approach (even if it was) if the woman who is being approached seems uninterested.

Moreover, it may be that Freud is correct in maintaining that telling sexual jokes is always a kind of sexual aggression, either imagined when jokes are told in all-male groups or real when they are told by one sex to the other. But there is a wide range in the kind of sexual aggression involved. Males and females both can use sexual jokes to insult and embarrass members of the opposite sex, they can use sexual jokes as a part of their sexual approach, or they can use sexual jokes merely as a friendly, light way of flirting with members of the opposite sex. When sexual jokes are used for friendly flirting, they usually do not indicate that the teller is really making a sexual approach to the other person; rather, the jokes are a way of saying "I think you're sexually attractive" or "I enjoy your company." In a way, this kind of joking is a sexual teasing that can be enjoyed by both sexes without necessarily leading to any sexual involvement. As with all kinds of teasing, however, there is involved an element of risk which can add to the pleasure of the situation but which may also hurt someone's feelings and lead to a hostile rather than friendly situation.

Nevertheless, despite the risks involved, sexual joking is very popular, since 37 percent of the jokes collected were sexual jokes.

It should be mentioned too that sexual jokes are also a release from society's stereotyped view of masculine sexuality. After his discussion of jokes as a release from socially expected aggressiveness, Eastman (1936:253) says, "Not only aggression, but sexuality also, is a cultural ideal. Its demands are vigorous and many people find it hard to meet them." Thus people can use sexual jokes also as a short vacation from the socially expected sexuality and lightly ridicule this cultural ideal. It is probably at least partially because society expects males to be more interested in sex than females are, that males tell more obscene jokes than females do, in order to release the tensions built up by their expected role as sexual aggressors.

Male to Mixed Groups

The *numbers* of jokes that are less openly hostile, like religious jokes, ethnic jokes, question-and-answer jokes, and jokes based on some kind of wordplay, are distributed fairly evenly to male audiences, female audiences, and mixed groups, although the *percentages* of these jokes that are told to the various audiences are not the same. Thus in the case of ethnic jokes, 34 were told to male audiences, 35 to female audiences, and 34 to mixed audiences; but only 11.76 percent of the jokes males told to males were ethnic jokes, while 14.97 percent of the jokes males told to females were ethnic jokes, and 15.87 percent of the jokes males told to mixed audiences were ethnic jokes. It may seem surprising to find ethnic jokes among the less-hostile jokes, but the ethnic jokes in this collection were relatively mild in their expression of hostilities, especially when compared with Negro jokes.

In general, males tell their least openly hostile and aggressive jokes to mixed audiences. Thus, they tell lower percentages of jokes about sex, authority, and deformity to mixed groups than to either men or women. And they tell higher percentages of absurd jokes and jokes based on wordplay to mixed audiences. One factor that enters into this difference in joke choice is that mixed-sex audiences are often larger than single-sex audiences, and jokes in which the content is hostile can be told in smaller, more intimate groups with less chance of offending anyone than in a larger group. In an intimate situation the audience is more likely to focus on the joke teller's intentions for telling a joke, while in a larger group the audience is more likely to focus on the content of the joke itself.

Female to Female

Like males, females tend to tell the majority of their most openly hostile jokes to same sex audiences. Thus, the percentages of the obscene jokes, scatological jokes, Negro jokes, morbid jokes, jokes about deformity, and jokes about authority figures are higher in all-female situations. Since women are not supposed to be openly aggressive, they feel more comfortable releasing these tensions in groups of other women who also feel the same restraints about showing hostility in joke-telling or in society at large. Telling jokes is also a way for women to protest against society's repression of female feelings of hostility, and thus can be done most safely with other women, without men knowing about it. Women who have told the more openly hostile jokes in mixed groups have usually felt social disapproval for this action. Often it is considered to be acceptable for a woman to tell an openly hostile joke to one or perhaps two males in a private situation, but not appropriate in a large group of all males or of both sexes, even though it might be thought appropriate for a male to tell the same joke in a mixed group. But women simply do not tell as many openly hostile and aggressive jokes as men do.

Also, women tell some of their most nonsensical and least hostile jokes to each other. While women tell only a slightly higher percentage of jokes that turn on a play on words than men do, women seem particularly to enjoy this form of joke, and they tell a higher percentage of jokes based on wordplay to other women than to males or to mixed groups. The play on words seems to be a particularly good disguise for whatever hostilities may be expressed in a joke, for tellers and audiences alike can focus on the wordplay rather than on the content of the joke. One should note here that males tell the lowest percentage of jokes based on wordplay to male audiences (13.86 percent), a considerably higher percentage to female audiences (18.18 percent), and an even higher percentage to mixed groups (22.22 percent). Thus in situations in which hostilities cannot be shown openly and in which disguise is needed, jokes involving a play on words are used.

Female to Male

Females, unlike males, tell their lowest percentage of obscene jokes to members of the opposite sex. It is interesting that when females tell jokes to males, Polack jokes seem to be the counterpart to the obscene jokes that males tell to females. In fact, 52.47 percent of the jokes women told to men were Polack jokes, and 47.59 percent of the jokes men told to women were obscene jokes. I do not mean to suggest that telling Polack jokes is a way of making sexual advances to men; rather, it is the female way of being aggressive with males in a joking situation, just as sexual jokes are used as a form of aggression when told by males to females. As Legman (1968, 1975) points out time and again, sexual jokes often thinly disguise male fear of and hostility toward women. Comparably, Polack jokes are almost always mildly hostile toward men. Even though the word "Polack," like the word "mankind," should be understood to include both sexes, it usually is not. Polack jokes are understood to be about males unless they specify females, as in jokes about the Polish bride. Thus, females can mildly ridicule males by telling jokes about the foolish Polack, and their hostility and aggression are sufficiently disguised to satisfy both themselves and the males. Polack jokes further disguise the hostility expressed toward males as hostility toward lower economic groups or toward ethnic groups.

Males do not appear to take offense at hearing Polack jokes from women, for as was mentioned previously, men tell a considerably higher percentage of Polack jokes to women than to any other audience. As with most jokes, women consider Polack jokes to be more aggressive and hostile than men do, so that in telling their Polack jokes to men, women feel they are being more aggressive than men perceive them as being. Women also tell higher percentages of jokes about filth and fools, question-and-answer jokes, and other forms of jokes not including narratives, to men than to other audiences. Women also tell a higher percentage of jokes involving death to males than to any other audience, which may further indicate that females use jokes as aggressive conduct toward males.

Female to Mixed Group

Again like males, females told mixed groups primarily those jokes that are only very mildly hostile. Thus they told more absurd jokes, ethnic jokes, and jokes about sports to audiences composed of both sexes. Women told no Negro jokes, only two morbid jokes, and one joke about authority to mixed groups. However, because women tell such a small percentage (16.59 percent) of their jokes in mixed groups, the numbers of any particular kind of joke are quite small. To the extent that joke-telling is a kind of sharing to be done with friends, women tend to do it in very small groups, which often excludes the larger mixed groups in which men perform.

CONCLUSIONS

While the joke-telling traditions of men and women are closely intertwined, there are many subtle ways in which they differ. This investigation showed that there are differences in the kinds of jokes told and in the kinds of audiences and situations chosen by each sex. And as I have discussed more fully elsewhere, there are differences in the ways in which men and women learn to become joke tellers and in the ways in which they tell their jokes (Mitchell 1976:1:98–139), as well as differences in interpretation and appreciation of jokes (Mitchell 1977). Many, if not most, of these differences occur because of our society's views of what is masculine and what is feminine, and joke-telling is one of the institutional structures that have evolved to reinforce the appropriate kinds of behavior in males and females. As a consequence, women's and men's attitudes toward joke-telling correlate with the different roles that women and men have been expected to play in this society.

First, the content of the jokes women told (in this study) was less openly hostile and aggressive than the content of the jokes men told, and, second, the ways in which women used their jokes (one aspect of context) were less openly hostile or aggressive than the ways in which men used their jokes. Third, women preferred to tell their jokes to audiences of the same sex, while men were more willing to tell their jokes to opposite-sex audiences and audiences of both sexes. And finally, both sexes are influenced in their choice of jokes by the sex makeup of the audience for whom they are performing.

NOTES

1. Some question-and-answer jokes, like riddles, give information in the question that supposedly will help the listener figure out the answer, as in "What's gray and comes in a red and white can? Campbell's cream of elephant soup." But the information given will not really help answer the question, and therefore it is a joke

on the audience. But most question-and-answer jokes simply ask a question and then give an absurd answer: "Why was the elephant standing on a marshmallow? So he wouldn't fall into the hot chocolate."

2. For the complete coding system used, see Mitchell (1976:1:9–15).

3. Violence would have been an interesting theme to include in order to learn what kinds of violence are most often pictured in jokes, to learn by whom and to whom the violence is committed, and to learn by whom and to whom jokes involving various kinds of violence are told. Unfortunately, I did not think of using this theme until after almost all the jokes had been coded.

4. For further discussion of exactly what kinds of jokes were considered obscene, absurd, etc., see Mitchell (1976:1:33–72).

5. It is difficult to specify the exact degree of tendentiousness or hostility for whole categories of jokes, but the following table is an attempt based on student and faculty ratings of jokes. The table shows the hostility classifications of various categories of jokes and indicates which sex tells more jokes in each category. In some instances the jokes in a particular category may range over more than one level of hostility. Thus, a single category may be rated as both tendentious and mildly tendentious, or as mildly tendentious and not tendentious.

	Tendentious (Most Hostile)	Medium Tendentious (Medium Hostile)	Not Tendentious (Least Hostile)
Males Tell Higher Percentages of These Jokes	Obscene	Obscene Religious Ethnic	
	Racial (Black) Death	Death Drinking	
Females Tell Higher Percentages of These Jokes	Deformity Morbid	Deformity	
		Polack Authority Sports Filth Riddle Wordplay	Sports Filth Riddle Wordplay Absurd

6. These conclusions were arrived at by taking a survey in which 28 female and 22 male undergraduates and 5 female and 5 male faculty members were asked to rate the hostility of the content of 60 jokes told by males and 60 jokes told by females. Half of each set of jokes were told in drinking situations, and half were told in nondrinking situations. The evaluators were not told anything about the jokes except that they had been collected from college students.

In this survey students and faculty were also asked to rate each joke according to how funny it was. Even though women are often accused of having a poor sense of humor and of telling lousy jokes, the majority of both males and females rated the jokes told by women as funnier. As with other women's communications, women's jokes are more highly valued when the evaluators do not know the jokes come from women.

7. See the discussion of the joke about a Texan who must drink a quart of whiskey, rape an Eskimo girl, and kill a polar bear, in Mitchell (1976:1:15–53).

· 11 ·

SEX ROLE REVERSALS, SEX CHANGES, AND TRANSVESTITE DISGUISE IN THE ORAL TRADITION OF A CONSERVATIVE MUSLIM COMMUNITY IN AFGHANISTAN

Margaret Mills

W HILE ORAL narrative traditions generally include both male main characters and female main characters, their distribution within the tradition may not be symmetrical. Analysis of my collection of contemporary oral narratives from Afghanistan in Dari Persian language suggests that men tend to tell stories about men, whereas women tell stories about women and men. In a sample of 450 fictional prose narratives (folktales and romances), 86 percent (249) of those told by men have male main characters. An additional 3 percent have two main characters, one of each sex. Only 11 percent (31) of men's

This discussion is based on fieldwork conducted in and around Herat and Kabul, Afghanistan, from 1974 to 1976, which yielded a collection of over five hundred recorded narrative performances, plus interviews and nonnarrative performances. I am grateful for financial support from the American Association of University Women Educational Foundation, the Fulbright-Hays Dissertation Grants program, the National Science Foundation, and Harvard University's Sheldon Fund. Parts of this chapter were presented at the Conference on Women and Folklore, University of Pennsylvania, Philadelphia, in March 1979, and at the 1979 annual meeting of the American Folklore Society. A full text and longer discussion of the *Āsh-e Bībī Murād* ceremony appears in Alan Dundes ed., *A Cinderella Casebook*, 1983, pp. 180–192.

stories concern female main characters exclusively, and one-third of that small group cast the women in male roles. By contrast, tales told by women are almost evenly divided between those with male main characters and those with female main characters, 48 percent (77) and 49 percent (79) respectively. Some 3 percent have dual main characters, one of each sex. (See Table 11.1 below.)

Similar patterns of sexual distribution of main characters have been observed even in the absence of an established oral tradition. Brian Sutton-Smith et al. (Sutton-Smith 1978) elicited stories from middle-class public school children in New York City, and among other differences in content, length, frequency, and so forth between girls' stories and boys' stories, found that girls used male figures more often than boys used female figures. Jack Santino (1979), discussing "Women Heroes and the Heroes of Women," speculated that women choose male heroes in part "because men have more options, and women want these options." The converse of this argument is that men do not narrate about women either because women do not have "options" or because men do not want women's options. The whole question of distribution of options by sex, however, is more complex than Santino's hypothesis would suggest, at least in the Afghan case.[1]

The range of options for action by men and women, as projected in this collection of Afghan tales, varies somewhat in representations by male and female narrators, and this asymmetry of options is underscored when characters adopt the dress, behavior, or social position of a member of the opposite sex. Not only the distribution of male and female characters between male and female narrators, but also the ways their respective main characters behave, reveal that male narrators are more consistently interested in sex role switching of various kinds than are women. One may or may not accept the hypothesis that sexual envy induces women to narrate about men, but it seems to me that the distribution of main characters' sex between male and female narrators in my sample indicates not a preoccupation of women with male social options but an avoidance by men of female narrative subjects. This interpretation also helps to explain men's tendency to cast women in masculine roles when they do tell stories about them, a tendency which is not at all pronounced among women narrators. If women envied men's social options, one would expect women narrators to masculinize women characters at least to the extent that men do.

The sample from which this discussion develops originated in a highly conservative society with distinct male and female social spheres. It may be argued that many women in such a society are conservative and unreceptive to variations in normal sex role distribution because a sort of "hostage mentality" makes them their own conceptual jailors. There is a second interpretation, however, which paradoxically inverts envy hypotheses: it may be that Afghan women simply *see* options for action (which Afghan men do not see) in the traditional female roles. To Afghan men, and perhaps to men of other cultures, it may be that in order to have "options" one must be or act like a male; for Afghan women, the choice of meaningful dramas is wider within the feminine sphere, with the result that they give equal time to male and female dramas and fantasize less about female annexation of male roles. (The discrepancy between men's and women's projections of male characters into female roles is less pronounced, but men also fantasize more about that possibility. See Table 11.1 below.)

Kay Stone observed in studies of European traditions in the New World that male narrators cast female heroes in masculine roles more often than women did (Personal communication 1976). Continued exploration of this topic in postindustrial societies where the sexual distribution of labor is in flux would provide a helpful comparison to the picture presented by oral tradition in a sexually conservative society like Afghanistan, where real-world sex role revisions have been minimal.

In the present discussion, sexual role switching is defined broadly to include transsexual disguise as well as undisguised performance of activities normally belonging to the other sex (e.g., spinning or cotton-carding by men, armed combat or acting as vizier or king by women). It includes both voluntary and involuntary role switching, including males threatened with rape, and a very few cases of actual sex change or acquisition of physical characteristics of the other sex. In the discussion devoted to texts, two cases of sex change / sexual marking are compared, one from a male narrator in a male-dominated performance context, the other from a woman in an all-female context. In both tales the consequences of involuntary sexual crossover are traumatic.

Disguise is a frequent adjunct to temporary sex role switching, more so for male characters than for females. In the sample under discussion, men assuming female roles disguise in nineteen out of twenty-four cases, while women taking male roles disguise in thirty-one out of fifty cases. Men threatened with homosexual rape are counted as instances of crossover, whether in female disguise or not. Role switching is more often involuntary for male characters. Temporary role switching by women is almost always voluntary, though often occasioned by desertion or banishment. Likewise, disguise as an animal or object is a voluntary and successful strategy for female characters in general, but it is more often forced on male characters (often by women they are trying to seduce) and results in sexual or other abuse or humiliation for males.

A full comparison of the dynamics of disguise as used by male and female narrators should address questions of status change (do characters of each sex disguise more frequently as higher or lower status than they are?), of voluntary versus involuntary disguise, and of disguise as animals and objects as well as humans. My preliminary observations suggest that all these features are distributed asymmetrically among male and female characters, as is their use by male and female storytellers. The most common form of disguise in this sample is that of a male disguising as a lower-status male (67 out of 232 cases). Males are portrayed in all types of disguise more often than females (158 cases, against 74 females), and male narrators' tales more often contain disguise themes than women's tales do (43 percent of the male-narrated tales contain disguise themes, versus 30 percent of the female-narrated tales). In this or other samples in which men's and women's tales are not equally represented, it is potentially deceptive to develop whole-sample figures for sexually linked behavior because of the underrepresentation of female characters in men's stories, described above. Any quantitative analysis of sexual themes must take into account the sex of the narrators. Also, the figures presented here are provisional since they are derived from synopses of texts in my field notes, not from full transcriptions of tales in all cases.

A full treatment of disguise cannot be undertaken here, but because of the frequent use of disguise in sex role manipulation and the continuing importance of veiling and seclusion (purdah) in Afghan society, I have suggested certain directions which that study might take. The issue of identity and anonymity is central to Afghans' social lives and enters into the dynamics of disguise, recognition, and sex role manipulation in Afghan folktales.

THE SOCIAL SETTING: SEXUAL SEGREGATION AND RESTRICTION OF MOBILITY

The seclusion of women is still the rule in modern Afghanistan. Girls are free to move from the private to the public areas of the house until about age eight, seen by nonkin male visitors and, like boys of all ages, acting as go-betweens for the women's quarters and the guest room where nonkin male guests are entertained. After about age eight, girls become more circumspect, avoiding adult male nonkin. Many girls are married between the ages of ten and twelve, although it is considered bad to consummate a marriage before menarche, around the ages of twelve to fourteen.[2] In Herat, in the west, some unmarried girls wear the semicircular, Iranian-style *chādor* veil in public, donning the baglike *chādrī* only when they marry. In other families, girls begin to wear the *chādrī* in public before they are married. Veiling is mainly an urban practice. In villages women generally keep to their houses and those of nearby kin. Women did not work in the fields in the Herat area in the 1970s, despite acute seasonal labor shortages caused by male labor migration to Iran.[3] Women's freedom of movement outside the house varies by family. In the city, some women visit the public baths, while others bathe only at home. A minority shop in the bazaar, but most shopping is done by men. Village women seldom come to the city except for medical care or to visit relatives. Within the neighborhood in both city and village, visiting is generally limited to kin. When two unrelated families share a compound, as sometimes occurred in Herat City, fictive sibling relationships may be invoked so that each family's women need not avoid the menfolk of the other family or go veiled about their household work, or the families may ally themselves by marriage. Compounds may also be subdivided by adding a mud wall to screen off each family's living area.

Children act as go-betweens in the neighborhood, sent from house to house to borrow bits of food, clothing, or equipment and gather news about other families' doings. Gossip is important for social control even when women do not meet face-to-face. One of my women friends complained of the racket and confusion caused by neighbor children in her compound, and I asked why she did not just shut her gate. She replied that that would cause talk about what she was doing, especially with foreign visitors. If children were free to come and go, the neighbors could see that she had nothing to hide. This paradoxical relationship between the seclusion of women and the actual lack of privacy in the community underscores the power inherent in success-fully concealed identity. Concealed identity, whether in male or fe-male guise, implies freedom of movement and freedom from very pervasive community control. Relative to men, women have greater everyday resources for concealing identity, through the veil.

Veiling is ambiguous in its very prescription under Islam (The Koran 2:59). The Koran directs the women of the Prophet Mo-hammed's family and other believers to cover their persons, not to conceal their identity but "so that they may be recognized and not annoyed." Modesty of dress as prescribed in the Koran identifies Muslim women and claims for them ethical status and freedom from annoyance as they go about legitimate business outside the home. Veiling, as it developed (in part from pre-Islamic practices), became an institution with some latitude for illegitimate activities. Even in the *chādrī*, the full veil, a woman is recognizable to her kin by the color of the veil and her footwear. But women can borrow a *chādrī* from one friend and shoes from another and go forth unrecognized by their families. Such disguise is only one of several real-world "options" unavailable to men. Although circumspection between the sexes is reciprocal (men are enjoined from looking at strange women or enter-ing strange houses without permission, or from disrobing before any-one but wives and servants, and then with restrictions), the fictive anonymity of women in public, not shared by men, gives them a potential tool for antisocial mobility which men do not have. The veil also has been used for political resistance, both in anti-French Alge-ria, where women smuggled arms and information, and in today's Afghanistan, where similar activities are reported. That many women see the veil as a source of power and immunity, not of oppression, is revealed in memorates about government attempts to abolish it. All this needs to be taken into account to understand women's conserva-tism concerning sex role manipulations.

Certain social roles offer some of the same ambiguity as veiling does. In general, women need not veil before any male who is not a potential marriage partner, either because of incest taboos (fathers, brothers, uncles, nephews, some male in-laws) or because of client relations (servants and the sons of servants). Certain categories are equivocal: girls in Afghanistan often do not veil before their male first cousins, though cousins are acceptable, even preferred, marriage partners. The Koran forbids believing women to marry non-Muslims but states that marriage to believing slaves is lawful if free believers are not available (2:220). The status of male servant thus mediates between kin and nonkin with regard to both veiling and marriage; hence its prominence in male-male disguise themes. Servants' guise is the commonest form of male disguise, and its usual purpose is to gain access to women.

This brief description of aspects of Muslim and Afghan social practice is intended to provide a background against which to view deviance from gender-specific behavior in folktale. Since veiling and seclusion are among the most prominent and fiercely defended forms of expressive behavior which articulate sexual-social identity, they must be kept in mind to understand men's and women's manipulations of male and female "options" in folktale.

STATISTICAL DISTRIBUTION OF SEX-ROLE
SWITCHING IN FOLKTALE

Table 11.1 indicates the asymmetrical distribution of sex role inversions in male-narrated and female-narrated tales. In the sample of 450 tales (289 told by men, 161 by women), men's tales show substantially more sex role manipulation of all types than do women's (21 percent of tales, versus 8.7 percent). Sex role inversions are most frequent in tales with female main characters told by men (35 percent of 31 tales), and tales with dual main characters, one male, one female, told by men (5 out of 9, or 56 percent). This concentration of sex role manipulation is more striking because men's tales about women are only 11 percent of the male-narrated sample. When men talk about women, women quite often are incorporated into the masculine social sphere.

Where role-switching occurs, men's and women's tales share a preference for women acting in male roles rather than for men acting in female roles, a fact which may support Santino's contention that

Table 11.1. Sexual Role-Switching in 450 Oral Prose Narrative Texts, by Sex of Narrator and Sex of Main Character

Sex of Narrator	Sex of Main Character	Number of Tales	Type of Role-Switching	Number of Tales	% of Sample
♂	♂	249	♀ → ♂	26	10.4
			♂ → ♀	15	6.0
	♀	31	♀ → ♂	11	35.0
			♂ → ♀	4	12.9
	Both (two main characters)	9	♀ → ♂	5	56.0
	Total	289	♀ → ♂	42	14.5
			♂ → ♀	19	6.6
			Total	61	21.0
♀	♂	77	♀ → ♂	1	1.3
			♂ → ♀	4	5.2
	♀	79	♀ → ♂	7	8.9
			♂ → ♀	1	1.2
	Both (two main characters)	5	♀ → ♂	1	20.0
	Total	161	♀ → ♂	9	5.5
			♂ → ♀	5	3.1
			Total	14	8.7

women covet male "options" and that men have more options. In the Koran and in social practice, men's legal dominance in the family is clearly established, so it is understandable that female activism should follow a male model. Yet from another point of view, it is the *women* who have the options, at least in fantasy, of annexing male social roles and, when convenient, reverting to the protected female role, whereas men cannot annex women's roles as successfully.

Overall, women's narratives do not develop themes of sexual role switching to the extent that men's narratives do. In particular, in women's tales with male main characters, there is only one-eighth the incidence of female-to-male crossover that there is in men's stories with male main characters (1.3 percent of the tales, against 10.4 percent for male narrators). In women's tales about female main characters, there is similarly minimal crossover of males into the female sphere (1.2 percent, against 12.5 percent of men's tales). One could say that women consistently tell stories about men in a masculine sphere into which women do not often intrude, and about women in a feminine sphere into which men do not intrude, whereas men fantasize considerably more cross-sexual intrusion. Furthermore, this intrusion is predominantly that of women into the masculine sphere of actions.

Phallic intrusion (bride-stealing by infiltrating the harem or, less often, homosexual rape) is the overt content of most male-to-female crossover where it does occur.

Overall, men's narratives (14.5 percent of 289 tales) show female-to-male crossover almost three times as often as do women's tales (5 percent of 161 tales). Although both men and women show a greater tendency to cast women in male roles when the story centers on a female character, this tendency is four times as pronounced among men (35 percent of 31 tales, against 8.9 percent of 79 tales by women). Male narrators' tales also show more male-to-female crossover overall, though the difference is not as pronounced (6.6 percent of tales against 3.1 percent of women's tales). Women's tales show the highest incidence of male-to-female crossover when the main character is male (5.2 percent of 77 tales), whereas men's tales show the most male-to-female crossover when the main character is female (12.9 percent of 31 tales). Aggregating male-to-female and female-to-male crossover, men's stories about men show 2.5 times as much sex role crossover as women's stories about men do, while men's stories about women show almost five times the rate of sexual crossover observable in women's stories about women.

DRAMATIC DIMENSIONS OF SEXUAL CROSSOVER

As mentioned above, most male-to-female crossover involved overt themes of sexual access. Men act like women in order to penetrate the private sphere to gain access to women, or involuntarily as victims of male aggression in the form of actual or threatened homosexual rape. By contrast, women most often act like men to gain mobility in the outside world, both to avoid sexual contact and to rescue family members (mostly male) who are confined or incapacitated. In the process of acting out "masculine" heroic roles, they may win brides, whom they turn over to the rescued spouse or other male ally. Women in male dress and masculine activist roles are universally heroic in both men's and women's tales. They usually choose male disguise, sometimes on the advice of a female ally. By contrast, women characters who initiate action in *men's* tales *without* assuming male dress or behavior are ambiguous figures, often mediators of disorder rather than order. The most common and ambivalent female initiator in men's stories is the go-between, the postmenopausal female who mediates between the inner world of the harem and the male hero or villain. Old widows acting as panderers and social disrupters are commonly described in tales as "seven steps ahead of Satan" in cleverness and evil intent; nonetheless, they as often aid heroes as villains. These intermediaries disguise not as men but as higher-status women (e.g., religious pilgrims) if they disguise at all. In actual social practice, the Koran exempts postmenopausal women from the injunction to veil in public if they are modest otherwise (24:59), and their public movements are correspondingly less restricted. One idiom in Persian for menopause is "to become a man" (*mard shodan*), yet while old, unattached women gain some of the mobility of men, they do not gain respect in folktale ideology.

Themes of obedience common in stories about female heroes are congruent with social norms governing women's behavior, but in women's tales obedience does not mean passivity. Female heroes, like male heroes, are effective executors of directions given by guides or mentors, often in direct contrast to the incompetence of other family members or rivals (see Synopsis B, below). Overall, in women's stories main characters, especially females, are less likely to assume opposite sex behavior or appearance in order to accomplish their tasks than they are in men's stories. Since assumption of male appearance and behavior reduces women's vulnerability (sexual and otherwise) and increases their mobility outside the domestic sphere, one can argue that women's comparative lack of use of this theme indicates less concern with the vulnerability of women cast in traditionally female roles. Women's female characters are able to do more as *females;* hence they imitate men less.

By contrast, male-to-female role switching usually increases the male character's vulnerability, either comically (a villain is humiliated or a trickster in disguise lampoons sex roles) or heroically (a hero places himself in danger by going unarmed, in female guise, into an adversary's harem). In addition, in the few instances of nonhuman disguise in this sample, males tend to be involuntarily disguised as animals (by trick or force in six out of fourteen cases) and humiliated, raped, or maimed as a result, whereas women generally don nonhuman disguise voluntarily and gain mobility and protection from it. (The vizier's wife in "Adel Kahn," Synopsis A [below], is an exception, with animal form imposed on a villainous female in retaliation for her inflicting it on her husband.) In general, renunciation of human status through disguise as animals or objects protects women but endangers men. Thus some asymmetry of "options" appears in male and female narrators' uses of other types of disguise besides cross-sexual ones.

Given the asymmetry of power distribution in everyday life, it is not surprising that females gain power over their own lives and those of others by assuming male roles in stories, but what is noteworthy is women storytellers' comparative lack of interest in these role manip-ulations. Their marked preference for women's strategies in tales about women suggests a conservatism with regard to annexing male social roles. This same conservatism shows in traditional women's reluctance to give up symbols such as the veil which to Western-educated outsiders epitomizes the restrictions on their social initia-tive. Older women in Herat discussing a 1963 attempt by the central government to abolish the veil recalled their feelings of humiliation and vulnerability when they were forced to appear in public unveiled. Likewise, stories still circulate in Iran concerning women's outrage at Reza Shah's efforts in the 1930s to outlaw the veil, partly enforced by soldiers who tore veils off women in the streets with bayonets. This phallic imagery is no accident: traditional women feel the loss of the veil as a form of sexual assault and do not aspire to public visibility to the extent that they equate it with sexual vulnerability. Men may fantasize about women in publicly visible roles (as in male dress in folktales) precisely because of that equation. When the female depen-dents of an overwhelmingly male secular power elite abandon the veil, as in prerevolutionary Iran, the action may be seen by male and female traditionalists not as an offer of greater security to all but as an arrogant statement of invulnerability by the few, a statement by one group of males to another concerning their ability to protect their women.

In the veil, women have a powerful symbol for the manipulation of public identity (family status) and privacy themes and a symbol of confinement and restriction which, paradoxically, can increase wom-en's mobility when manipulated in certain ways. Men see the restric-tive aspects of purdah and its implications as foremost, and fantasize women out of it, whereas women, more directly recognizing the poten-tial of the restrictive institution for manipulation in everyday life, fantasize less about its abandonment, either through sexual role switching or through other forms of disguise.

THE ARTICULATION OF MALE AND FEMALE SEXUAL IDENTITY: FICTIONAL SEX CHANGES IN TWO TALE TEXTS

Both male and female characters borrow behavior from the opposite sex in tales, but the borrowing is strategic and reversible in most cases. Exceptions are male characters forced into humiliating quasi-female positions. Actual sex changes are quite rare in tales, uniformly involuntary, usually temporary, and sometimes instructional for the sufferer. A legend of the Prophet Mohammed first appearing in a literary formulation by the thirteenth-century Indo-Persian poet Amir Khusrau[4] and probably of Indian origin, tells of a skeptic who ridiculed the Prophet's narrative of the *mi'rāj*, the Night Journey to Jerusalem and to Heaven and the Divine Throne. The skeptic scoffs that one cannot even get from Medina to Mecca in a single night. Shortly thereafter, the skeptic is miraculously turned into a woman, kidnapped, forced to marry and bear children, then returned to his former status and home, to find that only a few moments have passed in the life of his original family. This experience of the *nunc eternam* and the contingency of all human experience on God's will converts the skeptic to Islam.[5]

The two synopsized texts presented below contain other examples of sex change and sex branding.[6] "Ādel Khān" (Synopsis A) was told by a male, at the behest of a male host, to a male audience. The storytelling session was organized on my behalf during the earliest survey period of my fieldwork. My grasp of local dialect and my verbal interactions with the participants were minimal. Information acquired later about the social circumstances of the story session revealed considerable hostility between the storytellers and their host, the local subgovernor, who had effectively commanded them to perform. This tale's overt content of misogyny and male sexual anxiety, plus direct references to male and female genitalia, are more characteristic of performances in single-sex contexts. In retrospect, I would construe the main effect of my presence as providing an occasion for the storytellers, through traditional tales, to comment on the antireligious and Parchami Communist sentiments of the subgovernor, whom they opposed,[7] and to try to embarrass him. The dialogue was therefore male-to-male, with my presence one (perhaps minor) case in point in an ongoing disagreement about social rules.

Synopsis A: The Tale of Ādel Khān "the Just"
Told by Khalifeh Karim of Mirābād, Herat Province, Afghanistan, January 1975

A king named "Ādel Khān," "the Just," goes to the baths with his vizier. The king gives a barber who attends them three great jewels as payment. The vizier hints to the king that this is extravagant. The king is reluctant to take the jewels back. The vizier suggests that they each tell the worst misfortune of their lives, and the one who has suffered most will win the jewels. The king and barber agree, each man believing his own experience to be worse than anything the others can have seen.

The king, given the first turn, tells how as a young man he got lost on a hunting trip and came to a well where he dismounted to wash. Trying to fill a bucket from the well, he awakened a supernatural living in the well, who cursed him and turned him into a woman. As "she" wandered around the small oasis, dazed by this transformation, a young man rode up, immediately raped "her" and carried "her" off to his winter camp. There the king was kept for forty days, and used sexually twice a day. Finally the king begged "her" captor to take "her" out for some fresh air, pointing out that "she" was defenseless, probably pregnant, and not likely to flee. The young man took "her" back to the same spring where the transformation occurred. "She," sent to draw water for tea from the well, prayed to God to reverse the transformation. The same supernatural, awakened again by the falling bucket, praised the king for awakening him in time for prayers and granted "her" a wish. The king found his male parts restored and miraculously large. He thanked God, washed himself, and ran back to where his captor was lighting a fire. He dropped his trousers and threatened to rape his captor, who fled. The king then returned to his throne.

The vizier tells how he was married while young to a fine-looking girl who would have nothing to do with him. On his mother's advice he feigned sleep and learned his wife was leaving at night to visit a fortified dwelling (qal'eh) out in the desert. Again his mother explained that the girl had a demon (dīv) lover, and gave her son directions to gather friends, ambush, and kill the demon. The friends could then take what they wished from the demon's qal'eh, but the vizier must take only a small plain box from a certain room and give it to no one.

The vizier followed these directions, killed the demon, and brought the small box home. His wife greeted him enthusiastically and asked to see what he carried. As soon as he gave in and handed her the box, she struck him with it, turned him into a bitch in heat, and drove him from the house. For a week the vizier remained in this form, sexually attacked by all the dogs in town, until he finally reached his mother's house. His mother recognized him, went to her daughter-in-law's, and got the box. She struck her son and returned him to his own form. He then went home, struck his wife with the box, turned her into a bitch in heat, and turned her out. The wife remained in that form.

The king reckons this was worse than his experience, but the barber asks for his own turn. He tells that he once had a barbershop, but one day a beautiful woman passed by, lifting her veil to show him her face as she passed. Infatuated, he followed her off into the desert, leaving his shop open to any thieves or passersby. Finally he followed the woman into an isolated house and found her waiting for him. She told him, however, that she had sworn never to have sex in a ritually unclean state. He agreed to go and make ablutions in an anteroom where there were a pitcher and bowl, but as he poured the water over his penis, it fell onto the floor. He fled the scene.

He returned to the city, found his shop looted, and bought some poor meat for dinner with his remaining pocket money. It was Thursday, the evening often reserved for conjugal relations by Afghan Muslims,[8] and his wife wanted sex, but he feigned illness to put her off, claiming to have eaten "unpeeled, unwashed peaches" (peaches being a euphemism for female genitalia). The next night he again feigned illness to keep his wife away. The day after that the seductress again passed his shop and he followed her again, to try for some restitution. Sent to wash himself, he found his withered penis lying on the floor, prayed to 'Alī[9] for help, and found the penis came back to life in the wash water. Hurriedly clapping it in place, he fled, the seductress calling after him and he cursing as he went.

He went straight home, now cursing his wife for her sexual demands and vowing to take her in whatever activity he found her. She was working bread dough, and he pushed her down and loosened his pants, only to find that in his haste, he had put his penis and testicles on backwards. The barber, addressing the king and vizier, claims the jewels because his misfortune is permanent while theirs were temporary. They inspect him, find it is true, and agree he should keep the jewels.

The second text (Synopsis B), although a widely known and performed version of AT 510A ("Cinderella"), is examined here for its role in an all-female Ismaili Muslim ceremony, the *Āsh-e Bībī Murād*, in which a ritual meal (an *āsh* or soup among other items) is prepared by women as part of a petition to Bībī Fātimeh, the Prophet's daughter and wife of 'Alī.[10] The woman who sponsors the ceremony is supported by other women in her petition for the granting of a wish. Others may offer their own petitions along with hers. The story is told at the center of the ritual meal. The Ismaili community from which this particular ceremony (one of a class called *āsh* or *sofreh*) is reported is a village south of Mashhad in eastern Iran.[11]

Synopsis B: Field Notes on the *Āsh-e Bībī Murād*, "Soup for the Lady of Wishes," courtesy of Rafique Keshavjee, Dīzbād, Khorāssān, Iran, November 10, 1978

This *āsh* is a food offering and ritual meal offered by women to Bībī Fātimeh ("Bībī Murād," the "Lady of Wishes"), daughter of Mohammed and wife of 'Alī, for the fulfillment of a wish. The meal must be made by women of the *jamā'at*, the Ismaili Muslim congregation, in the *jamā'at khāneh*, the congregational house or mosque, which has a small kitchen. Ingredients for the meal must be begged from three to seven households (an odd number) containing women named Fātimeh, Zahrā, Sekīneh, or Zeinab (all revered female members of the Prophet's lineage). They must be begged by a female "for the sake of Bībī Fātimeh." The women beg silently after nightfall, from houses in their neighborhood, concealing their identities by hiding their heads under black *chādors*. The informant said that a fourteen-year-old boy in her household was so frightened by finding two silent, black shadows at the door that he fainted. Normally, visitors at the door say "Salām," and ordinary beggars appeal to God or 'Alī aloud. Visiting after dark is unusual in villages. Narrow streets are pitch-dark, and some families keep mastiffs chained by day but loose at night to patrol the compound.

The ingredients begged may include flour, greens, dried beans, sugar, carrots, meat, oil, chick-peas, water, lentils, or *qormeh* (stews of meat and/or vegetables). The begging must take place after the sunset prayer. Either men or women may give the ingredients, which are placed in a *chādor* the beggars spread on the ground. Women beg in pairs for safety. Items not obtained by begging are supplied by the *sāheb-e nazr*, the "master of the vow," who sponsors the ceremony. While others beg from surrounding households, the woman *sāheb-e nazr* places bowls of flour in three to seven places in her own house (again, an odd number) for five to ten minutes, then she "begs" from her own house, with the invocation "Yā, 'Alī!," gathering up the flour she has set out.

All the assembled foodstuffs are taken to the mosque at about nine p.m. A *sofreh*[12] is spread in the middle of the mosque, with the flour, a Koran, a woman's kohl (eyeshadow) container, salt in a saucer, powdered lump sugar, a mirror, a string of prayer beads, and a photograph of the Agha Khan, the spiritual leader of the Ismaili community.

All those women who have a wish sit with the sponsor in a circle around this *sofreh* and recite the Ismaili *do'a*, or congregational prayer, five to fifteen times. No males can be present. The women leave the materials assembled for the *āsh* in the mosque overnight.

At eight or eight-thirty the next morning, the women return to the mosque. If the petition has been accepted, traces of the prayer beads are seen in the flour, and fingermarks in the salt and sugar and on the *sofreh* itself. If no marks can be seen, the *nīat*, or wish, which is kept secret by the one making it, is no good. The informant stated that "those whose faith is pure" are able to see these traces.

The flour that has been on the *sofreh* (not all the flour) is now *tabarokī*, "blessed," and it is made into a special bread called *komāj*,[13] not to be eaten by men. Other flour is used to make noodles for the *āsh* or soup, which is cooked that morning. It is eaten at noon by ten to fifty women. Little boys can attend but should not, and they may eat the *āsh* and regular bread but not *komāj*. Adult males may eat neither *āsh* nor *komāj*. The *āsh* must be eaten in the mosque, each woman supplying her own bowl or using bowls from the mosque kitchen.

Before the *āsh* is eaten, a second *sofreh* is spread, with a lamp on it, and everything from the previous night's *sofreh* is moved to it.

Women with wishes bring sweets, dried fruits, and nuts, which they put on the second *sofreh*. A widow and a motherless virgin sit beside each other at this second *sofreh*. The widow has a bowl full of *āsh*, and the girl has an empty bowl. The widow, as she spoons *āsh* into the girl's bowl, recites the story of *Māh Pīshānī* ("Moon-Brow"). Every time the girl receives a spoonful of *āsh*, she must answer, "Yes."

The Story

A merchant enrolled his daughter in the *madraseh* (mosque school). The teacher, a female *ākhund*, or teaching mullah, was a widow and asked the girl about her family's circumstances, which were good. She asked the girl what they had in their house, and the girl replied, "Vinegar." The teacher convinced the girl that she, the teacher, was good and her mother was bad. She told the girl to tell her mother she wanted vinegar, and when she was getting it, to push her in and cover the storage jar. She was not to tell her father, just to say her mother fell in.

The mother was dead when the father found her. (Here the informant mentioned the widow's spooning *āsh* and the girl's answering "Yes.") Later the father found a yellow cow in his stable "in place of the murdered mother." The teacher and the father were married. The daughter was sent to pasture the cow. The new wife bore a daughter and began to mistreat the first daughter, giving her one rotten piece of bread to eat when she took the cow to pasture and raw cotton to clean and spin without tools while the cow grazed. In the fields the girl began to cry because she could not spin and could only hook the cotton fibers on a thorn and twist them with her fingers.

The cow asked why she was crying. She complained and said, "If I don't do this work, my stepmother won't let me back in the house." The cow asked for her bread. (The informant added that the listening girl continues to say "yes" at intervals.) The girl gave the bread to the cow, and then the cotton to eat, and the cow shat cotton thread until evening. The girl collected all the thread and took it back to her stepmother.

For three days, the stepmother gave the girl bad bread to eat and more cotton to spin. On the third day, when the girl gave the cow the cotton, the wind blew a piece down a well. The girl was about to go after it when the cow said, "When you go into the well, you'll see an old woman *bārzangī*.[14] Say 'Salām!' and ask for the cotton. She will say, 'Delouse my hair.' You should say, 'Your hair is perfectly clean. It's cleaner than mine.' "

The girl followed the directions. When the old woman asked, "What does my hair have in it?" the girl answered, "Nothing. Your hair is cleaner than my mother's." The old woman told her to take her cotton from a certain room. The daughter went in and saw that the room was full of jewels, but took only her cotton, swept the room, and left, saying goodbye. She started to climb out of the well, but when she was halfway up the *bārzangī* shook the ladder to see whether she had stolen anything. When no jewels fell from her clothes, the old woman prayed for her to have a moon in the center of her brow. When she reached the top, the *bārzangī* shook the ladder again and blessed her again, "May you have a star on your chin!"

The girl returned to the cow, who told her to cover her face so her stepmother wouldn't see. That night while she slept, her veil slipped, and the stepmother saw the moon and star. The next day, she sent her own daughter with the cow, with cotton to work and sweet nutbread to eat. The girl could not spin, but she guessed that the cow did the spinning, so she gave the bread to the cow, and the cotton, but the cow produced only a little thread.

On the third day, her cotton too blew down the well, and she followed and saw the old woman. She asked for the cotton without saying "Salām," and the old woman asked her to delouse her hair. The girl told her her hair was filthy, while her own mother's was clean. The old woman sent her to the room. She took some jewels, which fell from her clothes when the old woman shook the ladder. The old woman cursed her, first with a donkey's penis on her forehead,[15] then with a snake on her chin.

The girl went back to the cow, who saw the penis and snake but said nothing. They went home, and the mother cut off the penis and snake with a knife and rubbed the wounds with salt, but both objects grew back overnight. The stepmother realized the cow was behind this and feigned sickness, bribing doctors to tell her husband she must eat the meat of the yellow cow and have its skin thrown over her in order to recover. Meanwhile, the first daughter realized that the yellow cow was her mother, and she fed her candied chick-peas and bread. One day the cow wept and told her, "They'll kill me today. When they kill me, don't eat the meat. Collect all the bones in a bag, bury them, and hide them." The daughter pled with her father not to kill the cow, but the father said the cow was the only medicine for her stepmother.

The girl followed the cow's instructions after it was killed. The stepmother "recovered" and a few days later the stepmother and her daughter decided to go to a wedding. The mother cut off the penis and snake and put salt on the wounds, then mixed millet and *toğu* (another small seed), placed her stepdaughter beside an empty pool in the garden, and told the girl to sort the seeds and fill the pool with tears. The two left for the party. The girl sat and cried, then saw a hen and chicks enter the garden. The hen told the girl to put salt and water in the pool, take the horse and good clothes she would find in the stable, and go to the wedding, while the chicks separate the seeds. The hen added, "When you come back, one of your shoes will fall into the water. Don't stop—go quickly so your stepmother won't know you."

The girl found a horse, fine clothes, and gold shoes in the stable and rode to the wedding, covering her forehead and chin. They placed her at the head of the guests in the women's party when the dancing started. She danced, and the stepsister recognized her, but the stepmother said, "Impossible!" They left to see whether it was she, and Māh Pīshānī rushed to get home before them but dropped a shoe into some water. When she got home, she realized that the hen had become the horse. She put on her old clothes and sat down to separate the last seeds. The stepmother and stepsister saw the seeds and the full pool and the stepmother said, "I told you so!"

Two days later, a prince rode by the waterside, found the shoe, and decided to wed its owner. His father the king and the viziers tried the shoe on everyone, but it did not fit. Finally they reached Māh Pīshānī's father's house. The stepmother "cleaned and cut" her daughter's head, but the shoe did not fit. The first daughter was locked in the bread oven. A cock flew up on the oven[16] and began to crow,

A moon in the oven!	Māhi dar tannur,
A head is in there, ku-ku!	Sar ar unjeh, qu, qu!
Where is the foot, like glass?	Pā ku cī bolur
A head is in there, ku-ku![17]	Sar ar unjeh, qu, qu!

The stepmother and her daughter tried to catch the cock, who escaped and crowed twice more. The vizier insisted on looking in the oven and found the girl. The shoe fit and she married the prince.

After the story, the *āsh* is divided among the women present. No men may eat it, though the informant added, "They can have other *āsh*, later." Everyone present eats some *āsh*, and the sugar and other sweets are given as alms to complete the ceremony.

This telling of "Cinderella" is substantially identical to variants I found frequently performed farther east, in the Herat area, except that most of the performances I recorded lacked overt phallic imagery. There may be self-censorship in strangers' presence (see note 15). Two adolescent girls did include branding of the unkind sister with male genitalia. A third version by a twenty-nine-year-old married woman omitted phallic imagery but included scatological humiliation of the bad sister on her wedding night.[18] I did not find this tale in ritual context in Herat. *Sofreh* ceremonies may be more elaborate among Shi'a Muslims. Most of my informants were Sunni. Nonetheless, the use of the tale and particularly of its male symbols in an all-female ritual underscores symbolic dimensions also present in the story in nonritual circulation. It is offered here, like "Ādel Khān," not as a typical item but as a special case that contributes a polar term to the continuum of male and female narrative tradition. As "Ādel Khān" is told by a man for men, so "Māh Pīshānī" in this context is a tale told by and for women. The two tales illustrate not typical but extreme manifestations of the asymmetry prevailing in men's and women's uses of sex role inversions in folktale. They show a common horror of sexual crossover and marking.

The surface message of "Ādel Khān" expresses a hierarchy of male misfortune. All three disasters are sexual in nature. The first, the king's, was simply to *become* a woman for a brief period. This transformation occurred purely by chance: he had the ill luck to anger a supernatural. His misfortune is also totally mended. In fact, the private parts when restored are larger and better than the originals, and his first use of them is to terrify his tormentor. The female position here portrayed is one of powerlessness, captivity, and rape, and the king counts it the greatest misfortune of his life that he was briefly female. No hint of feminine acceptance or enjoyment of sex appears. Male sexuality is portrayed as pure aggression.

The vizier's misfortune, also involving a sex change, occurs through the disloyalty of his wife. Seduction of women is a form of male-male aggression in Afghan ideology (Nazif Shahrani, personal communication 1976). The superiority of wife-takers over wife-givers as a psychological theme can be traced to pre-Islamic Arabia as well. Mohammed sought to eradicate the idea that men should be ashamed of giving their women as brides by giving his daughter Fātimeh to 'Alī at a public party (Knabe 1977:43). The status hierarchy still survives in Afghan thought, expressed in bride-price among other things. Through his women's misbehavior, a man is himself raped, rendered feminine. The vizier's wife's malevolence directly expresses this equation. After her husband kills her demon lover, she arranges to have him suffer multiple rapes. Added to the humiliation of sexual vulnerability is the aspect of pollution: to the Muslim, dogs are unclean. "Son of a dog" (pedarsag) is a severe insult in Persian. The vizier, like the king, has full restitution and revenge, however, thanks to his mother, the only positive female character in the tale. Even she is a bit sinister, conversant as she is with her evil daughter-in-law's magic. At any rate, the vizier is pleased to condemn his wife to similar torment as a bitch in heat. Once again, the female physical state is deplored, and this episode adds the themes of female moral depravity and sexual disloyalty.

The third episode is another permutation of the masculine trapped by the feminine. The peril comes not from within the main character as a sex change, nor from the disloyalty of female relatives, but from pure, impersonal female sexual aggression in the form of a supernatural seductress. This episode manipulates the ideology of pollution connected with sex. For Muslims, both male and female, all sex is polluting and requires ritual ablutions before praying or entering a sacred precinct. (Pollution in varying degree follows other breaching of the body's boundaries, such as eating, elimination, menstruation, and childbirth. The hands, feet, and bodily orifices are washed after completion of polluting acts and/or before prayer.) It is significant that the seductress asks the barber to wash before sex, to render himself ritually pure for what is itself an impure act. This inversion of normal ritual order has a disastrous effect: his penis falls off.

It is also significant that the person involved is a barber, who by profession is in an ambiguous position vis-à-vis pollution. His work, polluting to himself, renders others clean (shaving, circumcision, sometimes cupping, bleeding, and minor surgery). In Afghanistan, India, and Iran, barbers are almost a separate class within theoretically classless Muslim society. In Afghanistan, barbers are often

members of the *jat*, regarded as a special ethnic group who traditionally dominate such professions as barbering, blacksmithing, music,
acting, prostitution, and sieve-making. They are endogamous and
widely scorned, yet their status has certain ambiguities. According to
tradition, the first Persian convert to Islam was Salmān, the Prophet's
barber, who is a revered figure in Shi'a Islam, the Iranian majority
religion. The fact that it is a barber around whom the manipulations
of the ideology of pure and impure become most complex in this tale,
thus resonates with a complex set of beliefs and practices concerning
purity and pollution with regard to the barber and his profession.

The barber is also the only one of the three who does not get full
restitution, nor is he able to punish his tormentor, unless escaping
her constitutes revenge. He is permanently marked: having inverted
the purification ritual, he also accidentally inverts the cure, attaching
his penis behind his testicles in his haste to escape.

Not only the supernatural seductress but also the barber's wife is
sexually importunate, expecting sex night after night while he pleads
illness. When he escapes, it is on his wife that he attempts to vent
his rage by raping her, until he discovers what has happened to his
privates.

Although the barber is not forced into a feminine sexual role, he
is sexually maimed and permanently marked by association with a
powerful female. Because his injury is permanent, the king and vizier
award him the prize for the greatest misfortune.

The three episodes also vary systematically in the degree to which
the victim's own will is implicated in his sexual predicament. The
king is concerned only with getting clean, with making the morning
ritual ablution, in fact, although this point is not stressed in the text.
His misfortune occurs through no will of his own. The vizier in turn
is trying only to assert his legitimate sexual rights over his wife by
removing his rival. The barber, however, shows illicit sexual initiative
when he follows his temptress. According to the Koran both partners
in adultery are equally culpable (24:2). Women showing their faces to
strangers briefly and thereby causing insane infatuation are a romantic
commonplace in Afghan oral tradition. This is the heavy artillery of
seduction, another reminder of the manipulative power of veiling.

When the various presentations of female sexuality and male experiences of it in "Ādel Khān" are summed up, it is clear that males
neither envy nor admire the female state. The female role in sex is

experienced by these men as rape victims, while those women who show sexual initiative are portrayed as importunate (the barber's wife), castrating (the seductress), and/or murderous (the vizier's wife). The message seems to be that it is tragic to be female and that one would have to be depraved to want to act like a woman. The only exception is the vizier's mother, who is both intelligent and capable of action supportive of a man. She completes the whore-mother dichotomy, but her role is relatively unstressed. She is also an old woman, presumably postmenopausal, who has "become a man" but remains socially attached and responsible to her family, not a disruptive social isolate like most old women in the tales.

Although "Ādel Khān" does not summarize Afghan male attitudes about women (men do tell stories about faithful and heroic women), the tale presents a coherent set of attitudes about women in which fear of being either female or, worse yet, a male in the power of females predominates. It is, I think, a summary statement of Afghan male views of women's "lack of options." Though it is received as comic by the Afghan audience, it is horrific comedy.

In the performance of "Māh Pīshānī" (Synopsis B) we have a story of, by, and for women. The story, generally called "Moon-Brow" ("Māh Pīshānī") or "The Yellow Cow" ("Gāu-e Zard"), was performed for me by both male and female storytellers, but the variants involving sexual marking of the unkind sister or her scatological humiliation were told by women. In this form of Type 510A, as in most forms, the dominant relations are between women: loyalty and disloyalty between mother and daughter, rivalry between stepmother and her offspring and the firstborn daughter. The telling of the tale in a ritual context by a widow to an orphan girl further emphasizes the themes of female abandonment and solidarity which dominate the tale itself. That the girl first betrays her own mother is important to the dynamics of female solidarity and redemption, as is the choice of this story as part of a solidarity ritual in which women join together to call on the spiritual "mother," deceased but present, in support of the desires of one or more of their number. The subject of the ritual sponsor's petition, though it may be known to other participants (and quite likely is, given the level of gossip in villages), is unspoken. Other women support her in at least putative ignorance of her purpose, yet another statement of a generalized female solidarity.

The marking of the wicked daughter with a donkey's penis and a snake, in contrast to the good daughter's radiant marks of female beauty, the moon and star, constitutes a strong rejection of male symbols, here equated with grotesque ugliness. This instance of transsexual marking must be understood in the context of a broader tendency of female folktale tellers not to develop themes of transsexual role manipulation. Male narrators more frequently cast characters in roles which entail their acting like or appearing to be members of the opposite sex. So far I have found *no* instances of sex change *per se* in tales told by women.[19] Sex changes are rare enough in tales told by men: besides "Ādel Khān," with its disastrous vision of such changes for men, I have heard two tales told by men in which females undergo permanent changes of sex or sex role which are construed as fortunate. In one example, told by an eighteen-year-old high school student, the heroine performs martial exploits in male disguise and wins a bride. The heroine has fled her home because of ill treatment and she has no spouse or other male ally to whom to award brides. Ultimately, the problem is solved when she is "cursed" with a sex change by an annoyed dragon. Two other male narrators told versions of a tale in which the wise daughter of the vizier is married to a prince who abuses her because she surpassed him in school. She tricks him into a quest for the princess of China in order to get rid of him, but ultimately has to rescue him, in the process winning the princess and three other brides. She turns them over to her husband and announces that henceforth she will be his vizier, as her father was his father's, rather than his wife.

In these male-narrated tales, sex change or permanent sex role change is part of the heroine's reward. In the absence of any such formulation by women narrators, the stepdaughter's marking with grotesque male genitalia and an equally phallic snake on her face in this version of "Māh Pīshānī" turns the idea of cross-sexual disguise on its head and elaborates the conceptual set of male : female : : public : private. When she is marked for scorn by the community of women celebrating the ritual, the unkind sister is not branded privately, as the barber was, but marked with *male* features in a manner that cannot be hidden even by that institution of female privacy and respectability, the veil. She receives sexual stigmata as a direct result of her own and her mother's attempts to exploit other females, human and supernatural, and as an indirect result of her mother's antisocial competition for a male. In this tale about women told exclusively for women, acquisition of male characteristics, far from being a reward, is a grotesque punishment for disloyalty to women. The female recourse of veiling cannot conceal this branding: the girl is forced into maleness and into public.

On the whole, "Māh Pīshānī" ignores male characters. The father and the prince are passive prizes of women's struggle, male brides. In a performance context from which males are excluded, the humiliation of an evil female is accomplished by the invocation of male symbols. If "Ādel Khān" reveals male fear both of women's biological situation and of their power for social disruption and sexual manipulation, "Māh Pīshānī" in this quintessentially female formulation reveals a view of marking (being made conspicuous) as both disastrous and masculine. Combined with the comparative lack of sex role crossover in women's stories, this suggests that penis envy has a much higher profile in men's stories than in women's stories and that women do not greatly covet male characteristics or male social roles, though men see them as doing so. If this interpretation is valid, one must recognize a certain conservatism among Afghan women, reflected in their choice of stories for entertainment and perhaps in other expressive behavior. Memorates about veiling and women's resistance to its abolition may be rooted in the same attitudes. Many conservative women do not favor "going public" by adopting male behavior, because in doing so they forfeit the power of anonymity, a power they have learned to exploit to give themselves mobility, and certain ways of manipulating the public, masculine sphere as well. These women's less-intense interest in disguise themes, also detectable in their storytelling, may be attributable to the fact that under current conditions women have considerable real-world power to conceal identity and thereby manipulate people and situations, whereas men, socialized to regard only the public sphere of male-male relations as "significant," and having little real privacy in the domestic world, fantasize more about the manipulation and concealment of sexual and other identity. A fuller consideration of disguise themes in general, both in Afghan tradition and cross-culturally, including comparisons to tale-telling communities where women are not secluded, might help to test whether the differential use of disguise and sex role manipulation themes between male and female narrators can be correlated with particular asymmetries in social practice, or whether it is a general characteristic of differences between male and female storytelling.

NOTES

1. The ethnic diversity of Afghanistan makes generalizations risky. My sample is from individuals speaking Persian as their first language, of Tajik, Pashtun, Turkic, and Hazara descent.

2. Since 1978 the Communist regimes have passed edicts setting the legal age of marriage for girls at sixteen and limiting the bride-price to a token sum (the former range was $200 to $2,000, 1 afghani = $.02 U.S., per capita income around $150). The regime lacks power to enforce this or other reforms, however.

3. These observations were made in peacetime in 1974–76. The impact of the war of resistance and the Iranian revolution on Herat's economy and labor patterns has been severe, but the author has no direct information on current conditions in 1984.

4. *Āïneh Iskandarī*, "The Mirror of Alexander," ca. 1290. Reference courtesy of Annemarie Schimmel. Michael Fischer (personal communication) and Henri Massé (1954:167) report Iranian variants in which 'Omar, as the skeptic, doubts the sanctity of 'Alī, the patron of the Shi'a Muslims.

5. The tale reappears in a Chinese version of the life of Mohammed, the *True Annals of the Prophet of Arabia* by Liu Chai-lien (Mason 1921). Eliade (1969:69–71) published a related tale from a Hindu context (from the *Matsya Purana* and the twentieth-century *Sayings of Śri Ramakrishna*). The Indian tale involves a change of spiritual status (from ascetic to householder) and also possibly a caste change (brahmin to vaiśya) but no sex change. A secular variant, "The Biggest Lie," was told by a Scots storyteller at the Seventh Congress on International Folk Narrative Research in Edinburgh, August 1979; the tale is apparently in oral circulation in Scotland.

6. Because of space limitations, it was necessary to synopsize where detailed textual analysis would have been more informative. Complete transcriptions are available from the author.

7. The series of tales told in this session and their shaping by social relations of the audience and tellers were discussed in detail in "The Uses of Memory," a paper delivered to the South Asia Seminar, University of Virginia, October 31, 1980.

8. Because men visit the baths before congregational prayer at the mosque on Fridays, Thursday is a convenient night to incur ritual pollution.

9. 'Alī, the cousin and son-in-law of the Prophet Mohammed, is the patron especially of the Shi'a branch of Islam, though revered by all. See the discussion of the status of barbers following the tale.

10. The objects and foodstuffs placed on the votive *sofreh* (a cloth on which food is served) are some of the same items used in marriage and in other rituals, in which *sofreh* are also displayed.

11. Data supplied by Rafique Keshavjee, an anthropologist and an Ismaili, who conducted research on village organization in the area. Being male, Dr. Keshavjee could not attend such an *āsh*. This description was given by an older woman who both attended and organized such ceremonies. It is a normative description by an insider, not the transcript of an actual ceremony.

12. In Persian, *sofreh* designates both the cloth on which everyday meals are served and a formal array of food and other items displayed on such a cloth for ritual purposes.

13. *Komāj* in general is a rich bread made with oil and sugar, in contrast to ordinary bread made only with flour, salt, and water. Sweet breads are generally party foods, not staples.

14. A monstrous, usually malevolent supernatural, according to one of my informants, "like a *dīv*, only bigger, worse." The name derives from *Zangbār*, "Zanzibar." Some informants associate *bārzangīs* with blacks, whom they for the most part have never seen. Color prejudice is widespread in rural Iran and Afghanistan.

15. The informant first told Dr. Keshavjee, "A piece of meat," then laughed and corrected herself. Some self-censorship seems at work.

16. A beehive-shaped structure of clay, about waist-high.

17. This translation is speculative. The speech is distorted to imitate a rooster's crow and is in local dialect. *Bolur* is old-fashioned blown glass, very thin and delicate.

18. In this connection women's cursing styles tend to be scatological while men's tend to be sexual in everyday speech.

19. *So far* in my collecting experience. I do not mean to imply *ex silentio* that women never tell such stories, only that they seem to be quite rare.

· 12 ·
WOMAN REMEMBERING:
LIFE HISTORY AS EXEMPLARY PATTERN
Elaine Jahner

T HE RELATIONSHIP between the individual elements of a person's life and the cultural and social milieu in which that life occurs
is always sensitive and difficult to characterize adequately. But an
understanding of the role of women in any culture must grow out of
an exploration of just that relationship. That is, we must find ways of
analyzing individual personal histories that will point toward their
many links with other aspects of the culture. The scholar who studies
life histories must be attentive to those features that turn on some
basic understandings the narrators have about their own lives. In this
analysis of Ann Keller's life story (which is presented at the end of
this chapter), I have tried to hear and pinpoint not merely the specific
content but the underlying and controlling rhythms of her personal
narrative. This kind of analysis can help show how individuals have
utilized the resources of their own creativity and courage to shape,
and in some cases to escape, the roles presented them by society.

Ann Keller is a Native American woman who is a member of the
Brule Sioux tribe.[1] The following analysis of her life story therefore
illuminates the lives of Sioux women, but it is also an example of the
process of relating a specific woman's experiences to their historical
and cultural context without minimizing the uniqueness of the person's life story. Ann Keller is in many ways representative of a group

of Native American women who are shaping the future for their people. She understands both the reservation and the urban viewpoint because she grew up, married, and raised her two children on Rosebud Sioux Reservation[2] before she moved to Lincoln, Nebraska, where she now lives and works. Her behavior as daughter, wife, mother, wage earner, and community leader illustrates the way many women have maintained aspects of the traditional way of life in the midst of important cultural changes that they themselves are working to bring about.

Ann Keller was born in 1917 on Rosebud Sioux Reservation. Because her family were all first-generation Christians, much of her own early experience combined Christian and traditional Indian customs. She first learned to speak English when she attended boarding school at St. Francis Indian Mission. Although her formal education is limited to eleven years of grade school and high school education, her avid curiosity about life and people has motivated her to participate in every informal learning experience that has been available to her. A few years after leaving school, she married, and the next seventeen years centered on her two children and her work at the local hospital. She worked in the hospital laundry partly because she needed the money and partly because she enjoyed working and wanted something outside her immediate housekeeping tasks. When she moved with her husband to Lincoln in 1960, her desire to learn and her genuine interest in people helped make the transition from the reservation to an urban way of life an essentially positive experience in spite of her struggles with poverty, hard work, and prejudice in strange surroundings. At the present time, Ann takes care of five grandchildren in addition to teaching the Lakota language to students at the University of Nebraska and at two state prisons. She also does general housecleaning to earn the money needed to maintain her household.

Such are the very broad outlines of the life of a creative and courageous woman. Which more specific features of her story can help us understand some of the basic unities in her life and, furthermore, how unity derives in part from her conception of the traditional role of women in a Sioux community? In order to answer this question, we must first consider some features of the pre-reservation Lakota worldview and the place of women within it, because that worldview is reflected in the present one.

Ethnographic literature about the Sioux stresses male dominance in almost all aspects of life, and it is true that the male as warrior had the more flamboyant role and thus the most easily observed role. But when we begin to analyze carefully the ceremonial data from the traditional culture, we see how much value the Lakota placed on the feminine realm of life, and how consistently they enacted ritually the interdependence of masculine and feminine. The feminine had to do with the natural possibilities of life-transformation. One early observer among the Sioux commented specifically on this aspect of femininity.

> Life appears in the grass by a transformation out of some other life-form in Mother Earth, hence it is a "miracle." Thus it is seen that many things the "scientist" regards as commonplace are regarded by these Indians as "miracles." A woman, at certain times, is "miracu-lous" (*wakan*) . . . for the reason that this status is, normally, con-nected with the transformation of some already existing life-form into a human life-form (child). This is the way they themselves under-stand this matter, as shown by their conversation among themselves. (Beede n.d.)

Woman as life-transformer is a central element in Lakota religion. It was a female, the White Buffalo Woman, who brought the sacred pipe to the Sioux. All accounts of the pipe stress that it represents all life. One very old text says, "The pipe is their heart; all hold firmly to it. . . . The Indians, in everything they undertake, they do it with the pipe." The same old text assigns the following words to the White Buffalo Woman: "I am bringing something so that the people will live; it is the Buffalo Calf Pipe. . . . I will assist all of the people by showing them good ways. I will go there" (Walker, 1980: 148–49). Men are pipe keepers; but the pipe itself is the gift of the feminine elements of the universe. A comparable relationship between mascu-line and feminine elements is shown in the symbolism of the sacred tree, which also represents the people, especially women. Black Elk expressed this relationship clearly:

> The woman is the life of the flowering tree, but the man must feed and care for it. One of the virgins also carried the flowering stick, another carried the pipe which gives peace, a third bore the herb of healing and the fourth held the sacred hoop; for all these powers together are woman's power. (Niehardt 1961:214)

Woman, or the feminine principle, has to do with establishing a center and drawing power toward that central point. Men experience the center as a focus, and then they move outward to put power to work for the community. It is consistent with this religious pattern that in actual everyday life the tipi belonged to the woman. It was also symbolically a microcosm, with the fire at the center representing the sacred (Brown 1971:23).

Consistent analysis of ceremonial data, then, belies observers' and ethnographers' statements about women as mere drudges completely subservient to men. But analysis of ceremonial data alone does not tell us much about how women related the quintessential feminine as shown in ritual to the way they dealt on a day-to-day basis with people around them. To understand something of this principle at work, we need to look at the role of woman as artist. Her artistic work was not an addition to her woman's work; it belonged to her definition of self. Women made articles of clothing, shelter, and decoration, and for many of these they created artistic designs. When we examine traditions in the visual arts, we notice that women executed predominantly abstract designs while men concentrated on concrete line drawings (see Wissler 1904). This division was a visual representation of the differing sexual roles. The abstract designs represented potentiality, spiritual power that could be put to use; the concrete line drawings represented actual deeds, ways in which power had been put to use for the group. Women were aware that in preparing their abstract designs they were working with potentialities for action and therefore for change.[3] Changes in design could be seen as important and fundamental implementations of change, and the designs kept the group aware of the need for constant adaptation. In their discussions of culture change, Ella Deloria and Peter Powell both mention the link between the belief system and woman's role as artist. Ella Deloria notes that in pre-reservation times change was continuous, and, as her prime example of change, she mentions that new ideas of art, "especially in the matter of design, were always appearing, 'dreamed' by certain women whom the tribe regarded as being supernaturally endowed" (Deloria 1944:75). Peter Powell includes more detail and points out that although there were designs "regarded as being merely pretty and created purely to delight the eye," the change from the simple bold designs using quills to the more complex designs of the 1880s and 1890s using beads was made in the belief that the women introducing the new designs had had visions directing them to do so (Powell 1977:46). As the sacred designs changed, so did the group's access to particular kinds of supernatural power.[4]

Another part of women's creative role had to do with the verbal arts. Women used the dynamics of even the simplest tale-telling event to explore some link between daily life (with its inevitable movement toward new ideas and customs) and the traditional ways. The Sioux hero tales tell of journeys that result in the hero's learning about new ways, and the Sioux legends discuss change in a historical context. Most of these legends have immense possibilities for stylistic additions that enable the storyteller to comment on immediate tribal concerns.

Thus, our examination of women's artistic role in Sioux culture leads us to the conclusion that women as designers and as storytellers affected significantly many of the basic directions in Sioux culture change and that women have traditionally understood their role to be one of integrating the forces of change into the fabric of daily life. In this context, Ann Keller's role seems traditional indeed, even though many aspects of her life may seem to be oriented toward the future rather than the past. The feminine aspect of culture is one of life-transformation, which of necessity leads to a future orientation. The content of Ann's story is individualistic and of the present, but group traditions affect its overall patterning. Both the ordering of events and the choice to eliminate certain realities so as to compose a particular kind of narrative are the result of traditional patterns rather than indications of personal preference. The process of discovering patterns, finding traces of the past in contemporary materials, is therefore of special importance in the study of personal narratives.

The overall pattern of Ann Keller's narrative shows one outstanding trait. There is a constant emphasis on the positive and a very careful elimination of that which cannot provide an example for others. Once, when my questioning led her to refer to an unfortunate time in her life, she asked that I not transcribe that reference even though the incident itself places her in a favorable light. She wanted no part of that event in the story of her life. We could assume that her concentration on the positive is a personal preference with no particular relation to her cultural tradition, but a careful reading of similar Lakota women's autobiographical accounts collected under comparable conditions shows the same tendency on the part of the women to use the events of their own lives to sketch a model or a pattern that can permit the audience to use experiences as positive example. This is not to say that the negative is ignored. It is subordinated to a pattern which is essentially positive in that it shows how women mastered adversity. The tendency to concentrate on the positive pattern was once so marked that when Ella Deloria (n.d.) recorded an autobiographical account that includes a lot of complaining, she saw fit to add a note to the account stating that it was atypical. We can then look at Ann Keller's remembrances as the gradual construction of an exemplary design showing how she participated in the overwhelming forces of change that affected her culture and through her participation shaped a personal and cultural identity that has meaning not only for her but for her grandchildren as well. Looked at in this way, her account is a powerful and revealing work of art, the result of choices which gradually create the picture of a heritage of freedom to choose and invent new designs, be they in life or in art.

The heart of Ann's narrative is the story of how her grandmother, and through her grandmother the old community, showed her how to respond to the complex challenges of reservation life. During the initial moments of her story, Ann introduces the leitmotif that becomes the controlling force of many of the scenes that have survived in her memory: the ever-present loving influence of her grandmother. Although the grandmother's influence was always a part of the child's life, her physical presence was not a constant. The grandmother taught the child that she had to learn to face new environments and make her own decisions. The first sections of Ann's story show this emphasis:

> I'll begin with my grandparents. I love my grandparents very much. They took over raising me and my sister when my mother died in 1918. My mother had died from influenza, so my grandparents insisted that they raise us. . . . I guess we caused my grandmother some hardship, but later on when my father had remarried and had married a woman who was a first cousin of my mother, my older sister Phoebe Rose had gone to live with them, but I stayed with my grandparents. I guess they just couldn't tear me out of their arms.

Ann's image is a strong one. It stresses the love she felt and adds to the intensity of what did happen to her. Learning to leave one kind of security to face new situations and to build new feelings of security is a fundamental part of Ann's story. Having begun by talking about her emotional ties to her grandparents, she goes on to describe being sent to a boarding school where children were allowed to see their relatives for only a few hours on Christmas Day.

For almost every Indian child in the plains, the boarding school reality spelled the difference between their lives and those of their parents and grandparents. Boarding school made children realize that they lived in a world of culture conflict. Although Ann says relatively little about her educational experience, she does stress that during the entire first year she was sick because she could not overcome her lonesomeness for her grandparents. Right after her first brief mention of the boarding school, she returns, seemingly without any obvious transition, to the memory of another event which underlines the lesson her grandmother was teaching her about the necessity of being independent.

> My childhood was a very, very happy one. When I was ten or eleven, my grandmother said to my father, "Come and take your daughter, take care of her now. She is asking questions. 'Where will I go when you die, Grandmother?'" So they sent me back to my father and mother, whom I came to love like a real mother. But it seems I had to see my grandparents every day or else I will die.

Incident by incident, Ann reveals her grandmother's own strength and independence and shows how the woman's example taught her. One episode is especially important in showing how the grandmother exercised her authority and what kind of example she set for the child she was raising. In discussing her grandmother's skill in moccasin-making, Ann says,

> She made moccasins like nothing, beaded or everyday moccasins or the kind you wear when you go out. . . . She did everything, but for some reason I never did learn, as close as I was to her. She just sort of let you make up your own mind.

Eventually Ann did begin to do beadwork, and her reputation would most likely please her grandmother, but at no point did her grandmother coerce her to learn the traditional beadworking skills. Women taught by story, by example, and by making possible rather than by coercion. Story, example, and the creation of possibilities continue to be part of what many women pass on to their children and grandchildren. Ann includes in her narrative a sketch of her grandmother as a storyteller.

> All day long she'd tell stories. . . . I was always close to her, so we'd sit down and she'd talk on and on and on, and we'd all look to sneak out for something to do, you know. Then we'd tiptoe back in, and

she'd just keep on talking. I think she sensed it as soon as we were not there, but she just keeps on talking. When we asked my grandfather to tell a story, we'd say, "Grampa, why don't you tell a story?" So he would start out, but she would take over, so he never says anything. He lets her take over. I wish I had just sat there and listened. I didn't. I don't know the stories. And she was real independent even though she was blind.

Almost every segment of Ann's story portrays some aspect of women's feelings of independence and their capacity to act decisively. In addition to her grandmother's example, Ann had the example of her aunts, one of whom assumed the role of community counselor. "She is constantly advising somebody, getting after them." Even though some people complained about the aunt's efforts to tell everyone else what to do, they also believed that her role was an important one and openly endorsed it on occasion. "When somebody dies, or there is a prayer meeting, they always choose somebody like big aunt who can get up and talk in front of a whole crowd. It doesn't bother her. Maybe that's why she goes around advising everybody."

The theme of independence that clearly moves in and out of Ann's narrative contradicts the commonly articulated descriptions of women's behavior as consistently subordinate to men and passive in nature. Ethnologists repeat the theme of subordination that they hear from male informants. James R. Walker noted that in the tipi, the man "was lord and his will was law governing all the inmates." Walker also mentions that "the animal instinct of preserving his female for his own use was strongly developed among the men of this people" (Walker, in press: "Oglala Sioux Indians"). Royal Hassrick (1964), perhaps more sensitive to the psychological dimensions of the relationship between the sexes, stresses the element of conflict that arose from men's attempts to subdue women. When we study the lives of specific women, though, we learn that women taught one another self-reliance, but they often encouraged men in the belief that men were, in Walker's terms, "lords of the tipi." One example of such unsanctioned but necessary independence among women occurs in Ann's narrative. She briefly mentions the destructive and unjust system of distribution of wages to Indian people during early reservation times. All money belonging to the Indian people was controlled by the Bureau of Indian Affairs superintendent, who required the people to come to him when they needed money for any expenditure. I asked Ann if women ever received the family money. Her answer was "No."

But then, after a significant pause, she added, "But my grandmother did." Women clearly did not and still do not often fit into passive roles of complete submission to men even though they often pay lip service to the importance of men's role as decision-makers. The description of women's roles that emerges from careful analysis of ceremonial and ritual literature comes much closer to the reality of women's experience than does the description that emerges from ethnographic statements based on men's comments.

Ann herself has consistently defined her own place in life. She decided, entirely on her own, to leave school when she was in the eleventh grade. A good student, she was offered opportunities to go to college, but she refused simply because the career options given her—teacher, nurse, social worker—did not appeal to her. Nor was she willing to accept marriage as an inevitable part of her life. She did marry, but in her narrative she pays little attention to the effect marriage had on her life.

> I had seen all kinds of married life that I didn't care for . . . , and I said that I'll never have that happen to me. I'll never have a bunch of children that I can't take care of. I had two, and of course I went to work at the Indian hospital. I stayed there for fifteen years. Then I resigned and came up here. I thought, "Oh my, what a beautiful city," but I was lonesome because I had never been away.

"Up here" is Lincoln, Nebraska, where Ann now lives and works. Lonesome or not, Ann quickly found work in Lincoln and kept on finding good jobs because she was determined to master the challenge of a new environment and because she enjoyed doing a job well. She had learned her grandmother's lesson. All work must be done as carefully as the worker constructs a beadwork design. One of Ann's jobs was working as a seamstress altering clothes at Lincoln's most exclusive department store. Working conditions were difficult. The women had to work in the basement with inadequate lighting, and they had to produce results that approached perfection. Nevertheless, Ann liked the work, for as she said, "I like to do good work. I like to do things just right, the way they should be done."

In Lincoln, Ann has worked with the Indian Center and with various educational institutions. In her way of approaching people's problems, there is immense sympathy but no sign of sentimentality. Often her sympathy is expressed through her humorous responses to potentially difficult situations. As a teacher in the state penitentiary and in the reformatory, she accomplishes more through her gentle and loving chiding of the men than most social workers can accomplish. Her capacity to use humor to steer people away from nonessentials is as much a part of her cultural heritage as her ability to speak Lakota.

Both in her own life and in her narration of that life's story, Ann always comes back to one essential pattern that makes life possible— the pattern of kinship, family relationships. That pattern is by its very nature fluid, requiring constant adjustments according to the demands of life. But the important thing is that it is a structure and that it keeps life's many and unpredictable demands from falling into hopeless disarray. Even little children have to learn that the life of the home and family have continuity that precedes the immediate generation. When Ann realized that her grandchildren needed her to give them this kind of personal security, she did not hestitate to give up her own work for a time to take care of them. She now lives with her daughter and gives them a day-to-day experience of the meaning of the extended family. Her sister occasionally lives with the family too and helps to care for the children. As Ann, her sister, and her daughter care for the children and plan for their education, it is clear that Ann is trying to do for her grandchildren what her grandmother did for her. If life has design, then it is woman's role to adjust parts of that design to assure continuity and to bring individuals into a fruitful relationship with continuing patterns. The Sioux woman assumes that life does have design and that the design is realized through the kinship pattern. She also assumes that she must actively shape that design; she must transform the materials of life so they fit into a productive pattern.

Many women, like Ann, even manage to transform the materials of their own lives into a story that shows the design of courage and independence. While Ann's story is long and includes episodes that give us a glimpse into past customs and events, it is as important for what is left out as for what is included. She leaves out most of the struggle and concentrates on the episodes that gave her strength to continue. Although she preferred that I question her occasionally, she knew that I wanted her to tell her story in whatever style she wanted. The result was a dramatization of how traditional attitudes can be a means of adapting to the present.

ANN KELLER'S LIFE HISTORY

Session One

I'll begin with my grandparents. I love my grandparents very much. They took over raising me and my sister when my mother died in 1918. My mother had died from influenza, so my grandparents insisted that they raise us. My father had already engaged a white couple in Valentine to take us and adopt us, and they in turn were to educate us, put us through college in exchange for Indian land; but my grandparents had objected to this very strongly, so my grandmother took care of us.

During that period my older sister spoke English. She wanted peaches, but it sounded like *pimiciciyaye*, meaning in Indian *bed* and *put me to bed*, so that's what she had done; but that wasn't what she wanted, so she cried and cried. So I guess we caused my grandmother some hardship, but later on my father had remarried and had married a woman who was a first cousin of my mother, and my older sister Phoebe Rose had gone to live with them, but I stayed with my grandparents. I guess they just couldn't tear me out of their arms.

So I stayed. And there was a law passed that children of age six were to be in school; but I didn't go to school until I was eight years old since I had been sick all the time. Now I come to realize my sickness was fright. The thought of going to school made me ill. So by the time I was eight, they took me to school. I went to school with long hair, moccasins. I don't know my dress, but I imagine it was long; and it was the first time I was among strangers, so you can see how frightened I was. When I was first in school, there was a law passed from Congress that applied to Indians, saying that the language will be English; so we were told not to talk Indian but English and to learn English. Anyone who was caught speaking Indian was punished, but it seems most of the time I was sick, so I was in the infirmary. There a nurse, a nun, Sister Bertrans—I came to love her, and another nun, Sister Assisia, was like a mother to me, a mother to most of the children of my age. Of course, the school I am speaking of was the St. Francis Indian Mission. It was run by the Franciscan nuns and Jesuit fathers. There I finally learned to speak English.

My childhood was a very, very happy one. When I was ten or

eleven, my grandmother said to my father, "Come and take your daughter and take care of her now. She is asking questions. 'Where will I go when you die, Grandmother?' " So they sent me back to my father and mother, whom I came to love also like a real mother. But it seems I had to see my grandparents every day or else I will die.

My father had worked in the fields. He had planted corn and everything a farmer does. So when he brings in his team of horses at the end of the day, I would say, "Papa, let's go and see Grampa." And he would say, "Sure, little girl, we will go." So we all piled into a wagon and went down the river. The river is the Little White River. My grandparents lived across the river. And that also gave my parents a chance to take a bath in the river after a hard day's work.

I don't remember my grandparents' ages, but it seems to my eyes that they were old until they died. They were a very hardworking people. Our main source of heat was wood which they gathered all summer and piled up. And when it was time to pick berries, my grandmother went to pick all types of berries—some chokeberries, buffalo berries, Juneberries, gooseberries, and cherries. Also when fall comes, the corn had to be fixed—dried corn, dried squash. Those were the days that I remember.

My parents never argued or said hard words. Maybe they do behind my back, but never in front of us.

When I was going to school (of course, I started school when I was eight on account of I was sick all the time), I came to find out maybe I was dying of lonesomeness for my grandparents.

[*Question: Did you like school?*]

Yes, I liked school. It was a boarding school, and at that time we didn't go home at any time. We didn't get out until the end of May or sometime in May, but our parents came to visit us on Thanksgiving. They camped out. They had campgrounds, and this was the only time we get to go home with them to the tent and stay with them until the next day.

[*Question: Do they camp at Christmastime too?*]

Yes, snow on the ground and all that, but what they do is shovel the snow away and put their tent up. Then after you get your fire and all that, your rugs down, it's nice and cozy. I can hear my father. He coughs quite a bit. We go to Midnight Mass. Everybody is Catholic. I hear him cough, and it makes me happy inside. You see, the visitors all go and receive communion first before all the students. So here goes my father. I always remember him. Brown suit. He only wears that on special occasions.

[*Question: What was his name?*]

Mark Kills Enemy.

So here we go, and my mother—of course, men and women don't sit together. Men have their special place and women over here. So here comes my mother, my grandmother, my aunts. They are all real holy. They go up like this. [Folds hands and bows head.]

Right away I begin to think about bean soup or corn or dried timpsila. Oh, it used to just make me drool to think about all those good foods that I'm going to eat, like fried bread and *wojapi*. Things that they don't serve at school, but I know that my mother will cook that. Dried meat.

[*Question: Didn't you see your parents until Midnight Mass?*]

No. We see them, but we can't go with them until after the Midnight Mass. Then they check us out, and we get to stay with them until five o'clock the next day.

[*Question: That's all, just one day?*]

That's all, but they all come to camp. Again that would be a meeting place of all the relatives, friends that they hadn't seen for months and months, you might say. The only time they all gathered together and met each other and visited each other in their tents.

I stayed in boarding school until the eleventh grade. It got better as the years went by. I think around 1936, 1935, they let you come home for a weekend. Then pretty soon the school put up a sort of addition, see, a sort of little sitting room where you could play cards or sew or whatever. They let you sit there, or if you want to smoke, you can. So that you won't go behind their backs. They restrict us from smoking, but most of us do it anyway, so they put up this recreation room. That is the only place you can smoke.

[*Question: What kinds of recreation did you have?*]

When I was little and first went to school, it seems to me that there was a piano somebody would play and they'd either dance or some would march to—I can't remember—Soosi, Soosa. They would play and give us some kind of little hats that you open up in all shapes. It has some kind of honeycomb so it doesn't go over your own head. It just perches up there. So a whole bunch of us would wear that. Then we'd march and play jacks. Some jump rope, or some just sit and talk, and some play school. All the schooling they get, and still on the outside they play school.

They were happy. Of course, we don't know the outside world, but we're happy with what we have—clothes or furniture. Of course, after the magazines show us, we know some things, but I only associated that with the rich people. I didn't know that everyone on the outside lived that way.

We wore the mission clothes. Those that could sew, the bigger ones, sewed for the younger ones. They made clothes different sizes so that when they come it would fit. The little ones got little clothes; the bigger ones, big and fat ones, got wide clothes. They gave us shoes to wear. Those that want to can buy their own shoes. They have a little storeroom that the nun comes and opens up in the afternoon. For some, their parents give them money. But see, it is put away so that you draw it out by buying something. I remember buying those all-day suckers. There were some square ones, suckers in all colors. I liked those. I would buy a bunch and pass them out to my friends. A dollar went a long ways. Those suckers were a penny, or two for a penny, in those days.

[*Question: Why did you leave in the eleventh grade?*]

Oh, you just think that this is enough. I had disagreements.

[*Question: What did you do after you left?*]

Oh, I stayed home. I didn't really do anything, but some of the officials from the agency were concerned, and they wanted to send me to school to become a social worker or a teacher or different things they were suggesting, but I never followed it up. I just didn't. If I had to live over again, I'd do a lot of things. I think for one that I'd come here when I am young and go to school or do something.

[*Question: When did you get married?*]

Oh, let's see. I was twenty-four. I had seen all kinds of married life that I didn't care for. My sister—her husband had run with other women. I had seen all that, and I said that I'll never have that happen to me. I'll never have a bunch of children that I can't take care of. I had two. And of course I went to work at the Indian Hospital. I stayed there for fifteen years. Then I resigned and came up here. I thought, "Oh my, what a beautiful city," but I was lonesome because I had never been away, and I was lonesome, so I went home every other weekend. Finally just once a month. Then after my mother died in 1964, I just stayed here for a long time. Then in 1970 or '71, I finally went home, and then for the big Indian powwows that they have.

Session Two

My father had two older sisters, and then next he was the youngest. There were three in that family. I have the name of the oldest one, in English. I have the second one's Indian name.

I can remember when we went berry-picking, my grandmother and I. She would take me home, and then she'd call out behind us. "Come, we're going home. Come back." Always that line. She'd call my spirit to come along home. She'd call every so often until we got home. But my legs still hurt, so she would go to the stove and take ashes and make a long line. Then she would cross it twice so it represents a dragonfly. Miraculously the pain is gone. So even to this day, every time I get a leg ache I do that and it goes away. Maybe it's because I believe it. A person has to believe in something before it works. Some go to church and some do things like this.

[*Question: Did you participate in Indian ceremonies?*]

Well, you might say no, because about the time that my mother was dying, my father was also dying. He had the flu. This is what my grandmother tells me. My father never talks about it, but he said he prayed "Let me live, and I'll become a Catholic." See, they were all Episcopals, I believe, so when my grandmother's only son became a Catholic (he didn't die) the whole family—aunts and everybody—became Catholic; so I was baptized again in the Catholic church, and we were converts. They're the best, I guess. They go to church every Sunday and all this and pray at mealtimes. But there was no Indian religion. It was all underground. If it flourished or if the authorities got wind of it, they— There is a law against that for the Indian, Indian religion. They finally let peyote in, but the other, it's just lately that they've let that come up. You couldn't practice it then. All kinds of missionaries came in to convert the Indians. And then most of them say, "Ah, it's the devil's work." Like the others and the Indian religion and the dancing.

They had powwows then. My grandmother danced. I guess that isn't a sin. It's just the other, the religious dancing.

My grandmother did beadwork too. This one John Anderson, the one that became famous for taking pictures. He bought all of my grandmother's beadwork. I think they have it in museums. I don't know what he did with it. I believe that there is some in the Rapid City museum. There is a big museum there. Her name was Julie Kills Enemy. How she got that name I don't know. Maybe she was baptized that and she just kept that. She was quite an artist. She made moccasins like nothing, beaded or everyday moccasins or the kind you wear when you go out. You put your best on. She did everything, but for some reason I never did learn, as close as I was to her. She just sort of let you make up your own mind.

It is just lately that I dance. I remember my two aunts. Oh, they dance quite a bit. But one, she just barely gets around, but when they say "dance," why she's there dancing. The oldest one. They always joked about her. She just barely went over the hill, but the minute she was out of sight, she'd walk real fast.

My little aunt, one was Big Aunt, the oldest one, and the other, Little Aunt. That was how we distinguished them instead of calling them by name. The second one is the one everybody loves; everybody loves her. The other one's a counselor. She is constantly advising somebody, getting after them, so that's how come we don't like her. But this one here, the oldest one, talks some English, but the middle one won't, never did speak English. After she got older, she lived at my house with me. One day she cleaned out the cupboard under the kitchen sink, so she had something to show to me when I came home from work. "Look," she said. She was proud of herself because she had done something for me. So then we laughed and laughed. I said, "You said, 'Look,' " I said. Then she said she didn't. It was the first time she used English, and she claimed she didn't. Maybe I just took it that way.

Indian women were sort of backwards. Their way is that they want to be in the background. When somebody dies, or there is a prayer meeting, they always choose somebody like Big Aunt who can get up and talk in front of a whole crowd. It doesn't bother her. Maybe that is why she goes around advising everybody.

And my grandmother used to tell me Indian men (I imagine this was when she was little), Indian men, they comb their wives' hair in the morning. And I think she in turn combs his hair. There was this couple, and I guess she was unfaithful to him, so he bent over to kiss her after he got her hair all combed, and he bit her nose off. He kept her until he died. I guess nobody would look at her, see. She was ugly.

[*Question: What other kinds of things did your grandmother tell you about women?*]

Oh yes, she'd tell stories. All day long she'd tell stories. Like I say, once she couldn't live alone, she went to my father and mother, so we got to be close to her. I was always close to her, so we'd sit down and she'd talk on and on and on, and we'd all look to sneak out for something to do, you know. Then we'd tiptoe back in, and she'd keep on talking. I think she sensed it as soon as we were not there, but she just keeps on talking. When we asked my grandfather to tell a story, we'd say, "Grampa, why don't you tell a story?" So he would start out, but she would take over, so he never says anything. He lets her take over. I wish I had just sat there and listened. I didn't. I don't know the stories. And she was real independent even though she was blind. There's a rope fixed for her like a railing out to the outhouse, and she goes where she has to go, and she comes back real slow so that she'll have that fresh air. She has a cane. Sometimes she wanders away. I let her go. Then pretty soon I'd say, "Grandma, let's go home now." She'd agree. I grab her hand then. I guess her disagreement or whatever it is, she feels she lost it by walking.

Oh, there was no laziness about her. She did everything. She did all the berry-picking. She'd say, "Well, this is ripe now." So I would go. (I was a little girl, I might be three years old, five years old, six, in there.) First we'd have— Oh, what do you call them? A canning kettle. Well, that's what she'd take and fill that up with berries, and then she'd pack it on her back. Here I am going along, crying because my legs hurt. So she'd perch me, and carry me on her back along with her berries, and we'd go home. But all the while, when we'd start home, she'd call me by name. In Indian she'd call, "We're going home now. Come, we're going home." That way she says my spirit comes back. We might leave the spirit back there and take me home; then I'd be sick and all that. She calls me, so all of me comes home.

My father was a farmer. Once the BIA [Bureau of Indian Affairs] superintendent came and told us there was money in the bank, that we can use it. It was our own money. When we want money, we've got to put in for a purchase order. They fill it out for you, and you have got to take it to the store. No money involved. They just take and buy your food and whatever it is you want. There's a bank there, a government bank, I guess, and they keep the money there. Requests, cash requests, that's the way you get money. And so you go to the store, and they charge you ten cents to cash the check. And you sign it, and of course, if you want to spend it there or take all the cash, well, that's up to you.

[*Question: Did women go to get a cash request?*]

No. [*Pause.*] But my grandmother did. Of course women can, I guess, but almost always the man of the house goes. Once a month they release money to different ones that do have money. Some don't, but some do, from land sales or lease sales. Oh, they give you just so much. They drag it out. So we have some kind of money anyway. They released the money to my father, and they got the carpenter to come and look our place over, and they come and fix it up. Of course, it was a log house, so by the time they got through, it was that wide— stucco on the outside. So we had a nice house to live in. They put floors in.

[*Comment: I bet your stepmother liked that.*]

Oh, she loved it, but I really didn't consider her my stepmother. My father didn't like that word, so we just called her mother. Oh, she was a real good woman. She wasn't aggressive either. She was sort of— Of course, Indians are not aggressive. They take things in stride.

[*Question: What was your wedding like?*]

Well, you can have a church wedding if you want to, or you can go to the justice of peace. That was in my time. I don't know about my parents' wedding. I don't know how they got married. They didn't have showers and all that in those days. I never like big deals. I'd rather be married by the justice of the peace. Then the couple comes home, and the parents are squabbling and getting after them, but they are married already. They want to give a big church wedding, but the couple doesn't want it, so they elope. In the Indian way you choose each other and have a little ceremony with some Indian food, and sing, and dance, whatever. No papers signed or anything. It is just mutual agreement, I guess. And they stay with each other until they die. Of course, there are some that leave each other. It isn't really legal, I guess, in the white man's eyes, but it is to the couple. Maybe that is why it worked so well. Now everybody, the minute they get married, they are fighting and divorcing.

Session Three

I'll just tell you about the Indian Center here in Lincoln. Of course, somebody had told my daughter Barbara to go up there. And here they hired her as a secretary, and so I used to go up once in a while whenever I had free time. It was at Ninth and O Street, right above Maria's, so I used to go up there during my lunch hour. The ladies sold lunch usually on Thursday, and soon they sold it quite cheap. They sold meat and corn soup—the usual—fry bread, fried potatoes, all that. And for a while there I was on the board, but there wasn't too many there at all.

[*Question: Are there other women on the board?*]

Yes, about four.

It seems like we would get a million dollars to start a new Indian Center. Next week they're going to Denver. I'm real excited. They have the alcoholic program and of course the Indian Center itself, and they are trying to develop other programs like recreation and education programs. They had a breakfast program for the children, but they took it away because they said it was duplicating. The school serves them breakfast, you know. Indian children are very shy, and they wouldn't eat at school, but they did at the Indian Center because they are among their own people. But again I don't see that. They want to learn to live in a city. They have to learn to do like the rest. That's the way I see it.

[*Question: What were some of the jobs you had here in Lincoln?*]

When I came here to Lincoln, I was scared, but I wanted to go to work. I worked at the laundry for a while. Then I got a job at [an exclusive store], sewing. We worked down in the basement there. We have to match the colors of the threads just right. The light wasn't too good there, so it was hard to see. But I liked it. I like to do good work. I like to do things just right, the way they should be done.

I cleaned for First Methodist Church for a while too. I liked that. The people were real nice to me. I've learned a lot of real valuable lessons from this group. I like to get out and meet people.

NOTES

1. The Brule Sioux are one band of the western Sioux. Since they speak the L dialect of the language, they are also called Lakota to distinguish them from N and

D speakers called sometimes the Nakota and Dakota. Sometimes people refer to the entire Sioux tribe as the Dakota, although the general method is to use the term "Sioux" to refer to the whole tribe. The various groups have reservations in North and South Dakota, in Nebraska, and in Montana.

2. The Rosebud Sioux Reservation, home of the Brule Sioux, was established on February 27, 1877, and the Rosebud Agency was established the following year. During this period the Brule Sioux under Chief Spotted Tail were moved to Rosebud. (See Hamilton, Hamilton, and Anderson 1971.)

3. James R. Walker has recorded one interesting incident that illustrates women's perceptions of their art. He noted that in doing beadwork Lakota women first mixed together all the various colors of beads to be used in a design, picking out each bead individually as it was to be used. He asked their reasons for this apparently impractical usage. They answered that it was "because glass beads are made by white men who do not know how to control their potencies, and by mixing the beads their potencies are equalized so that no bead may have the power to overcome other beads, and the potency of the design will not be disturbed." (See Walker, 1982: 107.)

4. Powell (1977) also speaks of the importance of beadworkers' societies among the Lakota Sioux.

REFERENCES

Abrahams, Roger D. 1976. Comments at Sex Roles and Fieldwork panel, annual meeting of the American Folklore Society, New Orleans.

———. 1978. "American Sense of Community: Circling the Square or Hitting the Road." *Festival of American Folklife Program Book, 1978*, pp. 5–6.

Alvirez, David, and Bean, Frank D. 1976. "The Mexican American Family." In *Ethnic Families in America: Patterns and Variations*, ed. Charles H. Mindel and Robert W. Habenstein, pp. 271–292. New York: Elsevier.

Anonymous. 1908. *The Mrs. Gunness Mystery: A Thrilling Tale of Love, Duplicity, and Crime*. Chicago: Thompson and Thomas.

———. 1974. "Newsmakers." *Newsweek*, November 11, p. 72.

Ardener, Edwin. 1972. "Belief and the Problem of Women." In *The Interpretation of Ritual: Essays in Honour of A. I. Richards*, ed. J. S. La Fontaine, pp. 135–158. London: Tavistock.

Arreola, Juan José. 1964. *Confabulario and Other Inventions*, trans. George D. Schade. Austin: University of Texas Press.

Babcock, Barbara A. 1978a. "Introduction." In *The Reversible World: Symbolic Inversion in Art and Society*, ed. Barbara A. Babcock, pp. 13–36. Ithaca, N.Y.: Cornell University Press.

———. 1978b. " 'Liberty's a Whore': Inversions, Marginalia, and Picaresque Narrative." In *The Reversible World: Symbolic Inversion in Art and Society*, ed. Barbara A. Babcock, pp. 95–116. Ithaca, N.Y.: Cornell University Press.

Balassa, Iván. 1963. *Karcsai mondák*. Budapest: Akadémiai Kiadó.

Baldwin, Karen. 1976. "Rhyming Pieces and Piecin' Rhymes: Verse and Family Poem-Making." *Southern Folklore Quarterly* 40:209–238.

Bausinger, Hermann. 1958. "Strukturen des alltäglichen Erzählens." *Fabula* 1:239–254.

———. 1968. *Formen der "Volkspoesie."* Berlin: E. Schmidt.

———. 1975. "Alltägliches Erzählen." In *Enzyklopädie des Märchens*, ed. Kurt Ranke, 1:323–330. Berlin: Walter de Gruyter.

Beauvoir, Simone de. 1953. *The Second Sex*, trans. H. M. Parshley. New York: Knopf.

Beede, Aaron McGaffey. N.d. Unpublished manuscript. Chicago: Newberry Library.

Bernard, Jessie. 1971. *Women and the Public Interest*. Chicago: Aldine.

Berne, Eric. 1973. *What Do You Say After You Say Hello? The Psychology of Human Destiny*. New York: Bantam.

Berze Nagy, János. 1957. *Magyar népmesetipusok*. 2 vols. Pécs: Baranya Megye Tanácsának Kiadása.

Bettelheim, Bruno. 1976. *The Uses of Enchantment: The Meaning and Importance of Fairy Tales*. New York: Knopf.

Boatright, Mody C. 1958. "The Family Saga as a Form of Folklore." In *The Family Saga and Other Phases of American Folklore*, pp. 1–19. Urbana: University of Illinois Press.

Bourke, John G. 1894. "Popular Medicine, Customs, and Superstitions of the Rio Grande." *Journal of American Folklore* 7:119–146.

Brandes, Stanley. 1975. "Family Misfortune Stories in American Folklore." *Journal of the Folklore Institute* 12:5–17.

Brown, Joseph E., ed. 1971. *The Sacred Pipe: Black Elk's Account of the Seven Rites of the Oglala Sioux*. Baltimore: Penguin.

Brunvand, Jan H. 1968. *The Study of American Folklore*. New York: W. W. Norton.

Bullough, Vern L., and Bullough, Bonnie. 1973. *The Subordinate Sex: A History of Attitudes Toward Women*. Urbana: University of Illinois Press.

Cardozo-Freeman, Inez. 1978. "Serpent Fears and Religious Motifs Among Mexican Women." *Frontiers* 3:10–13.

Cole, Arthur Harrison. 1932. "The Rise of the Factory in the American Carpet Manufacture." In *Facts and Factors in Economic History: Articles by Former Students of Edwin Francis Gay*, pp. 380–401. Cambridge, Mass.: Harvard University Press.

Cooper, Susan. 1975. Review of *Womenfolk and Fairytales*, by Rosemary Minard. *New York Times Book Review* April 13, p. 8.

Cutting-Baker, Holly; Gross, Sandra; Kotkin, Amy; and Zeitlin, Steven. 1976. *Family Folklore*. Washington, D.C.: Smithsonian Institution and the National Park Service.

Dégh, Linda. 1966. "Approaches to Folklore Research Among Immigrant Groups." *Journal of American Folklore* 79:551–556.

——— . 1969. *Folktales and Society: Story-Telling in a Hungarian Peasant Community*, trans. Emily M. Schossberger. Bloomington: Indiana University Press.

De La Torre, Lillian. 1954. "The Coffee Cup." In *Butcher, Baker, Murder Maker: Stories by Members of the Mystery Writers of America*, pp. 60–81. New York: Borzoi Books.

——— . 1955. *The Truth About Belle Gunness*. New York: Fawcett.

Delgado, Sylvia. 1971. "Young Chicana Speaks upon Problems Faced by Young Girls." *Regeneración* 1:5–7.

Deloria, Ella. N.d. "Dakota Autobiographies." Unpublished manuscript. Philadelphia: American Philosophical Society Archives.

——— . 1944. *Speaking of Indians*. New York: Friendship Press.

Dixon, Elizabeth, and Mink, James V., eds. 1967. *Oral History at Arrowhead: Proceedings of the First National Colloquium on Oral History*. Los Angeles: Oral History Association.

Dobie, J. Frank. 1935. *Tongues of the Monte*. Garden City, N.Y.: Doubleday.

Dobos, Ilona. 1964. "Az 'igaz' történetek müfajának kérdéséröl." *Ethnographia* 75:198–217.

Dorson, Richard M. 1964. *Buying the Wind: Regional Folklore in the United States*. Chicago: University of Chicago Press.

——— . 1967. *American Negro Folktales*. Greenwich, Conn.: Fawcett.

Dundes, Alan, ed. 1982. *Cinderella: A Folklore Casebook*. New York: Garland Press.

Eastman, Max. 1936. *Enjoyment of Laughter*. New York: Simon and Schuster.

Ehrenreich, Barbara, and English, Deirdre. 1973. *Complaints and Disorders: The Sexual Politics of Sickness*. Glass Mountain Pamphlet, No. 2. Old Westbury, N.Y.: Feminist Press.

Eliade, Mircea. 1969. *Images and Symbols*. New York: Sheed and Ward.

Farrer, Claire R. 1975a. "Introduction: Women and Folklore, Images and Genres." *Journal of American Folklore* 88:v–xv.

——— , ed. 1975b. *Women and Folklore*. Austin: University of Texas Press.

Fernandez, James W. 1974. "The Mission of Metaphor in Expressive Culture." *Current Anthropology* 15:119–45.

Fiedler, Leslie A. 1966. *Love and Death in the American Novel*. New York: Dell.

Fishman, Joshua A. 1966. *Hungarian Language Maintenance in the United States*. Bloomington: Indiana University Press.

Flores, Francisca. 1971. "Conference of Mexican Women." *Regeneración* 1:1–4.

Franz, Marie-Louise von. 1972. *Problems of the Feminine in Fairytales*. New York: Spring Publications.

Freud, Sigmund. 1963. *Jokes and Their Relation to the Unconscious*, trans. James Strachey. New York: Norton.

Gardner, Richard A. 1974. *Dr. Gardner's Fairy Tales for Today's Children*. Englewood Cliffs, N.J.: Prentice-Hall.

Garrett, Kim. 1961. "Family Stories and Sayings." *Publications of the Texas Folklore Society* 30:273–281.

Georges, Robert. 1969. "Toward an Understanding of Storytelling Events." *Journal of American Folklore* 82:313–328.

Girardot, N. J. 1977. "Initiation and Meaning in the Tale of Snow White and the Seven Dwarfs." *Journal of American Folklore* 90:273–300.

———. 1979. "Response to Jones: 'Scholarship Is Never Just the Sum of All Its Variants.' " *Journal of American Folklore* 92:73–76.

Glassie, Henry. 1967. "William Houck: Maker of Pounded Ash Adirondack Pack-Baskets." *Keystone Folklore Quarterly* 12:23–54.

———. 1968. *Pattern in the Material Folk Culture of the Eastern United States*. Philadelphia: University of Pennsylvania Press.

———. 1974. "Structure, Function, Folklore, and the Artifact." *Semiotica* 7:313–351.

Goffman, Erving. 1959. *The Presentation of Self in Everyday Life*. Garden City, N.Y.: Doubleday.

———. 1967. *Interaction Ritual*. New York: Doubleday.

Goldstein, Kenneth. 1964. *A Guide for Field Workers in Folklore*. Hatboro, Pa.: Folklore Associates.

Gottschalk, Louis; Kluckhohn, Clyde; and Angell, Robert. 1945. *The Use of Personal Documents in History, Anthropology, and Sociology*. New York: Social Science Research Council.

Grebler, Leo; Moore, Joan W.; and Guzman, Ralph C. 1970. *The Mexican-American People, the Nation's Second Largest Minority*. New York: Free Press.

Green, Rayna D. 1977. "Magnolias Grow in Dirt: The Bawdy Lore of Southern Women." *Southern Exposure* 4:29–33.

Grimm, Jacob, and Grimm, Wilhelm. 1974. *The Complete Grimm's* [sic] *Fairy Tales*, trans. Margaret Hunt and James Stern, intro. Padraic Colum, folkloristic commentary Joseph Campbell. New York: Pantheon.

Hamilton, Henry W.; Hamilton, Jean Tyree; and Anderson, John. 1971. *The Sioux of the Rosebud: A History in Pictures*. Norman: University of Oklahoma Press.

Handlin, Oscar. 1951. *The Uprooted: The Epic Story of the Great Migrations That Made the American People*. Boston: Little, Brown.

———. 1959. *Immigration as a Factor in American History*. Englewood Cliffs, N.J.: Prentice-Hall.

Hartman, Mary S. 1978. *Victorian Murderesses: A True History of Thirteen Respectable French and English Women Accused of Unspeakable Crimes*. New York: Schocken.

Hassrick, Royal. 1964. *The Sioux*. Norman: University of Oklahoma Press.

Hawes, Bess Lomax. 1968. "La Llorona in Juvenile Hall." *Western Folklore* 27:153–170.

Heuscher, Julius E. 1974. *A Psychiatric Study of Myths and Fairy Tales: Their*

Origin, Meaning, and Usefulness, 2d ed. Springfield, Ill.: Charles C. Thomas.

Holbrook, Stewart H. 1941. *Murder Out Yonder: An Informal Study of Certain Classic Crimes in Back-Country America*. New York: Macmillan.

Holstein, Jonathan. 1972. *American Pieced Quilts*. New York: Viking Press.

———. 1973. *The Pieced Quilt: An American Design Tradition*. Greenwich, Conn.: New York Graphic Society.

Horney, Karen. 1967. *Feminine Psychology*. New York: W. W. Norton.

Hough, Emerson. 1920. "Round Our Town." *Saturday Evening Post* February 14, pp. 18–19.

Hughes, Robert. 1979. "The Old Lady of Eagle Bridge." *Time* April 2, p. 94.

Hummel, Charles F. 1976. "Floor Coverings Used in Eighteenth-Century America." In *Imported and Domestic Textiles in Eighteenth-Century America*, ed. Patricia L. Fiske, pp. 61–92. Washington, D.C.: Textile Museum.

Ice, Joyce, and Shulimson, Judith A. 1979. "Beyond the Domestic: Women's Traditional Arts and the Creation of Community." *Southwest Folklore* 3:37–44.

Jason, Heda. 1977. "A Model for Narrative Structure in Oral Literature." In *Patterns in Oral Literature*, ed. Heda Jason and Dimitri Segal, pp. 99–139. The Hague: Mouton.

Johnson, Robbie Davis. 1973. "Folklore and Women: A Social Interactional Analysis of the Folklore of a Texas Madam." *Journal of American Folklore* 86:211–224.

Jones, Michael Owen. 1967. "The Study of Traditional Furniture: Review and Preview." *Keystone Folklore Quarterly* 12:233–245.

———. 1968. "Two Directions for Folklorists in the Study of American Art." *Southern Folklore Quarterly* 32:249–259.

———. 1971. "The Concept of 'Aesthetic' in the Traditional Arts." *Western Folklore* 30:77–104.

———. 1975. *The Hand Made Object and Its Maker*. Berkeley: University of California Press.

Jones, Steven. 1979. "The Pitfalls of Snow White Scholarship." *Journal of American Folklore* 92:69–73.

Jordan de Caro, Rosan. 1973. "A Note About Folklore and Literature (The Bosom Serpent Revisited)." *Journal of American Folklore* 86:62–65.

Kalčik, Susan J. 1975. " ' . . . like Ann's gynecologist or the time I was almost raped': Personal Narratives in Women's Rap Groups." *Journal of American Folklore* 88:3–11.

Kavablum, Lea. 1973. *Cinderella: Radical Feminist, Alchemist*. Guttenberg, N.J.: The author.

Kearney, Michael. 1969. "La Llorona as a Social Symbol." *Western Folklore* 28:199–206.

Kiefer, Monica. 1948. *American Children Through Their Books, 1700–1835*. Philadelphia: University of Pennsylvania Press.

Kiev, Ari. 1968. *Curanderismo: Mexican-American Folk Psychiatry*. New York: Free Press.

Kinsey, Alfred C., et al. 1965. *Sexual Behavior in the Human Female*. New York: Pocket Books.

Kirtley, Bacil F. 1960. "La Llorona and Related Themes." *Western Folklore* 19:155–168.

Knabe, Erika. 1977. *Frauenemanzipation in Afganistan*. Afganische Studien, No. 16. Meisenheim am Glan: Anton Hain.

Kotkin, Amy J., and Cutting-Baker, Holly. 1977. "Model Course Outline: Family Folklore." Baltimore: Maryland Arts Council Folklife Program.

Kovács, Ágnes, and Maróti, Lajosné. 1966. *A rátótiádák tipusmutatója: A magyar falucsufolók tipusai*. Budapest: Neprajzi Muzeum.

Langlois, Janet Louise. 1977. "Belle Gunness, The Lady Bluebeard: Community Legend as Metaphor." Ph.D. dissertation, Indiana University.

———. 1978. "Belle Gunness, the Lady Bluebeard: Community Legend as Metaphor." *Journal of the Folklore Institute* 15:147–160.

Langness, L. L. 1965. *The Life History in Anthropological Science*. New York: Holt, Rinehart, and Winston.

Leach, Edmund R. 1964. "Anthropological Aspects of Language: Animal Categories and Verbal Abuse." In *New Directions in the Study of Language*, ed. Eric H. Lenneberg, pp. 23–63. Cambridge: M.I.T. Press.

Leddy, Betty. 1948. "La Llorona in Southern Arizona." *Western Folklore* 7:272–277.

———. 1950. "La Llorona Again." *Western Folklore* 9:363–365.

Legman, Gershon. 1964. *The Horn Book: Studies in Erotic Folklore and Bibliography*. New Hyde Park, N.Y.: University Books.

———. 1968. *Rationale of the Dirty Joke: An Analysis of Sexual Humor*. New York: Grove Press.

———. 1975. *No Laughing Matter: Rationale of the Dirty Joke: 2nd Series*. New York: Breaking Point.

Lengyel, Emil. 1948. *Americans from Hungary*. Philadelphia: Lippincott.

Lieberman, Marcia R. 1972. " 'Some Day My Prince Will Come': Female Acculturation Through the Fairy Tale." *College English* 34:383–395.

Little, Nina Fletcher. 1967. *Floor Coverings in New England Before 1850*. Sturbridge, Mass.: Old Sturbridge Village.

———. 1975. *Country Arts in Early American Homes*. New York: E. P. Dutton.

Lurie, Alison. 1970. "Fairy Tale Liberation." *New York Review of Books* December 17, pp. 42–44.

———. 1971. "Witches and Fairies: Fitzgerald to Updike." *New York Review of Books* December 2, pp. 6, 8–11.

Lüthi, Max. 1970. *Once Upon a Time: On the Nature of Fairy Tales*, trans. Lee Chadeayne and Paul Gottwald. Bloomington and London: Indiana University Press.

Mainardi, Patricia. 1973a. "Quilts: A Great American Art." *Ms*. December, pp. 58–62.

———— . 1973b. "Quilts: The Great American Art." *Feminist Art Journal* 2:18–23.

Martin, Wendy. 1971. "Seduced and Abandoned in the New World." In *Woman in Sexist Society: Studies in Power and Powerlessness,* ed. Vivian Gornick and Barbara Moran, pp. 329–346. New York: New American Library.

Mason, Isaac, trans. 1921. *The Arabian Prophet.* Shanghai: Commercial Press.

Massé, Henri. 1954. *Persian Beliefs and Customs,* trans. Charles A. Messner. New Haven: Human Relations Area Files.

Meadow, Kathryn P. 1977. "Name Signs as Identity Symbols in the Deaf Community." *Sign Language Studies* 16:237–245.

Mendoza, Vicente T., and Mendoza, Virginia R. R. de. 1952. *Folklore de San Pedro Piedra Gorda, Zacatecas.* Mexico: Secretaría de Educación Pública.

Miller, Elaine K., ed. 1973. *Mexican Folk Narrative from the Los Angeles Area.* American Folklore Society Memoirs, No. 56. Austin: University of Texas Press.

Minard, Rosemary, ed. 1975. *Womenfolk and Fairy Tales.* Boston: Houghton Mifflin.

Mitchell, Carol A. 1976. "The Difference Between Male and Female Joke Telling as Exemplified in a College Community." 2 vols. Ph.D. dissertation, Indiana University.

———— . 1977. "The Sexual Perspective in the Appreciation and Interpretation of Jokes." *Western Folklore* 26:303–329.

Mitchell, Lucy Sprague. 1948. *Here and Now Story Book.* New York: Dutton.

Moore, Joan W. 1967. *Mexican-Americans: Problems and Prospects.* Madison: University of Wisconsin Institute for Research on Poverty.

Moore, Powell A. 1959. *The Calumet Region: Indiana's Last Frontier.* Indianapolis: Indiana Historical Bureau.

Morgan, Kathryn L. 1973. "Caddy Buffers: Legends of a Middle Class Negro Family in Philadelphia." In *Mother Wit from the Laughing Barrel: Readings in the Interpretation of Afro-American Folklore,* ed. Alan Dundes, pp. 595–610. Englewood Cliffs, N.J.: Prentice-Hall.

Mukarovsky, Jan. 1970. *Aesthetic Function, Norm, and Value as Social Facts.* Ann Arbor: University of Michigan Press.

Murphy, Yolanda, and Murphy, Robert F. 1974. *Women of the Forest.* New York: Columbia University Press.

Neumann, Siegfried. 1967. "Arbeitserinnerungen als Erzählinhalt." In *Arbeit und Volksleben: Deutscher Volkskundekongress 1965 in Marburg,* pp. 274–284. Göttingen: Otto Schwartz.

Nie, Norman H. 1975. *Statistical Package for the Social Sciences.* 2d ed. New York: McGraw-Hill.

Niehardt, John. 1961. *Black Elk Speaks.* Lincoln: University of Nebraska Press.

Olch, Peter D., and Pogue, Forrest C., eds. 1972. *Selections from the Fifth and Sixth National Colloquia on Oral History*. New York: Oral History Association.

Park, Robert E. 1950. *Race and Culture*, ed. E. C. Hughes et al. Glencoe, Ill.: Free Press.

Partridge, Virginia P. 1976. "Techniques Found in Eighteenth-Century Floor Coverings in America." In *Imported and Domestic Textiles in Eighteenth-Century America*, ed. Patricia L. Fiske, pp. 96–102. Washington, D.C.: Textile Museum.

Peacock, James L. 1969. "Society as Narrative." In *Forms of Symbolic Action: Proceedings of the 1969 Annual Spring Meeting*, ed. Robert F. Spencer, pp. 167–177. Seattle: University of Washington Press for the American Ethnological Society.

Perez, Soledad. 1951. "Mexican Folklore from Austin, Texas." *Publications of the Texas Folklore Society* 24:71–127.

Poe, Harold W. 1963. "Gnista." Unpublished play script.

Powell, Peter J. 1977. "Beauty for New Life: An Introduction to Cheyenne and Lakota Sacred Art." In *The Native American Heritage: A Survey of North American Indian Art*, ed. Evan Maurer, pp. 33–56. Chicago: Art Institute.

Princiotto, Peter. N.d. "Oral Life History of an Italian-American Grandmother." Unpublished semester paper (78-8): Northern Virginia Folklore Center, George Mason University.

Randolph, Vance. 1958. *Sticks in the Knapsack and Other Ozark Folk Tales*. New York: Columbia University Press.

———. 1976. *Pissing in the Snow and Other Ozark Folktales*, introduction, Rayna Green, annotations by Frank Hoffmann. Urbana: University of Illinois Press.

Rendon, Armando B. 1973. "Chicano Culture in a Gabacho World." In *Introduction to Chicano Studies: A Reader*, ed. Livie Isauro Duran and H. Russell Bernard, pp. 350–362. New York: Macmillan.

Riddle, Almeda. 1970. *A Singer and Her Songs: Almeda Riddle's Book of Ballads*, ed. Roger D. Abrahams, music edited by George Foss. Baton Rouge: Louisiana State University Press.

Rincón, Bernice. 1971. "La Chicana: Her Role in the Past and Her Search for a New Role in the Future." *Regeneración* 1:15–18.

Ritchie, Jean. 1955. *Singing Family of the Cumberlands*. New York: Oxford University Press.

Roach, Susan, and Weidlich, Lorre. 1974. "Quilt Making in America: A Selected Bibliography." *Folklore Feminists Communication* 3:17–28.

Roberts, Leonard. 1974. *Sang Branch Settlers: Folksongs and Tales of a Kentucky Mountain Family*. American Folklore Society Memoirs, No. 61. Austin: University of Texas Press.

Rogers, Kathrine M. 1966. *The Troublesome Helpmate: A History of Misogyny in Literature*. Seattle: University of Washington Press.

Rosaldo, Michelle Zimbalist, and Lamphere, Louise, eds. 1974. *Women, Culture, and Society*. Stanford: Stanford University Press.

Rosenberg, Tobias. 1946. *La serpiente en la medicina y en el folklore*. Buenos Aires: Tridente.

Roth, Rodris. 1967. *Floor Coverings in Eighteenth Century America*. Washington, D.C.: Smithsonian Press.

Rowe, Karen. N.d. "Cinderella Meets Gulliver: Jane Eyre's Education in Romance." Unpublished paper.

Santamaría, Francisco J. 1959. *Diccionario de mejicanismos*. Mexico: Editorial Porrua.

Santino, Jack. 1979. "Women Heroes and the Heroes of Women." Unpublished paper.

Senour, Maria Nieto. 1977. "Psychology of the Chicana." In *Chicano Psychology*, ed. Joe L. Martinez, Jr., pp. 329–342. New York: Academic Press.

Sexton, Anne. 1971. *Transformations*. Boston: Houghton Mifflin.

Sherzer, Dina, and Sherzer, Joel. 1976a. "Mormaknamaloe: The Cuna Mola." In *Ritual and Symbol in Native Central America*, ed. P. Young and J. Howe, pp. 21–42. University of Oregon Anthropological Papers, No. 9. Eugene: University of Oregon.

——— . 1976b. "Towards a Semiotic Analysis of Cuna Molas." *Punto de Contacto* 1:4–13.

Sims, Barbara. 1974. " 'She's Got to Be a Saint, Lord Knows I Ain't': Feminine Masochism in Country Music." *Journal of Country Music* 5:17–23.

Spiller, Harley. 1979. "Cinderella in the Schools." Unpublished paper.

Stone, Elizabeth. N.d. "Frolicks of a Distempered Mind: Early Publication of Fairy Tales in England and America." Unpublished paper.

Stone, Kay. 1975. "Things Walt Disney Never Told Us." *Journal of American Folklore* 88:42–50.

Strecker, John K. 1926. "Reptiles of the South and Southwest in Folk-Lore." *Publications of the Texas Folklore Society* 5:56–69.

Sullerot, Evelyne. 1971. *Woman, Society, and Change*. New York: McGraw-Hill.

Sutton-Smith, Brian. 1978. "Stories of Little Girls." Unpublished paper.

Thompson, Stith. 1946. *The Folktale*. New York: Dryden Press.

Toor, Frances. 1947. *A Treasury of Mexican Folkways*. New York: Crown.

Vlach, John. 1973a. "The Fabrication of a Traditional Fire Tool." *Journal of American Folklore* 86:54–57.

——— . 1973b. *Philip Simmons: Afro-American Blacksmith*. Folklore Preprint Series, 1, no. 2. Bloomington: Folklore Publications Group.

Walker, James R. N.d. "Arts of the Sioux Indians." Unpublished manuscript. Denver: Colorado State University Archives.

——— . 1980. *Lakota Belief and Ritual*, ed. Elaine Jahner and Raymond J. DeMallie. Lincoln: University of Nebraska Press.

——— . 1982. *Lakota Society*, ed. Raymond J. DeMallie. Lincoln: University of Nebraska Press.

——— . 1983. *Lakota Myth*, ed. Elaine A. Jahner. Lincoln: University of Nebraska Press.

Warner, Marina. 1976. *Alone of All Her Sex: The Myth of the Cult of the Virgin Mary*. New York: Knopf.

Weigle, Marta. 1978. "Women as Verbal Artists: Reclaiming the Daughters of Enheduanna." *Frontiers* 3:1–9.

Wilgus, D. K. 1970. "Country-Western Music and the Urban Hillbilly." *Journal of American Folklore* 83:157–179.

Willems, Emilio. 1955. "On the Concept of Assimilation." *American Anthropologist* 57:225–226.

Wissler, Clark. 1904. *Decorative Art of the Sioux Indians*. Bulletin of the American Museum of Natural History, no. 18, part 3. New York: American Museum of Natural History.

Wooldridge, Clifton. 1908. *Twenty Years a Detective in the Wickedest City in the World*. Chicago: The author.

Zeitlin, Steven J.; Kotkin, Amy J.; and Cutting-Baker, Holly. 1982. *A Celebration of American Folklore*. New York: Pantheon Books.

CONTRIBUTORS

Karen Baldwin is Associate Professor of English and Director of the East Carolina University Folklore Archive, Greenville, North Carolina.

Linda Dégh is Distinguished Professor of Folklore and Chair of the Folklore Institute of Indiana University, Bloomington. She earned her Ph.D. at the Eötvös Loránd University in Budapest, where she was associate professor until she came to Indiana. Her book, *Folktales and Society*, earned the International Pitré Prize in 1969. Specializing in folk narrative study, and in the folktale and the legend in particular, she has been conducting research in rural and urban communities in Europe and North America among different ethnic cultural groups. She is the author of 12 books and about 150 essays.

Elaine A. Jahner is Professor of English and Native American Studies at Dartmouth College. She has edited *Lakota Myth* and coedited with Raymond J. DeMallie *Lakota Belief and Ritual*. She is the author of numerous scholarly articles.

Geraldine N. Johnson is a Training Coordinator for the United Planning Organization, a community action agency in Washington, D.C. She is the author of many articles on woven rag rugs.

Rosan A. Jordan is Associate Professor at Louisiana State University, where she teaches courses in folklore and English.

Susan Kalčik is Research Coordinator of the Smithsonian Institution's Development Office and Chairperson of the Smithsonian Institution Women's Council. Her research and publications are in ethnicity, women's culture and the expressive aspects of everyday life.

Janet L. Langlois is Assistant Professor in the English Department at Wayne State University in Detroit and Director of the university's Folklore Archive.

Margaret A. Mills is currently Assistant Professor of Folklore at the University of Pennsylvania.

Carol Mitchell is an Associate Professor at Colorado State University where she teaches literature and folklore. She has published articles on joke lore and on folklore and literature.

Susan Roach serves as Adjunct Professor of English at Louisiana Tech University in Ruston, Louisiana, where she is directing a survey of folklife in north central Louisiana. She is also a consultant on Louisiana folklife and currently completing her dissertation in folklore at the University of Texas on traditional quiltmaking in north Louisiana.

Kay F. Stone is Associate Professor of Folklore in the English Department, University of Winnipeg.

Margaret R. Yocom, Associate Professor of English and American Studies at George Mason University in Fairfax, Virginia, is currently the folklorist for the Eskimo Heritage Program sponsored by Kawerak, Incorporated of Nome, Alaska.

Publications of the American Folklore Society
New Series
General Editor, Marta Weigle

1. Stanley Brandes, *Metaphors of Masculinity: Sex and Status in Andalusian Folklore*
2. Roger deV. Renwick, *English Folk Poetry: Structure and Meaning*
3. Brian Sutton-Smith, *The Folkstories of Children*
4. Henry Glassie, *Passing the Time in Ballymenone: Culture and History of an Ulster Community*
5. Steven Feld, *Sound and Sentiment: Birds, Weeping, Poetics, and Song in Kaluli Expression*
6. Mark Slobin, editor and translator, *Old Jewish Folk Music: The Collections and Writings of Moshe Beregovski*
7. David J. Hufford, *The Terror That Comes in the Night: An Experience-Centered Study of Supernatural Assault Traditions*
8. Rosan A. Jordan and Susan J. Kalčik, eds., *Women's Folklore, Women's Culture*